Paralegal Careers

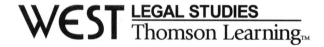

Paralegal Careers

Angela Schneeman

Africa • Australia • Canada • Denmark • Japan • Mexico • New Zealand • Philippines
Puerto Rico • Singapore • Spain • United Kingdom • United States

NOTICE TO THE READER

Publisher does not warrant or guarantee any of the products described herein or perform any independent analysis in connection with any of the product information contained herein. Publisher does not assume, and expressly disclaims, any obligation to obtain and include information other than that provided to it by the manufacturer.

The reader is notified that this text is an educational tool, not a practice book. Since the law is in constant change, no rule or statement of law in this book should be relied upon for any service to any client. The reader should always refer to standard legal sources for the current rule or law. If legal advice or other expert assistance is required, the services of the appropriate professional should be sought.

The Publisher makes no representation or warranties of any kind, including but not limited to, the warranties of fitness for particular purpose or merchantability, nor are any such representations implied with respect to the material set forth herein, and the publisher takes no responsibility with respect to such material. The publisher shall not be liable for any special, consequential, or exemplary damages resulting, in whole or part, from the readers' use of, or reliance upon, this material.

West Legal Studies Staff:
Business Unit Director: Susan L. Simpfenderfer
Executive Editor: Marlene McHugh Pratt
Acquisitions Editor: Joan M. Gill
Editorial Assistant: Lisa Flatley
Executive Marketing Manager: Donna J. Lewis
Channel Manager: Eleanor J. Murray
Executive Production Manager: Wendy A. Troeger
Production Editor: Betty L. Dickson
Cover Design: Connie McKinley

Library of Congress Cataloging-in-Publication Data

Schneeman, Angela.
    Paralegal careers / Angela Schneeman.
        p.   cm.
    Includes bibliographical references and index.
    ISBN 0-7668-0950-1
    1. Legal assistants—Vocational guidance—United States.   I.   Title.

KF320.L4 S357 2000
340'.023'73—dc21   99-053556

Preface

Students who are considering a career as a paralegal will have questions about the profession: Who are paralegals? What do they do? Where do they work? How much can I expect to earn as a paralegal? How can I find a paralegal position? *Paralegal Careers* answers those questions and more. It is the ideal text for any course that focuses on paralegal careers, including courses typically taught at the beginning of a paralegal student's education, and courses taught to aid paralegal students who are beginning the job search. This text introduces students to the paralegal profession and imparts the information they will need to make the transition from the classroom to the office.

For individuals who are exploring the possibility of a paralegal career, *Paralegal Careers* includes the information and tools necessary to make a well-informed decision. In addition, information on obtaining a quality paralegal education will assist the reader in forming a plan for a paralegal education.

THE STATUS OF THE PARALEGAL PROFESSION

The paralegal profession is still new and evolving. Because the profession is constantly defining itself, students may have unclear or unrealistic expectations about a career as a paralegal. *Paralegal Careers* provides the most recent data on the paralegal profession, combined with the personal experience of the author and several other paralegals, to give the student insight as to the realities of the profession.

TEXT ORGANIZATION

Paralegal Careers covers the following topics vital to an understanding of the paralegal profession:

- The Paralegal Profession—The introductory chapter to this text includes a look at the history, current status, and probable future of the paralegal profession, and defines *paralegal, legal assistant,* and related terms.
- Paralegal Employers—Who employs paralegals? The chapter on paralegal employers focuses on the major types of paralegal employers and the possible advantages and disadvantages to working for law firms (large, medium, and small), corporations, and the government, as well as being self-employed.
- Paralegal Specialties—What do paralegals do? *Paralegal Careers* includes an in-depth discussion of the major paralegal specialties with descriptions of the work performed by specialists in each area. Emphasis is given to those specialties where significant growth is expected.
- Paralegal Salaries and Benefits—How much do paralegals earn? Information gleaned from the most recent salary and benefit surveys is tabulated and discussed in detail.
- Paralegal Associations—A discussion concerning the major paralegal associations, benefits of membership, and the contributions of the associations to the profession includes resources for paralegals interested in joining a state or local group.
- Paralegal Regulation—The pros and cons of paralegal regulation, the various means of regulation, and the positions of several important paralegal groups are included in the Paralegal Regulation chapter. A state-by-state look at the latest developments, including introduced legislation, is also included.
- Paralegal Skills—The chapter in this text on paralegal skills identifies the important skills for paralegals, including those that paralegal employers look for. A separate section on each skill defines what is expected of paralegals and where students can acquire any skills they do not already have. Several resources are included in this chapter, including Web sites and reference books.
- Job Search—How can the student land his or her first paralegal position? This book includes an in-depth discussion on finding a paralegal position, with information concerning where to find a position, how to prepare a resume, and how to interview for a position effectively. Several Internet references are given. In addition, Appendices include several sample resumes and cover letters in various styles.

Each chapter is filled with examples, charts, graphs, practical advice, and resources to help the student make the transition from the classroom to the office. A glossary defines important terms in each chapter.

A special *Career Track* section at the end of each chapter asks students to do some self-evaluation and career planning by applying the information learned throughout the previous chapter to their own personal situations.

The *Focus on Ethics* within each chapter is a brief description of some of the major ethical issues faced by paralegals. The *Focus on Ethics* feature, as well as the discussion of the model codes of ethics adopted by the two national paralegal associations, emphasizes the importance of ethics to a paralegal's career.

Several *Paralegal Profiles* of working paralegals who hold diverse positions are included throughout the text to give the student a better understanding of what paralegals do and how diverse the field actually is. These profiles include paralegals who work in small, medium, and large law firms, as well as for government agencies, and corporate legal departments. Their specialties include family law, litigation, ccorporate law, tax law, and more.

The accompanying *Instructors Guide* includes additional resources, suggested activities, and suggestions for class discussions.

Finally, this book ties into a companion Web page on West Publishing's Web site at **www.westlegalstudies.com.** This unique resource includes new information and developments in several topics addressed in this text that are of great importance to the paralegal instructors, paralegal students, and paralegals. The site will be updated quarterly. Links to several useful Web sites can also be found on this page.

I would like to thank the NFPA, NALA, and AAfPE for allowing me to include excerpts and data from several of their invaluable studies and surveys. Also, my special thanks go to everyone at West and Delmar who helped with each step of this project, especially Joan Gill, Lisa Flatley, and Betty Dickson.

I would like to thank the following reviewers:

Wendy Edson	Konnie G. Kustron
Hilbert College	Eastern Michigan University
Jean Hellman	Mary Lowe
Institute of Paralegal Studies	Westark College
Melynda Hill-Teter	Richard Shaffran, J.D.
Contract Paralegal	UCLA Extension
Julia Ingersoll	Sybil Taylor Aytch
Pierce College	Smock & Weinberger

Angela Schneeman

Please note the Internet resources are of a time-sensitive nature, and URL addresses may often change or be deleted.

Introduction

If you are considering a new career as a paralegal—Congratulations! You are contemplating a career in one of the fastest growing, most dynamic professions of the new millennium.

Whether you have experience working in the legal field or it is all new to you, you probably have many questions concerning the paralegal profession. Some of these questions may include:

- Exactly what is a paralegal?
- Where do paralegals work?
- In what areas of law do paralegals specialize?
- What kind of salary and benefits can I expect as a paralegal?
- What assistance is available to paralegals throughout their careers?
- Do I need to be licensed to be a paralegal?
- What skills will be important to me as a paralegal?
- How do I find my first job as a paralegal?

This text will answer all of these questions—and more. Chapter 1 starts by defining the term *paralegal* and exploring the history, evolution, and predicted future of the paralegal profession

Next, Chapter 2 describes the various paralegal employers and the advantages and disadvantages to working for each.

Paralegals specialize in numerous areas of law. Chapter 3 explores several of these specialties and the duties and work environment of the paralegals who specialize in each of them.

Chapter 4 includes highlights of the most recent paralegal salary and benefit surveys. This information will be updated quarterly at the companion web site to this text found on the Internet at **www.westlegalstudies.com.**

Paralegal associations can offer assistance in many forms to you throughout your career as a paralegal. Chapter 5 includes information on both of the national as well as the state and local paralegal associations.

Currently you do not need a license to work as a paralegal in any state in the country. However, Chapter 6 explores the trend toward the almost certain regulation of paralegals on some level.

Chapter 7 takes a look at the skills that will be important to you in your work as a paralegal—according to paralegals *and* paralegal employers.

Chapter 8 will assist you in your job search and offer helpful suggestions for finding employment at any point in your career.

Finally, this book will point you to additional resources to answer all your questions—now and throughout your career as a paralegal.

Contents

The Paralegal Profession

"Teachers open the door, but you must enter by yourself."

CHINESE PROVERB

The paralegal profession is one of the fastest growing and most dynamic professions in the United States. In the 1980s, the U.S. Department of Labor proclaimed the paralegal profession *the* fastest growing profession in the country and predicted that there would be 100,000 paralegals in the United States by the beginning of the new century. In fact, according to the latest statistics, there are currently nearly 130,000 paralegals employed in the United States.[1] In addition, the Bureau of Labor Statistics predicts that the paralegal profession will continue to grow at a *much faster than average* rate, at least through the year 2006 (Figure 1–1).

Attorneys have benefited from the growth of the profession because paralegals assist them in offering affordable, quality legal services to clients. Paralegals have benefited because the profession offers well-paid, interesting, and rewarding work. In addition, the public has benefited because paralegals have made quality legal services more available and more affordable. To fully understand the nature of the paralegal profession and the contributions paralegals have made to the work force and to society, it is helpful to have an understanding of what a paralegal does and to have some

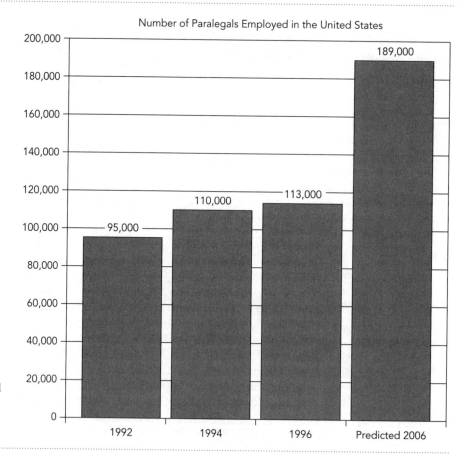

FIGURE 1–1
Growth of the Paralegal Profession (From the Statistical Abstract of the United States [1995, 1996, 1998])

knowledge of the history and emergence of the paralegal profession. This chapter will examine those aspects of the profession—plus take a look at the predicted future for paralegal careers in the United States.

Paralegal Profile

PROFILE ON CRISTI A. MALONE

My attorney frequently asks my opinion on issues of our cases, and she allows us to work as a team. I like being involved in the day-to-day work-up of a case.

Name and Location:	Cristi A. Malone, Pensacola, Florida
Title:	Certified Legal Assistant
Specialty:	Plaintiff personal injury, including automobile accidents and premises liability cases
Education:	Associate of Science in Legal Assistance from Pensacola Junior College. Currently working on Bachelor of Arts Degree in Legal Administration at the University of West Florida.
Experience:	6 Years

Cristi Malone is a personal injury paralegal in Pensacola, Florida. When she is not on the job, she is busy with her duties as vice president of the Pensacola Legal Assistants Association or volunteer work. Somehow she still finds time to enjoy boating, swimming, and camping with her husband and two daughters.

Cristi works for an 18-attorney law firm that employs 15 paralegals. She reports to one attorney who specializes in premise liability law. Her work involves maintaining client files in personal injury and premise liability cases. She is responsible for monitoring the medical treatment and condition of each client and submitting appropriate information to the insurance adjuster. After the client's medical treatment and analysis are complete, she prepares drafts of demand letters and packages for attorney review. If a settlement cannot be reached for a client, Cristi assists with several aspects of litigating the client's case, including drafting the complaint and trial preparation.

Cristi enjoys working on the legal team. It is not unusual for the attorney to whom she reports to ask her opinion on a case, and she is very involved with all aspects of each client's file. Cristi's research and contribution to each client file can have a real impact on the outcome of a client's case and a client's life. Currently, Cristi is working on a premises liability case where the client, a truck driver, had a toxic chemical sprayed on him. The client suffered burns on his neck, back, and throat from inhaling the chemical. Cristi is researching the chemical and its possible long-term effects.

Christi's advice to paralegal students:

If at all possible, intern. Even if the company or firm you intern for does not have a position available when you graduate or complete your internship the experience is invaluable. Office policies vary from place to place but the practice is basically the same within the same state.

PARALEGAL AND LEGAL ASSISTANT DEFINED

There are several widely accepted definitions of the term **paralegal**, which is usually considered interchangeable with the term **legal assistant.** The **American Bar Association (ABA)**, the **American Association for Paralegal Education (AAfPE)** and the two national paralegal associations (the **National Federation of Paralegal Associations [NFPA]** and the **National Association of Legal Assistants [NALA]**) each have their own definition (Figure 1–2).

These definitions are very similar, but they have a few notable distinctions:

- Under the ABA and NALA definitions, a paralegal performs specifically delegated work *for which a lawyer is responsible.* Under these definitions, the paralegal works under the supervision of an attorney.
- The NFPA definition, adopted in September 1997 to "reflect the diversity of the NFPA's membership and the profession,"[2] includes paralegals who are not working under the direct supervision of an attorney but who are practicing within the law through administrative, statutory, or court authority.

In addition to those mentioned above, several definitions with slight variations have been adopted by several courts, state legislatures, and state bar associations. Appendix A to this text is a list of state-approved definitions of the terms *paralegal* and *legal assistant.*

Most of these definitions provide that paralegals:

- Have specialized knowledge gained through training or several years of experience.
- Perform substantive legal work that may otherwise be done by an attorney.

THE ABA'S DEFINITION

Adopted at the August 1997 Annual Meeting:

A legal assistant or paralegal is a person, qualified by education, training or work experience who is employed or retained by a lawyer, law office, corporation, governmental agency or other entity and who performs specifically delegated substantive legal work for which a lawyer is responsible.

THE NATIONAL ASSOCIATION OF LEGAL ASSISTANTS' DEFINITION

The National Association of Legal Assistants (NALA), prefers the title *legal assistant* and the following definition:

Legal assistants, also known as paralegals, are a distinguishable group of persons who assist attorneys in the delivery of legal services. Through formal education, training and experience, legal assistants have knowledge and expertise regarding the legal system and substantive and procedural law which qualifies them to do work of a legal nature under the supervision of an attorney.

THE NATIONAL FEDERATION OF PARALEGAL ASSOCIATION'S DEFINITION

The other national paralegal association, the National Federation of Paralegal Associations (NFPA), prefers the term *paralegal* and the following definition:

A person qualified through education, training or work experience to perform substantive legal work that requires knowledge of legal concepts and is customarily but not exclusively performed by a lawyer.

This qualified person may be retained or employed in a traditional capacity by a lawyer, law office, governmental agency, or other entity or is authorized by administrative, statutory or court authority to perform this work; or

This qualified person may be retained or employed in a non-traditional capacity, provided that such non-traditional capacity does not violate applicable unauthorized practice of law statutes, administrative laws, court rules or case law.

THE AMERICAN ASSOCIATION FOR PARALEGAL EDUCATION'S DEFINITION

Paralegals perform substantive and procedural legal work as authorized by law, work which, in the absence of the paralegal, would be performed by an attorney.

Paralegals have knowledge of the law gained through education, or education and work experience, which qualifies them to perform legal work.

Paralegals adhere to recognized ethical standards and rules of professional responsibility.

FIGURE 1–2
Paralegal and legal assistant definitions

- Work under the supervision of an attorney or within the law through administrative, statutory, or court authority.
- Do not practice law.

All paralegals have specialized knowledge gained through training or several years of experience. The majority of paralegals have four-year college degrees, although there are other options as well. For more information on choosing a quality paralegal education program, see Appendix B to this text.

The substantive work done by paralegals is work that typically would be done by attorneys, such as drafting documents and researching the facts or law pertaining to a specific case. Paralegals do not perform work that must be done exclusively by attorneys, such as representing clients in court or giving legal advice.

The vast majority of paralegals work under the direct supervision of an attorney. There are, however, a growing number of paralegals who work independently to perform work under administrative, statutory, or court authority. The work performed by these individuals is not considered the practice of law. Paralegals who do not work under the supervision of attorneys must be very careful to avoid the **unauthorized practice of law.** There is currently much debate concerning the regulation of paralegals who do not work under the direct supervision of attorneys. Paralegal regulation is discussed in Chapter Six of this text.

OTHER RELEVANT TITLES DEFINED

In addition to the terms *legal assistant* and *paralegal,* it is helpful to be familiar with some related terms. These terms are titles for special types of paralegals or titles for other relevant positions.

Contract Paralegal. A paralegal who works for several different attorneys, law firms, or corporations, either as a freelance paralegal or through one or more temporary agencies.

Freelance Paralegal. A self-employed paralegal who works for several different attorneys, law firms, or corporations under the supervision of an attorney.

Independent Paralegal. A self-employed paralegal who works directly for the public to provide legal services not considered to be the practice of law. Also known as a *legal technician.*

Legal Nurse Consultant. An individual who has training as both a nurse and as a paralegal who often works for personal injury law firms, medical malpractice law firms, or the legal department of insurance companies.

Legal Technician. A self-employed paralegal who works directly for the public to provide legal services not considered to be the practice of law. Also known as an *independent paralegal.*

Paralegal Manager. A person responsible for hiring and supervising paralegals who spends little or no time working on client cases as a paralegal. Also known as a *legal assistant manager.*

Traditional Paralegal. A paralegal who works under the direct supervision of an attorney.

THE MANY FUNCTIONS OF PARALEGALS

One reason a single definition for the term *paralegal* or *legal assistant* seems so elusive is the diverse nature of the profession. The work of two paralegals in different firms can be incredibly dissimilar. Among other things, your employer and the type of law in which you specialize will affect your work and working conditions. If you work for a merger and acquisitions department of a large Wall Street law firm in New York City, you may have the same title as a paralegal who works in a small immigration law firm in a border town in Texas, but you will have little else in common. Most paralegals work for private law firms, but growing numbers of paralegals work for the legal departments of corporations, for nonprofit organizations, and in the public sector for federal, state, or local administrative agencies.

THE HISTORY AND EVOLUTION OF THE PARALEGAL PROFESSION

Although attorneys have been around for centuries, paralegals are a relatively new phenomenon. This section examines the evolution of the paralegal profession and paralegal education, as well as the reasons for the rapid growth and expansion of the profession.

THE BEGINNING

The paralegal profession had its formal beginning in the United States in the 1960s. Paralegals were hired in the mid-1960s to assist federally funded lawyers in poverty programs as part of President Lyndon Johnson's "War on Poverty." Soon the benefits of hiring paralegals became apparent throughout the private sector of the legal community, and law firms began hiring paralegals as well. Many of the first paralegals were either experienced legal secretaries or college graduates who were trained by the attorneys within the law firms for which they worked.

In the beginning, the paralegal profession was met with resistance from some attorneys who did not understand the advantages of hiring paralegals as opposed to hiring more attorneys or legal secretaries. While it is true that attorneys can practice law and paralegals cannot, paralegals proved their economic value to law firms by performing tasks competently that are not considered to be practicing law. Attorneys found that their expertise was not necessary for *all* the functions they were performing and that some of the tasks they were performing could be done more efficiently by paralegals.

Paralegals established themselves as experts in procedure. Whereas an attorney's education focuses heavily on law and legal theory, a paralegal's education is more oriented toward procedure and *how to get things done.* Attorneys give clients legal advice and decide what course of action to take on behalf of a client. The contribution paralegals make to the legal services team is often that of being an expert on procedure, or how to accomplish the goals established by the attorneys. Because paralegals are paid less than attorneys and because their salaries can be recouped by billing clients, law firm decision makers quickly realized the economic benefits of hiring more paralegals. Since the 1960s, law firms and other paralegal employers have

More Attorneys	Legal Secretaries or Administrative Assistants
Paralegals may be hired at a lower salary. Paralegals do not have partnership expectations. Paralegals can provide more affordable legal services to clients. Paralegals may be more qualified, and willing to perform, routine procedural tasks.	Paralegals have specialized training to allow them to perform more substantive tasks. Paralegals can perform routine tasks with less supervision. Paralegal time may be billed to the client. Paralegals are often more qualified to work directly with the client (under the supervision of an attorney).

FIGURE 1–3

Why law firms hire paralegals instead of:

increased their paralegal staff and their use of paralegals to maximize productivity while minimizing client expenses. Paralegals have proved their worth by providing valuable assistance to attorneys and increasing client satisfaction and firm profits (Figure 1–3).

Paralegals also had to overcome the resistance to their profession presented by attorneys who felt that well-trained legal secretaries adequately fulfilled all their paralegal needs. In fact, many of the first paralegals were former legal secretaries who gained recognition through additional training and education. Paralegals demonstrated that they were able to work with less supervision than legal secretaries and that their training and professionalism made them more competent to meet with clients and conduct client interviews. In addition, because paralegal time is customarily billed to clients, paralegals profit the law firm in a way that legal secretaries cannot.

THE EVOLUTION OF THE PARALEGAL PROFESSION

The paralegal profession has evolved over the years and has gained respect and recognition from the legal community and the public. Two factors in the successful growth and expansion of the profession are the efforts of the two national paralegal associations and the quality education offered by a growing number of schools.

Recognition by the Legal Community. In 1968, the ABA first recognized the importance of paralegals with the creation of its Special Committee on Lay Assistants (now called the **Standing Committee on Legal Assistants**). The Committee was charged with "developing, encouraging, and increasing the training and utilization of nonlawyer assistants to enable lawyers to discharge their professional responsibilities more effectively and efficiently."[3] The Committee developed **Model Guidelines for the Utilization of Legal Assistant Services** to provide guidance to attorneys for the effective use of paralegals. Many states have followed this model in adopting their own guidelines. The Committee now oversees the ABA approval process for paralegal education programs.

Recognition for paralegals came from the U.S. Supreme Court in 1989. The Court found that "By encouraging the use of lower cost paralegals rather than attorneys whenever possible, permitting market rate billing of paralegal hours encourages cost effective delivery of legal services and, by reducing the spiraling cost of civil rights litigation, furthers the policies underlying civil rights statutes."[4] When awarding attorneys' fees, most courts now routinely allow compensation for the contribution of paralegals.

In 1992, the ABA established the Commission on Nonlawyer Practice to conduct research, hearings, and deliberations to determine the implications of nonlawyer practice for society, the client, and the legal profession. The Commission examined nonlawyer activity in law-related situations by paralegals and legal technicians, as well as self-represented persons and document preparers. The Commission issued its Report with Recommendations in 1995. Within the conclusion of this report were the statements that ". . . nonlawyers, both as paralegals accountable to lawyers and in other roles permitted by law, have become an important part of the delivery of legal services, and that their expertise and dedication to the system have led to improvements in public access to affordable legal services."[5]

The ABA currently grants legal assistant associate memberships to paralegals who are sponsored by an attorney member and who meet certain requirements. As of 1998, there were over 900 paralegal associate members of the ABA. Many states have followed the lead of the ABA by inviting paralegals to become members of their associations as well.[6]

During the 1980s and 1990s, the profession continued to grow and mature, despite some growing pains. Over the years, paralegals have worked to earn the respect of attorneys and the public alike and to demonstrate the unique contributions they can make to a legal services team.

The Evolution of the National Paralegal Associations. As the number of paralegals in the United States grew, so did the need for those paralegals to network and organize. Paralegals organized several state and local associations, and in the 1970s two separate national paralegal associations were formed. These paralegal associations provided a way for paralegals to share ideas and promote their professional standing throughout the country.

In 1974, the National Federation of Paralegal Associations (NFPA) was formed by a group of eight local paralegal associations. The NFPA has five official goals:

- To advance, foster, and promote the paralegal profession with absolute dedication
- To monitor and participate in developments in the paralegal profession
- To maintain a nationwide communication network among paralegal associations and other members of the legal community
- To advance the education standards of the paralegal profession

- To participate in, carry on, and conduct research, seminars, experiments, investigations, studies, or other work concerning the paralegal profession

The NFPA currently has more than 55 association members located throughout the United States and Canada and representing more than 17,000 individual members.

The National Association of Legal Assistants (NALA) was established by 800 charter members in 1975 for the following stated purposes:

- To increase the professional standing of legal assistants throughout the nation
- To provide uniformity in the identification of legal assistants
- To establish national standards of professional competence for legal assistants
- To provide uniformity among the states in the utilization of legal assistants

The NALA currently has individual memberships and 90 state and local affiliated associations representing a total of over 18,000 members.

In addition to the two national associations, many associations have formed at the state and local levels. Although membership in a paralegal association is not mandatory for paralegals, membership in an association offers numerous benefits to paralegals and paralegal students. The paralegal associations promote professionalism, offer continuing legal education to paralegals, set ethical guidelines for paralegals to follow, and offer assistance in many forms to paralegals. The associations have done much over the years to shape public opinion of paralegals, both with attorneys and with the public in general. The paralegal associations are explored further in Chapter Five of this text. Appendix C to this text is a directory of paralegal associations.

The Evolution of Paralegal Education. Paralegal education has also evolved through the years (Figure 1–4). In the 1960s and early 1970s, most paralegals were experienced legal secretaries or college graduates who were trained by the attorneys for whom they worked. Gradually, proprietary schools, colleges, and business schools began offering paralegal programs, and in the early 1970s the ABA began approving paralegal programs. The American Association for Paralegal Education (AAfPE) was formed in the 1980s to organize educators and paralegal education programs. The AAfPE currently has approximately 285 institutional members.

In 1970 there were only four paralegal training programs throughout the United States. Today, there are more than 800 educational programs for paralegals, over 200 of which are approved by the ABA. Education options for paralegals include two-year, four-year and postgraduate degree programs, as well as certificate programs. Paralegal programs are offered through traditional classroom settings and, more recently, through distance learning programs.

1960s	Paralegals hired to assist federally funded lawyers in poverty programs as part of War on Poverty.
1960s	Profession grows as attorneys recognize the benefits of hiring paralegals.
1968	American Bar Association forms the Special Committee on Lay Assistants.
1971	The ABA recognizes the term *legal assistant* and renames committee to the ABA Standing Committee on Legal Assistants.
1973	The ABA approves the Guidelines for the Approval of Legal Assistant Education Programs.
1974	The National Federation of Paralegal Associations is formed.
1975	The National Association of Legal Assistants is formed.
1981	The American Association for Paralegal Education is formed.
1986	ABA defines *legal assistant*.
1987	NFPA defines *paralegal*.
1989	Supreme Court holds that paralegal time must be included in the reimbursement of attorneys' fees in *Missouri v. Jenkins*, 491 U.S. 274 (1989).
1991	ABA Standing Committee on Legal Assistants develops Model Guidelines for the Utilization of Legal Assistant Services.
1992	ABA establishes the Commission on Nonlawyer Practice to determine the implications of nonlawyer practice for society, the client and the legal profession.
1995	The Commission on Nonlawyer Practice issues its Report with Recommendations, recognizing that "nonlawyers, both as paralegals accountable to lawyers and in other roles permitted by law, have become an important part of the delivery of legal services, and that their expertise and dedication to the system have led to improvements in public access to affordable legal services."
1996	Nearly 130,000 paralegals are employed in the United States.
1997	ABA defines *legal assistant* and *paralegal* as someone who "performs specifically delegated substantive work for which a lawyer is responsible."
1997	NFPA adopts definition of *paralegal* that includes paralegals who are not working under the direct supervision of an attorney, but who are practicing within the law through administrative, statutory, or court authority.
1999	It is predicted that there will be as many as 189,000 paralegals working in the United States by the year 2006.

FIGURE 1–4
*Time line of the
evolution of the
paralegal profession*

REASONS FOR THE CONTINUED GROWTH OF THE PARALEGAL PROFESSION

The paralegal profession has grown at ever-increasing rates because paralegals have adapted to fit the changing environment of the practice of law. The increased use of paralegals has allowed attorneys to offer legal services of a higher quality, make legal services more available to the public, and make legal services more affordable.

Improving the Quality of Legal Services. Paralegals improve the quality of services offered to clients by relieving attorneys of tasks they need not necessarily perform. This allows attorneys to focus their attention on matters that do require their attention, such as complex research, negotiations, advising clients, and representing clients in court.

In each area of law, paralegals assist attorneys to make them more efficient. For example, a litigation paralegal may organize all exhibits and other court documents so that the attorney is better organized and prepared for presentations in court. A corporate paralegal may prepare and organize all documents for a merger and acquisition closing, leaving the attorney free for negotiations and answering substantive questions raised by the client. A paralegal's knowledge of procedure can assure that tasks undertaken on behalf of a client are completed as quickly and efficiently as possible.

Paralegals are often in a position to improve client relations by acting as a liaison between the client and the busy attorney. Paralegals can give the client personal attention and see to it that clients' phone calls are returned promptly and their questions answered.

Paralegals are necessarily detail-oriented, taking care of small, but important details that may be overlooked by the busy attorney. Overall, proper utilization of paralegals allows attorneys to offer superior quality legal services to their clients.

Making Legal Services More Available. Paralegals are often in a position to offer their assistance to individuals who would not otherwise have legal services available to them. Many paralegals are employed by courts and government agencies that do not have the funding to hire an adequate number of attorneys to assist their indigent clients. For example, some courts employ paralegals as **pro se** clerks to assist indigent clients as they select and complete the proper legal forms. Legal technicians and independent paralegals often assist individuals with tasks that do not require the practice of law but may be intimidating for individuals who are unfamiliar with the legal system. Paralegals and attorneys are working together toward the goal of providing legal services to all in need of them.

Making Legal Services More Affordable. The main reasons for the increased hiring of paralegals are economic. Law firms have found they can hire paralegals, get their work completed competently and efficiently and bill their clients less, all the while retaining their profit margin. For example, if a client has been quoted a fee of $350 for a simple will, and it takes approximately 3.5 hours to meet with the client, draft the will, and see to its execution, the firm's time could be spent in one of two ways:

Meeting with client	1 hour	Attorney rate	$100/hr.	$100
Drafting of simple will	2 hours	Attorney rate	$100/hr.	$200
Meeting with client for execution of will	1/2 hour	Attorney rate	$100/hr.	$ 50
Total cost of billable time to law firm:				$350

When an attorney who bills $100 per hour handles the task exclusively, the firm might bill $350 to the client, but this is exactly the amount of billable time that it costs the firm. However, when a paralegal is involved, the scenario can look quite different.

Meeting with client	1 hour	Attorney rate	$100/hr.	$100
Draft simple will	2 hours	Paralegal rate	$50/hr.	$100
Review simple will	1/2 hour	Attorney rate	$100/hr.	$ 50
Meeting with client for execution of will	1/2 hour	Paralegal rate	$50/hr.	$ 25
Total cost of billable time to law firm:				$275

In this case, the cost of billable time to the law firm is $275. The law firm can choose to pass the savings on to the client and bill at a more competitive rate of $275, or the firm can bill at the usual rate of $350 and enjoy the extra profit. The average billing rate of paralegals in the United States is between $40 to $80 per hour,[7] which is significantly less than the average billing rate for attorneys. The salary paid to the paralegal is also substantially less than what the attorney is paid. In the second scenario, the attorney's time can be focused on matters that may be taken care of only by a licensed attorney, thus benefiting the lawyer, the law firm, and the client.

These factors are not fleeting in nature. All indications are that the paralegal profession will continue to grow into the twenty-first century.

THE FUTURE OF THE PARALEGAL PROFESSION

The incredible success of the paralegal profession is due in large part to the flexibility of the profession and of individual paralegals. The adaptability of paralegals has allowed them to grow and change as the profession has matured, and this also will serve paralegals well into the future. It is predicted that the paralegal profession will continue to rank among the top 20 fastest growing occupations in the United States, and that by the year 2006, there will be as many as 189,000 paralegals in the United States, an increase of over 68 percent from 1996.

Some trends paralegals will likely encounter include increased responsibility; improved utilization, salaries, and benefits; more emphasis on specialization; state regulation; technological advances; the increasing popularity of contract and temporary paralegals; and new opportunities in **Alternative Dispute Resolution (ADR)**.

INCREASING LEVELS OF RESPONSIBILITIES AND IMPROVED COMPENSATION

The increasing demand for quality legal service at an affordable price will likely continue to feed the evolution of the paralegal profession. The level of responsibility assumed by paralegals, as well as job satisfaction, will most certainly continue to rise.

Attorneys and law firms are still learning the best means for using paralegals. As the experience of law firms and other paralegal employers grows and more information is shared, paralegals will be more efficiently utilized. Information on how best to utilize paralegals is becoming available to attorneys from several sources, including bar associations, paralegal associations, paralegal educators, and the courts. The information being provided includes guidance on the type of work best assigned to paralegals, ethical concerns in working with paralegals, avoiding the unauthorized practice of law by paralegals, and the overall team approach to law practice. As more information becomes available on how to utilize paralegals within law firms and organizations, paralegals will find increasing satisfaction in their work.

Paralegal salaries will likely continue to rise as well. Improved utilization and increased responsibility, coupled with a growing demand for qualified paralegals, will lead to improved salaries and benefits for paralegals.

MORE EMPHASIS ON SPECIALIZATION

Specialization, which is currently impacting the way that law is practiced in the United States, will surely help to define the position of the future paralegal. The ever-increasing complexity of practicing law, as well as the need to keep legal costs affordable, has encouraged attorneys to specialize more than they ever have in the past. It is not unusual for an attorney to specialize in one area of law and to practice in that area almost exclusively. Many law firms have attorneys who specialize in various areas of law. Some firms have built their reputations on the expertise of their attorneys in one or more areas of law.

As attorneys specialize at an increasing rate, so do paralegals. "The demand for expertise has led many paralegals to develop knowledge and skills in highly technical or specialized subject areas."[8] The growing demand for specialists in various areas of law will mean that more and more paralegals will develop a very specific competence in a certain area of law. Some of the specialties that may be in great demand in the future include complex litigation, environmental law, intellectual property, product liability, alternative dispute resolution, elder law, and Internet research.

STATE REGULATION

Currently, paralegals are not required to be licensed, certified, or registered with the state in which they work. However, many experts believe that the paralegal profession will be regulated at the state level before long. Legislation has been introduced in several states that would require the registration, certification, or licensing of paralegals. Much of the legislation so far has been aimed at independent paralegals or legal technicians rather than traditional paralegals. However, in the future, state legislation may be adopted that will establish qualifications for all paralegals and require them to be licensed, certified, or registered. Paralegals who are regulated will need to meet requirements established by each state in which they work. These will include minimum education requirements, continuing education requirements, adherence to rules of ethics, and such other requirements established by each state.

INCREASING USE OF TECHNOLOGY

The introduction of technology to the practice of law and its rapid growth has aided the expansion of the paralegal's role in the legal team. Nearly all paralegals use computers daily. Much of the time paralegals have previously spent in law libraries is now spent on the computer, using CD-ROM technology or the Internet. An increasing amount of the time paralegals spend drafting documents is spent at the keyboard, rather than dictating to a secretary or writing longhand. Electronic timekeeping, document, database, and case management software have all increased productivity and changed the way paralegals spend their time. These are all trends that are sure to continue into the future.

Paralegals who are proficient with the latest technology will be able to assist attorneys and clients with more functions than ever before. Rapid changes in technology and the current trend toward paperless litigation will require paralegals to keep current with the technological advances made in the practice of law. Paralegals who have the skills required to design and manipulate databases will be in increasing demand in litigation law firms and corporate law departments.

Technology also may offer the paralegal of the future more flexibility. Laptop computers and other advances (especially improved telecommunications) already allow some attorneys and paralegals to put in a full day's work without leaving home.

INCREASING USE OF CONTRACT AND TEMPORARY PARALEGALS

The increasing use of contract and temporary paralegals to accommodate the fluctuating workloads of law firms and corporate legal departments will more than likely continue into the future. Contract and temporary legal staffing is a rapidly growing business. Some estimates put the growth of this relatively new business at 25 percent annually. More and more paralegals are opting to work on a contract basis or for temporary legal service agencies. Contract and temporary work allow paralegals more flexibility than traditional employment and offer the opportunity for a vast array of experiences.

NEW OPPORTUNITIES FOR PARALEGALS IN ALTERNATIVE DISPUTE RESOLUTION

Many indicators point to the continuing increase of Alternative Dispute Resolution (ADR) to resolve legal disputes in the future, and paralegals are adapting to this trend. ADR involves resolution of legal disputes without

FIGURE 1–5
*Possible furure trends
for the paralegal
profession*

- Increase in paralegal responsibilities
- Improved utilization of paralegals
- Increase in number of paralegal positions
- Improved salaries and benefits
- Increase in specialization
- State regulation
- Increase in use of technology in law firms
- Increase in use of contract and temporary paralegals
- New opportunities for paralegals in alternative dispute resolution (ADR)

litigation. The most popular forms of ADR include **arbitration** and **mediation.** With the rising costs of litigation and crowded court calendars, the use of ADR is growing at an unprecedented rate. Some family courts not only encourage the use of mediation, they *require* that couples who have filed for divorce attempt mediation to work out issues such as property division, custody, and child support. The increasing use of ADR may mean less litigation, but it does not mean less work or fewer opportunities for paralegals. Paralegals can assist with all facets of ADR, and many paralegals have chosen to specialize in ADR. Some even work as mediators.

The paralegal profession will continue to grow and change to accommodate the changes in the practice of law (Figure 1-5). According to the Bureau of Labor Statistics, "employment of paralegals is expected to grow much faster than average—ranking among the fastest growing occupations in the economy through the year 2006—as law firms and other employers with legal staffs increasingly hire paralegals to lower the cost, and increase the availability and efficiency, of legal services."[9]

Focus on Ethics: *The Importance of Legal Ethics*

When can you divulge information shared with you by a client? What should you do if your personal interests conflict with the interests of a client? Is it okay to give legal advice to clients on routine matters? These are all questions of ethics—the types of ethical dilemmas you will frequently be faced with as a paralegal.

Every day of your life you make ethical decisions, and every day of your career as a paralegal, you will be making important ethical decisions. Most of these decisions will be easy, and will be made with little thought. You will make many decisions by relying on your education, experience, good judgment, and common sense. However, there are some decisions that you will be forced to make based on other criteria. Your common sense alone will not always be enough to help you make the right, moral, legal, and ethical decisions in the complex environment in which you will be working. Rules of ethics, especially those dealing with client rights, are not always intuitive. Your instinct and gut feeling may tell you one thing when the rules of ethics may prescribe another. For example, your personal ethics may tell you that the right thing is to turn in your client when he or she is evading justice, but the rules of ethics may prescribe another course of action.

As a paralegal it will be important to you to be familiar with all rules of ethics that apply to you and to follow those rules at all times. The ethical decisions you make will have an impact on you, your employer, your clients, and the public. Unethical behavior can cost you your reputation and your job. It could also subject you to lawsuits and even criminal prosecution in some instances. Your unethical behavior can also cause the attorneys to whom you report to be subject to discipline, including being disbarred.

Both the National Association of Legal Assistants and the National Federation of Paralegal Associations have established rules of ethics for their members. In addition, the rules of ethics applicable to the attorneys you work for will generally apply to you as well. It is important that you have an understanding of all these rules of ethics. The study of legal ethics and professional responsibility, which is an integral part of any paralegal's education, will assist you in making appropriate decisions when dealing with clients, the courts, the public, and the business of law practice that you will be concerned with every day.

CAREER TRACK

The career track sections at the end of each chapter of this text are designed to help you think through the information you have learned in each chapter and to determine how you can use the information as you begin your career as a paralegal.

Now that we have taken a look at the history and possible future of the paralegal profession—how does it compare to your preconceptions and expectations? How do the predictions of the future of the paralegal profession meet with your predictions for your future career? Remember, the paralegal profession is still defining itself, and as a future member of the profession, you can have a hand in shaping it.

GLOSSARY

Alternative Dispute Resolution (ADR) A procedure for settling a dispute by means other than litigation, such as arbitration, mediation, or minitrial. (*Black's Law Dictionary, 7th Edition*)

American Association for Paralegal Education (AAfPE) Association of paralegal educators and institutions that educate paralegals formed in 1981. The AAfPE currently has approximately 285 members.

American Bar Association (ABA) A voluntary national organization of lawyers. Among other things, it participates in law reform, law-school accreditation, and continuing legal education in an effort to improve legal services and the administration of justice. *(Black's Law Dictionary, 7th Edition)*

Arbitration A method of dispute resolution involving one or more neutral third parties who are usually agreed to by the disputing parties and whose decision is binding. *(Black's Law Dictionary, 7th Edition)*

Contract Paralegal A paralegal who works for several different attorneys, law firms, or corporations, either as a freelance paralegal or through one or more temporary agencies.

Freelance Paralegal A self-employed paralegal who works for several different attorneys, law firms, or corporations under the supervision of an attorney.

Independent Paralegal A self-employed paralegal who works directly for the public to provide legal services not considered the practice of law. Also known as a *legal technician.*

Legal Assistant A person with specialized knowledge gained through education and training who performs substative legal work not considered to be the practice of law, under the supervision of an attorney, or within the law through administrative, statutory, or court authority. Also known as a *paralegal.*

Legal Nurse Consultant An individual who has training both as a nurse and a paralegal who often works for personal injury law firms, medical malpractice law firms, or the legal department of insurance companies.

Legal Technician A self-employed paralegal who works directly for the public to provide legal services not considered the practice of law. Also known as an *independent paralegal.*

Litigation The process of carrying on a lawsuit (the attorney advised his client to make a generous settlement offer in order to avoid litigation). A lawsuit itself (several litigations pending before the court). *(Black's Law Dictionary, 7th Edition)*

Mediation An alternative dispute resolution process in which a neutral third person, the mediator, helps disputing parties to reach an agreement. The mediator has no power to impose a decision on the parties, unless participation is voluntary.

Model Guidelines for the Utilization of Legal Assistant Services Guidelines adopted by the American Bar Association's Standing Committee on Legal Assistants in 1991 to provide guidance to attorneys for the effective utilization for paralegals.

National Association of Legal Assistants (NALA) National association of legal assistants (paralegals) formed in 1975; currently represents over 18,000 members through individual memberships and 90 state- and local-affiliated associations.

National Federation of Paralegal Associations (NFPA) National association of paralegals formed in 1974; currently has more than 55 association members representing more than 17,000 individual members.

Paralegal A person with specialized knowledge gained through education and training, who performs substantive legal work not considered to be the practice of law, under the supervision of an attorney, or within the law through administrative, statutory, or court authority. Also known as a *legal assistant.*

Paralegal Manager A person responsible for hiring and supervising paralegals who spends little or no time working on client cases as a paralegal. Also known as a *legal assistant manager.*

Pro Se For oneself; on one's own behalf; without a lawyer (the defendant pro se) (a pro se defendant). Also termed *pro persona; in propria persona. (Black's Law Dictionary, 7th Edition)*

Standing Committee on Legal Assistants Committee formed by the American Bar Association, which currently oversees the ABA approval process for paralegal education programs.

Traditional Paralegal An individual who works as a paralegal under the direct supervision of an attorney.

Unauthorized Practice of Law (UPL) The practice of law by a person, typically a non-lawyer, who has not been licensed or admitted to practice law in a given jurisdiction. *(Black's Law Dictionary, 7th Edition)*

ENDNOTES

[1] Bureau of Labor Statistics, National Occupational Employment and Wage Data, 1997.

[2] National Federation of Paralegal Associations Web site, *NFPA Statement on Issues Affecting the Paralegal Profession,* October 1999, **http://www.paralegals.org.**

[3] American Bar Association Web site, American Bar Association, *ABA Standing Committee on Legal Assistants History,* October 1999, **http://www.abanet.org/legalassts/history.html.**

[4] *Missouri v. Jenkins,* 491 U.S. 274, 109 S.Ct. 2463, 105 L.Ed.2d 229 (1989).

[5] ABA Commission on Nonlawyer Practice, *Nonlawyer Activity in Law-Related Situations A Report with Recommendations,* 1995.

[6] The states of Alaska, California, Colorado, Connecticut, Florida, Illinois, Kansas, Michigan, Minnesota, Montana, Nevada, New Jersey, New Mexico, North Carolina, North Dakota, Ohio, Rhode Island, Texas, Utah, Virginia, and Wisconsin currently have paralegal members.

[7] National Federation of Paralegal Associations, *1997 Paralegal Compensation and Benefits Report* (1997).

[8] National Association of Paralegal Associations Web site, *NFPA Statement on Issues Affecting the Paralegal Profession,* **http://www.paralegals.org** (October 1999).

[9] Bureau of Labor Statistics, National Occupational Employment and Wage Data, 1997.

[10] Selected definitions from *Black's Law Dictionary, Seventh Edition,* Copyright © 1999 West Group, Eagan, Minnesota, USA, with permission.

Feature: Working With Attorneys

Because there are as many different personalities as there are attorneys, it is difficult to generalize about rules to follow when working with attorneys. After you are on the job long enough to get to know the attorneys for whom you work, you will be the best judge of how to work with them. However, if you are just starting out in a new position and have never worked in a law firm environment before, here are some general rules to follow until you get your bearings.

COURTESY AND PROFESSIONALISM

When you begin working for an attorney, the attorney will assess your ability to meet with other people, especially his or her clients. It is important that your manner remain courteous and professional. Be careful to use proper grammar, dress appropriately, and speak clearly.

BE PREPARED WHEN ASKING QUESTIONS

Attorneys are taught to analyze facts. If you are working with an attorney on a file and you have a question, ask! Before you ask your question, however, review the situation carefully to be sure that you are aware of all the facts. Before the attorney can answer your question, he or she will need to know all the circumstances surrounding the issue.

BE ASSERTIVE WHEN NECESSARY

Busy attorneys can at times be very focused on their work. If you have a question or need to talk about something, it may take persistence to get the attorney's full attention. However, if there is a problem that the attorney must know about, it is up to you to be assertive enough to get the message across.

If you have performed research and come to a conclusion, do not be intimidated if the attorney starts to question you about your conclusion. Be assertive. Possibly the attorney is just playing devil's advocate and wants to make certain that you are sure of yourself and your position.

Being assertive also means knowing when to say no. If an attorney gives you an assignment and asks for it tomorrow morning, do not say yes unless you can have it ready by tomorrow morning. If you have other assignments that will prevent you from completing the task on time, say so by explaining the situation to the attorney. He or she can give you a different due date or give the assignment to someone else who has more time. Do not get caught in a power struggle. When an attorney wants you to give priority to his or her assignment, in preference to an assignment you have already received, ask him or her to discuss it with the other attorney and let the two of them come to an agreement.

COMMUNICATE

One of the most important rules in dealing with attorneys and the practice of law is to communicate. When you are working on a file with a particular attorney, be sure to let him or her know of all developments. The type of communication you use will be determined by the type of message you are sending. If you just need to update an attorney as to routine progress on a file, perhaps you can combine it with the progress or status of other files and send a progress report to save the attorney's time. When using a memo to communicate important facts to an attorney, you may want to follow up by mentioning it to him or her a few days later to make sure the memo was received and reviewed. If, however, there is an emergency, you will need to speak face-to-face as soon as possible—even if it means locating an attorney at a meeting.

Honesty is another important part of communication, including admitting to any mistakes you may make. In almost every instance, any mistake you make is best corrected by admitting it and looking for alternative solutions as soon as possible. Trying to cover up the mistake may only cause problems to escalate.

Paralegal Employers

"We don't work for each other, we work with each other."

STANLEY C. GAULT

INTRODUCTION

Although most paralegals work in private law firms, law firms are not the only employers of paralegals. Corporations and government agencies, as well as law firms of all sizes, employ paralegals. In addition, a growing number of paralegals work in less traditional settings such as for other types of businesses, for themselves, or for temporary agencies (Figure 2–1).

As a paralegal, the type of employer you choose to work for will have a significant impact on your career. It will impact your working conditions and environment, your pay, and the types of responsibilities assigned to you. This chapter examines the working environment you may expect from each major type of employer, as well as the pros and cons of working for law firms, corporations, government offices, temporary agencies, and yourself.

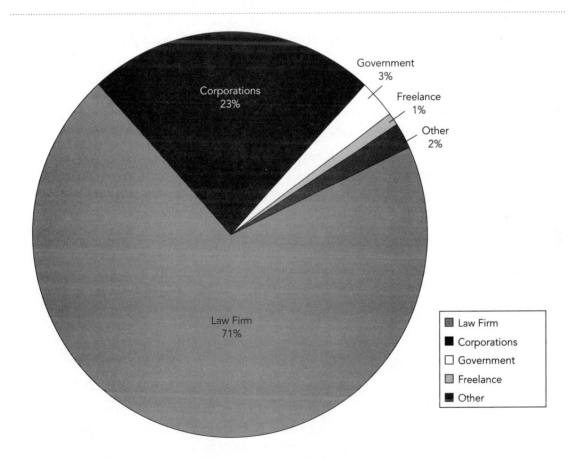

FIGURE 2–1
*Paralegal employers (*From the 1997 NFPA Paralegal Compensation and Benefits Report)

Paralegal Profile

PROFILE ON JOHN OSBORN

The most interesting part of my job is my clients. The client base is out of this world. Some clients are Silicon Valley entrepreneurs, CEOs in business, or just well-established socialites in San Francisco. I get a glimpse of my clients' personal lives, whether preparing an estate plan or dealing with a death in the family.
It is never boring!

Name and Location:	John Osborn, San Francisco, California
Title:	Senior Paralegal
Specialty:	Tax, Estate Planning, Probate, and Nonprofit Law
Education:	Some College. Paralegal Certificate from George Washington University in Washington, D.C.
Experience:	8 Years

John Osborn is an active, high-profile paralegal. He has served as a director on the board of various paralegal associations since becoming a paralegal, and he is now president of the San Francisco Paralegal Association.

John currently works for a large San Francisco law firm that employs over 400 attorneys and 150 paralegals. John's work involves researching, analyzing, and presenting estate plans to meet the needs of the firm's clients. He is responsible for preparing numerous types of documents, including wills, trust agreements, and partnership and limited liability company agreements. John assists clients with their estate planning and tax planning needs by forming family limited partnerships, limited liability companies, and entities for philanthropy, including public, private, and supporting foundations. His work in the probate area includes the preparation of all forms of estate tax returns, probate forms, and forms for the transfer of property. In addition, he works directly with clients in identifying, analyzing, and gathering estate assets, as well as arranging for the appraisal of estate assets.

John likes the diversity of his position, and he enjoys his co-workers and clients. John feels that although the members of his team possess different titles and different strengths, they work well together. John's work with clients often gives him the opportunity to meet with and help dynamic and interesting individuals who are on the cutting edge of technology.

One of the most interesting projects John has worked on is the formation and operation of a nonprofit entity dealing with emerging technology-based and new media art. John helped to establish a nonprofit organization that conducts activities that promote projects, institutions, and individuals, as well as providing an international forum for the discussion of this art medium.

Although John enjoys his position, like many paralegals, he finds time-keeping and interruptions to be among his greatest frustrations. Being cost-effective for the firm's clients can also be a challenge at times—often due to circumstances beyond his control.

John's advice to paralegal students:

Do not be afraid. You will find a job as a paralegal. You will get juicy projects after you have paid your dues. Do not quit or give up. Start with what you know. Believe in yourself. Do your best and take pride in your work product. Learn, learn, and learn it again. I believe everyone learns on the job. You learn how different firms and attorneys operate and how they interpret the law. I am still continuing to learn. As part of our representation of clients, we set up entities for philanthropy, including public, private, and supporting nonprofit organizations. I have become quite versed in the organizational process and continued operation of such entities. I learned almost all of this on the job.

LAW FIRMS

In a 1997 survey of paralegals by the National Federation of Paralegal Associations (NFPA), more than 71 percent of the respondents indicated that they work in private law firms.[1] Nearly all law firms with more than 100 attorneys employ paralegals. More than 60 percent of law firms with between 4 and 10 attorneys employ paralegals, and nearly 30 percent of all firms with 1 to 3 attorneys employ paralegals.[2] Paralegals who work in law firms of any size have some common ground in their environment. The personnel employed in a law firm are unique to the setting, and so are the billing requirements that usually are imposed on paralegals.

LAW FIRM PERSONNEL

The personnel of a law firm depends, in large part, on the size and structure of the firm. An individual attorney in solo law practice is referred to as a **sole practitioner.** Law firms with more than one attorney are owned and headed by the **partners** or **shareholders** of the firm. Nonattorneys may not have an ownership interest in law firms. Reporting to the partners or shareholders are attorneys within the firm who do not have an ownership stake,

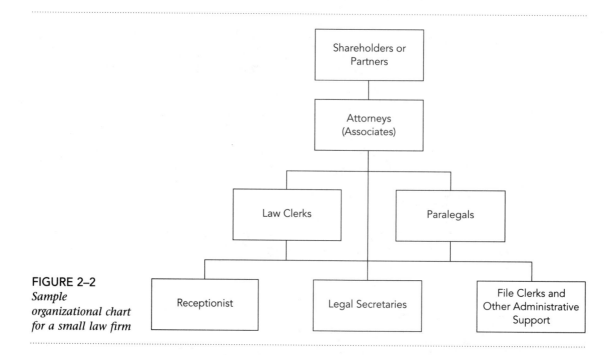

FIGURE 2–2
Sample organizational chart for a small law firm

usually referred to as the firm's **associates.** If the firm employs law students who work on a part-time basis while finishing their education, those employees are referred to as **law clerks.** In addition to law clerks and paralegals, the nonattorney personnel of law firms usually include the **law office administrator,** paralegal manager, and additional administrative and clerical staff, including **legal secretaries,** word processors, receptionists, records managers and file clerks (Figure 2–2).

ETHICAL CONSIDERATION

The Rules of Ethics for attorneys restrict law firm ownership to attorneys. Nonattorneys may not have an ownership interest in a law firm.

Larger law firms may have several more classifications and titles for their employees. They may have additional classes of attorneys, such as junior partners and senior associates. They also may have an entire administrative staff instead of just a law office administrator. The clerical staff may include messengers and data entry personnel (Figure 2–3).

Paralegals. If you are considering a position in a law firm, it is helpful to know where paralegals typically fit in the law firm's environment. Certain generalizations can be made about a law firm's paralegals, including who paralegals report to, who paralegals have authority to delegate to,

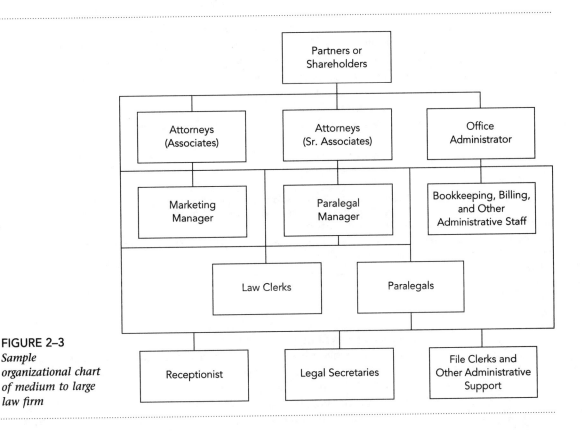

FIGURE 2–3
Sample organizational chart of medium to large law firm

how much time paralegals are expected to spend in the office, and what type of office space is assigned to paralegals.

The number of paralegals in a firm depends on the size of the firm and the nature of the practice. Paralegals may be departmentalized in terms of specialty, or they may all make up the "paralegal department" of a firm.

Most paralegals report to one or more attorneys within the law firm, as well as the law office administrator or the paralegal manager (if there is one). This means that you may be required to answer to several different individuals within the firm. To avoid conflicts between you and the individuals you report to, it will be important for you always to get deadlines on each project you are assigned. If your workload will not allow you to meet a deadline, say so at once, and ask the two assigning attorneys to place a priority on their work to resolve the conflict (Figure 2–4).

You can expect to have the authority to delegate work to legal secretaries, file clerks, and other individuals who offer clerical assistance in the office, such as messengers and the receptionist. Paralegals are rarely assigned their own legal secretary. More often, they share a secretary with one or more associates or partners of the law firm and are expected to complete some of their own secretarial tasks. This is becoming more and more common with the increasing use of computers in the law firm. Whereas in the

- Be sure that you and the attorney agree on a realistic due date for the assignment.
- Ask questions about any aspects of the assignment that are unclear to you.
- Be sure to find out who should be billed for your time.
- Always take notes when an attorney is giving you an assignment. Keep the notes with the file while you are working on it.
- If you need additional resources to complete your assignment efficiently and on time, say so.
- Organize your questions while you are working so you can ask the attorney all the pertinent questions at one or two meetings, instead of constantly asking the attorney questions.
- When working on longer assignments, keep the attorney apprised of your progress. Progress reports in memo format are usually sufficient when the assignment is progressing as expected.
- Volunteer to perform any related tasks that may present themselves and to tie up any loose ends to your assignment.

FIGURE 2–4

Tips on taking assignments from attorneys

past a secretary was needed to type each piece of correspondence that left the law office, now it is more common for paralegals and attorneys to compose short correspondences on their own computers and give them to their secretary for copying, mailing, and filing.

Full-time paralegals usually are required to spend at least 40 hours per week in the office, although additional time may be required to meet deadlines and sometimes to meet billable hour requirements. Most paralegals report that they work in excess of normal working hours *at least* once per week.[3] Most of your day likely will be spent in the office working on client files. You will probably have regular contact with your firm's clients and may be invited to attend client meetings or asked to conduct them. Some of your assigned tasks may take you out of the office to file documents at the courthouse or other government offices, to attend meetings at a client's home or office, to attend closings, or to assist an attorney in court.

Your assigned office space will depend, in large part, on the size and location of your firm. Most paralegals who work in law firms have their own small but private offices; in firms where office space is at a premium, paralegals may share offices or be located in modular office space.

The paralegal staff of larger law firms is often divided into classifications, such as Paralegal (for newer paralegals), Paralegal I (for paralegals with at least two years of experience who have shown competence) and Paralegal II (for paralegals with more than five years of experience who have shown a superior level of competence). These individuals also may be referred to as Senior Paralegals.

The following is a brief description of several of the positions that may be held by individuals you will encounter and work with in a law firm.

The Law Firm Partners or Shareholders. Depending on whether the law firm is a **professional corporation,** a **professional limited liability company,** or a **partnership,** the firm's *shareholders* or *partners* are the attorneys who own the law firm. Sole practitioners are the only owners of their firms, but very large law firms may have dozens of partners or shareholders. The exact role played by the partners or shareholders will depend on the size and focus of the law firm. In larger law firms, several partners or shareholders may constitute an executive committee. One of the partners may be designated as the managing partner to work with the office administrator and the executive committee to handle office administrative matters.

In many large firms, partners or shareholders devote the majority of their time to speaking engagements and courting new clients. Their actual practice of law and work on client files is reserved for the largest, most important cases or matters. In law firms where this is so, paralegals may have little involvement with the firm's partners or shareholders. Most of their contact will be with the firm's associates who actually oversee the majority of work on client files.

Law firms may also have attorneys who are "of counsel." Attorneys of counsel are usually semi-retired partners or shareholders who have maintained their contacts with the firm and work on a part-time basis.

The Law Firm Associates. Attorneys who do not have an ownership interest in a law firm generally are referred to as the firm's associates. These individuals typically are hired with the promise of becoming a partner or shareholder of the firm if their performance is adequate, within a set number of years. There usually is no guarantee that an associate will be invited to become a partner or shareholder. It is a goal that associates are constantly seeking to achieve.

The associates in a law firm usually have responsibility for files and delegate assignments to the paralegals in the firm. Associates in large law firms often are required to bill a very high number of hours per year, and they work under a certain amount of pressure from the partners to whom they report. Most associates are very appreciative of the efforts paralegals make to assist them, as long as the work is done correctly and on time. Remember, if you are a paralegal working with an associate on a particular file, the associate ultimately will be responsible for your work. Your supervising attorneys have a legal, ethical, and moral obligation to supervise your work.

ETHICAL CONSIDERATION

Attorneys have an ethical duty to supervise the work and ethical conduct of their nonattorney assistants.

New associates often rely on the more experienced paralegals in the firm to "show them the ropes." Although attorneys may come out of law school with a superior theoretical knowledge of the law, their knowledge of procedure and just exactly where things are and how to get things done may be inferior to the paralegal's. Most new associates appreciate any assistance in these matters that paralegals can give them.

Law Clerks. Law clerks are law students who work in a firm to gain experience before graduating law school or passing the bar exam. Law clerks usually are hired for summer positions and part-time positions during the school year, often with the aim of being hired as associates after graduating and passing the bar exam. The utilization of law clerks varies significantly from firm to firm. In most firms, law clerks' work involves intensive legal research and writing. Paralegals and law clerks may be assigned to work together on certain projects, especially those involving legal research. Law clerks are seldom assigned client files, and they rarely meet with clients.

Case Assistants. Case assistants, sometimes called *paralegal assistants,* are relative newcomers to the law office. They are unique to large law firms and firms that specialize in complex litigation. Case assistants help paralegals with the clerical tasks associated with large cases, including document organization and indexing. Many of these tasks are done by computer with specialized software. At times new paralegals will begin their careers as case assistants to get the experience needed to qualify for paralegal positions.

The Law Office Administrator. The position of the law office administrator or law office manager will depend on the size and management structure of the law firm. In most small to medium-size firms, the office administrator is responsible for all administrative functions of the law firm, including personnel, marketing, and budgeting. Paralegals typically report to the office administrator on all personnel matters and questions concerning office policy. The office administrator reports to the partners or shareholders of the firm, the managing partner, or the executive committee. The law office administrator is responsible for overseeing the entire nonattorney staff of the law firm. At times, the associates of a law firm also report to the law office administrator on certain matters.

Paralegal Manager. Larger law firms that employ several paralegals often have a paralegal manager on staff. Paralegal managers are responsible for coordinating the assignments of the paralegals in their departments and, at times, for acting as liaisons between the paralegals and the attorneys when problems arise. Paralegal managers may report to the law office administrator, directly to the law firm's partners or shareholders, to the managing partner, or to the management or executive committee.

The duties of a paralegal manager may include:

1. Hiring and supervising paralegal personnel
2. Delegating assignments and managing the work flow to the paralegals within a firm
3. Scheduling and conducting meetings of the paralegal personnel within a firm
4. Acting as liaison between the paralegals and the attorneys within a law firm
5. Designing and implementing policies and systems for the paralegal personnel within a law firm

The Law Office Librarian. Every law office has some type of law library, and every law library has at least one individual who performs the functions of a law librarian. A knowledgeable law librarian can be a valuable asset to all law firm personnel. If you are routinely assigned research projects, chances are you will get to know the librarian very well. Do not be afraid to ask for help from the librarian when you need it. Law librarians are usually very knowledgeable and willing to help. You can repay the favor to the librarian by carefully following all procedures for using the law firm library.

In many small- to medium-sized law firms, no actual librarian is employed, and the task of library maintenance falls to the firm's paralegals. In that event, it will be especially important for you to become familiar with the law firm library as soon as possible so that you can assist with library maintenance if you are asked to do so.

Increasingly, law librarians are becoming handlers and managers of information, rather than handlers of books. In many firms, the law librarians offer training and assistance with all types of research, including research performed on-line and with CD-ROM technology.

Information Technology Manager. Depending on the size of the law firm, and the extent of the technology used in the office, the firm may employ an Information Technology Manager (IT manager). In larger firms, the IT manager may have several individuals to assist him or her with various aspects of this position. This person is generally responsible for the hardware and software technology in the office and for seeing that the computers are functioning properly. When something malfunctions, the IT manager (or someone on his or her staff in larger firms) will be responsible for correcting the problem or for calling in other technical experts to see that the problem is corrected.

The IT manager may also be responsible for researching and recommending new hardware and software options for the law firm.

Other Administrative Staff. Larger law firms may employ several additional administrative staff members, including a personnel manager, marketing manager, billing manager, and accountants. These individuals—who may even have staff of their own—perform some of the individual functions performed by the office administrator in smaller firms. For example, in a law firm with 20 attorneys, the office administrator may have responsibility for hiring paralegals. He or she may place an ad in the paper or contact employment agencies, review resumes, screen candidates, and make recommendations to the attorneys who will be responsible for the paralegal's work. In a law firm of 200 attorneys, the office administrator would not have the time to perform all the functions of hiring all the paralegals required to staff the firm. This task would likely fall to a personnel manager and his or her staff.

Legal Secretaries. Never underestimate the importance of a good legal secretary. If you are starting a new position within a law firm, a knowledgeable, experienced legal secretary can be an invaluable asset. He or she can help to familiarize you with office procedures, the firm's files and clients, and the basic procedures followed in preparing legal documents.

Typically, paralegals do not have their own personal legal secretaries but instead perform some of their own secretarial duties and share the services of a secretary with one or more other paralegals and/or associates. With the increased use of technology in the law firm, it is not uncommon to see as many as five attorneys and paralegals sharing the services of one legal secretary. Sharing a secretary with a busy attorney can be challenging to the paralegal when both the paralegal and the attorney have deadlines to meet and secretarial work to be done. Try to be courteous by giving your secretary as much time as possible to complete assignments. Your secretary may be responsible for typing your correspondence and certain legal documents, or for sending them through the firm's word processing department. He or she also may be responsible for taking your phone calls when you are out of the office or otherwise unavailable.

Other Clerical Staff. Most law firms employ either a few or several other individuals in various clerical capacities. These individuals may include word processors, messengers, receptionists, file clerks, billing clerks, and data processors. As a paralegal in a law firm, you and your secretary both will require the services of these individuals regularly. Every clerical employee has certain procedures to follow. To get optimum assistance from the clerical employees in your firm, you should make certain you are aware of the firm's clerical procedures and follow them as closely as possible. For example, the billing clerk will have a deadline for turning in your timesheets. Meeting that deadline will ensure that the billing clerk does not need to look for you every billing cycle, and that you do not hold up the billing for the law firm. File clerks will have certain procedures for requesting files. Following these procedures carefully whenever possible may pay off in added assistance from the file clerk when you need a file that has been lost or when you need a file immediately.

BILLING REQUIREMENTS

The vast majority of law firms do most of their billing based on time spent by attorneys and paralegals on each client's file. Attorneys and paralegals have set billing rates, and clients are billed accordingly. Billing rates usually are based on the market and the attorney's or paralegal's experience and level of expertise. The average hourly partner rates at law firms is between $180 and $247. For associates, the average hourly rate is from $134 to $173.[4] The average rate for paralegals is between $40 and $80 per hour. The highest rates tend to be billed at the large law firms. It is important to a law firm's bottom line that all individuals with billing responsibility, including paralegals, closely track their **billable hours** and meet their set requirements for annual billable hours.

Paralegals who work in law firms are required to account for time spent on client matters, as well as work a requisite number of billable hours (Figure 2–5). Billable hours are hours and fractions of hours that are spent working on a client's file that will later be billed to that client. In addition to their bill-

1. Most firms require that you track your time in six-minute intervals (one tenth of an hour).
2. Budget your time carefully starting with a determination of your annual billable hour requirements.
3. Do not forget to allow time for vacations and holidays.
4. Keep copies of all time sheets.
5. Do not procrastinate when it comes to recording your time. You will be surprised how much you may forget after several interruptions.
6. Record all of your billable hours. Whether you have spent too much time on a certain matter is for the billing attorney to decide.
7. Always be honest.
8. Manage your time carefully.

FIGURE 2–5

Tips for timekeeping

able hours, paralegals are usually assigned several administrative responsibilities that are considered nonbillable. Nonbillable time includes time spent on training, continuing education, marketing, form file maintenance, billing, miscellaneous administrative matters, pro bono work, and personal matters.

Approximately 88 percent of all paralegals who work in law firms are required to bill their time (Figures 2–6 and 2–7). According to one survey, the average number of hours billed by paralegals in 1997 was 1,413, or approximately 6 1/2 hours per working day with 2 weeks vacation per year.[5] The number of billable hours required of the paralegal tends to be tied to the paralegal's salary. In a recent survey by the NFPA, it was found that paralegals who had targeted billable hours of between 500 and 750 hours per year had an average salary of $24,777. Paralegals who had targeted billable hours of 2,001 or more hours per year had an average base salary of $35,813.[6] For information on the latest trends in billing requirements for paralegals, see the companion Web site to this text at **www.westlegalstudies.com.**

Many law firms tie annual bonuses to the paralegal's meeting or exceeding his or her billable hour goal. In some firms, pay raises are at risk if paralegals do not meet or exceed their billing goals. Paralegals may even expect a decrease in pay for falling below the norm.

FIGURE 2–6
How an experienced paralegal profits a law firm

Number of Hours Billed Annually	1,500
Hourly Billing Rate	$ 80
Annual Income from Hours Billed	$120,000
Paralegal's Annual Salary	($40,000)
Payroll Taxes and Benefits (25% of Salary)	($10,000)
Office and Clerical Overhead	($25,000)
Profit to the Law Firm	$45,000

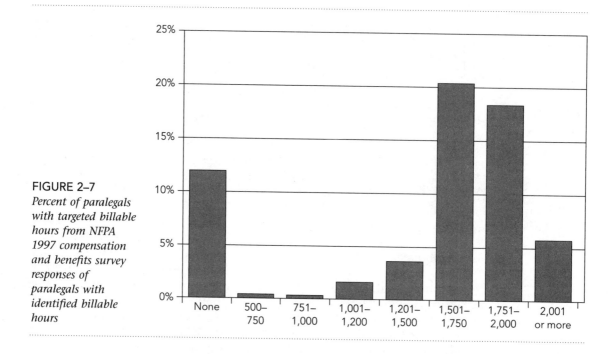

FIGURE 2–7
Percent of paralegals with targeted billable hours from NFPA 1997 compensation and benefits survey responses of paralegals with identified billable hours

THE LARGE LAW FIRM

Large law firms employ more paralegals than any other category of employer. Large law firms are the most likely to have paralegal departments and to have paralegals who specialize in certain areas of law.

According to recent surveys, paralegals who work in large law firms earn significantly more than their counterparts in smaller firms. The *Legal Assistant Today* 1998-99 Salary Survey reported that the average compensation for paralegals working for sole proprietors was $32,212. The average salary of paralegals working for firms with 11 to 25 attorneys was $37,727, and the average salary of paralegals working for firms with more than 100 attorneys was $41,232. When considering this data, you must keep in mind that most larger firms are located in large metropolitan areas where salaries and the cost of living tend to be higher.

In addition to enjoying better pay and benefits, some paralegals find large law firms to be more exciting, challenging, and rewarding. Large law firms offer vast resources in comparison to smaller firms, including extensive law libraries, research materials, and additional support staff that are unavailable in smaller firms. Large law firms usually have more clerical personnel to whom paralegals may delegate clerical and nonbillable tasks.

However, paralegals in large law firms may have to meet demanding billing requirements that commit them to long hours of hard work. Probably the most common complaint of paralegals in large law firms is that their employers have unreasonably high billable hour expectations.

FIGURE 2–8
Advantages and disadvantages of working for a large law firm

ADVANTAGES	DISADVANTAGES
• Higher pay is common • Better benefits usually are offered • Vast resources of the law firm • Additional clerical assistance • Exciting and fast-paced atmosphere	• High billable hour requirements • Overspecialization • Stressful working conditions • Extensive overtime may be required

Many paralegals complain that they are assigned a number of tasks of a more clerical nature that are not considered billable work, yet they are expected to put in billable hours comparable to the associates in the firm (Figure 2–8).

According to a recent survey, the median annual billable hours worked for paralegals in a small firm (fewer than nine attorneys) was 1,319 hours per year compared with 1,401 hours per year for paralegals in firms of 75 or more attorneys.[7] In comparison, associates in firms with fewer than nine attorneys billed an average of 1,693 hours and associates in firms of 75 or more attorneys billed an average 1,864 hours. It is not unusual for the larger firms in large metropolitan areas to require both their paralegals and associates to bill in excess of 2000 hours per year.

THE SMALL OR MEDIUM-SIZED LAW FIRM

Paralegals in the smaller or medium-sized law firm often work more closely with the attorneys. Unlike their counterparts in large law firms, paralegals in smaller firms usually report directly to the attorneys of the firm, with no paralegal manager as an intermediary. In small law firms with only one or two paralegals, paralegals report to certain attorneys within the firm or handle certain types of matters with which the attorneys need assistance.

One reason many paralegals prefer small law firms is that, compared with most large law firms, smaller law firms usually do not have high billing requirements that necessitate long work hours. In addition, many paralegals feel that smaller law firms offer a more congenial, less stressful working atmosphere and a chance to experience working in more than just one area of law. Paralegals who work for small firms often experience more variety in their work and less specialization. They may also have more client contact and more opportunities to work closely with the firm's partners and other senior attorneys.

One disadvantage, however, is that small firms are often unable to offer salaries and benefits competitive with those of large law firms (Figure 2–9).

Although law firms all have many common elements, it is important to realize that each law firm has its own distinct "personality" and culture. The success or failure of your first paralegal position can depend on the right match between your personality and expectations and the personality and expectations of your law firm employer.

FIGURE 2–9
*Advantages and
disadvantages of
working in a small
law firm*

ADVANTAGES	DISADVANTAGES
• Lower billing requirements are common • More variety in work • More congenial, relaxed • working atmosphere	• Lower salaries and fewer benefits are common • Fewer resources are available • May be required to do more clerical work

CORPORATE EMPLOYERS

In addition to law firms and governmental agencies, corporate law departments are a major employer of paralegals. Roughly 20 percent of all paralegals work in corporate law departments. Corporate law departments tend to have low turnover, and paralegals working within corporations generally report high job satisfaction.

THE CORPORATE LAW DEPARTMENT

The exact role of the paralegal in the corporate law department will depend, in large part, on the role of the attorneys to whom the paralegal reports. In some corporations, the resources of the law department are used mainly as a resource for in-house advice and to coordinate and supervise the work of outside counsel, where the bulk of the legal services are performed. In other corporations, the attorneys have a much more *hands on* role, and little work is delegated to outside counsel. Obviously, in corporations where most of the work is done in-house, paralegals will have a much more involved role. In a corporate law department, the attorney's client is the corporation and the several departments or divisions within the corporation.

Paralegals may specialize within a law department just as they do within a law firm. For example, it is not uncommon for a law department to have several sub-departments, including:

- Litigation Department
- Securities Department
- Corporate Department
- Employee Benefits Department
- Intellectual Property Department
- Contracts Department
- Mergers and Acquisitions Department

As a paralegal in a corporate law department, you will probably report to one or more attorneys in the department in which you work, and possibly a senior paralegal or a paralegal manager. Depending on your exact responsibilities, you may also work closely with individuals in other departments (Figure 2–10). For example, if you work in the intellectual property

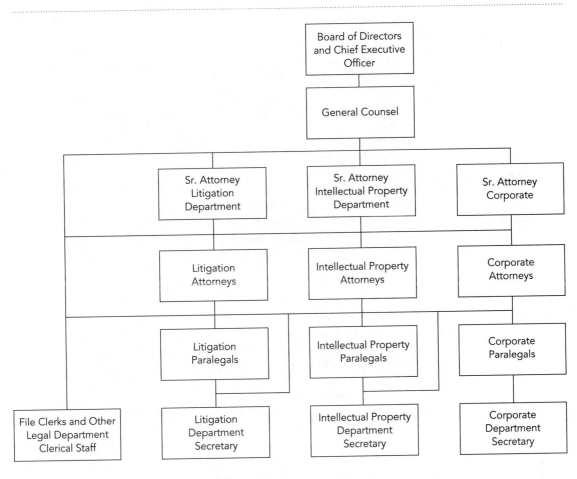

FIGURE 2–10
Sample legal department organizational chart

division of the law department, you may find yourself working closely with individuals from the product development department of the corporation.

There will probably be a legal secretary to assist you, although you may be required to share your secretary with the attorneys you report to and do some of your own secretarial work when necessary.

There are usually two or three levels of paralegal positions in a corporate legal department, such as associate paralegal (0 to 2 years experience), paralegal (2 to 5 years experience) and senior paralegal (more than 5 years experience). As paralegals advance through the levels, they experience an increase in pay and responsibilities.

Duties of paralegals within a corporate law department vary greatly depending on the circumstances and the paralegal's specialty. Some of the more important functions performed by paralegals within a corporate law department include:

- Administrative duties, such as acting as liaison between the in-house attorneys and outside counsel
- Procedural responsibilities, such as filings with governmental agencies on behalf of the corporation or incorporating subsidiaries
- Reviewing and preparing legal documents
- Performing legal and factual research
- Subsidiary maintenance
- Shareholder relations

Paralegals in a corporate law department usually have small private offices, but they may be assigned to cubicles if space is limited.

If you work in a corporate law department, you are an employee of the corporation. As such, you will have dealings with individuals throughout the corporation. You may have dealings with the personnel department and payroll department on a regular basis. Most of your personal contact will be with the other members of the legal department. The following is a brief description of the titles of individuals you are likely to be working with in a corporate law department:

General Counsel. The **general counsel** is the lead attorney in the corporate law department. The general counsel has the primary responsibility for all legal affairs of the corporation, including advising the board of directors and officers of the corporation on legal matters. All attorneys report to the general counsel, who may be an officer of the corporation.

Often, the general counsel will serve in the capacity of corporate secretary of the corporation. The corporate secretary is an officer of the corporation and is required to approve and sign numerous corporate documents, including stock certificates, bylaws, and corporate minutes. The corporate secretary is also responsible for holding annual meetings of the directors and shareholders of the corporation.

Senior Attorney. Senior attorneys are experienced attorneys who have either been with the corporation for a number of years, or have been hired from a law firm or other corporation with a number of years of experience. Senior attorneys often head the several divisions of the law department, and the other attorneys in that department report to the senior attorney.

Attorney. Attorneys in the law department report to either a senior attorney in their department or they report directly to the general counsel of the corporation.

Law Clerk. Similar to law firms, corporate law departments often employ law students to assist with legal research and similar functions in the law department. The law clerks usually report to the attorneys in the legal department, and they may be assigned to work closely with paralegals on certain projects.

Paralegal Manager. Some larger law departments have paralegal managers to assist with administrative functions and the utilization of the paralegals in the law department. Other law departments have senior paralegals who hold the paralegal meetings and act as liaison between the paralegals in the department and the attorneys.

Other Administrative Personnel. In addition, several other administrative personnel may be working within the corporate law department, including a law librarian and an information technology manager. The function of the law librarian will be similar to that of a law librarian in a law firm. The information technology manager responsible for the technology-related functions in a corporate law department may also have responsibility for functions within other departments or even the entire corporation, depending on its size.

Legal Secretary. The secretaries in a law department may be assigned to a division of the law department or to one or more attorneys and paralegals. They will be responsible for much of the routine correspondence, handling phone calls, scheduling appointments, and other administrative tasks.

File Clerk and Other Clerical Personnel. In the law department of a large corporation, where the attorneys and paralegals often need files from storage as well as files from other departments, the law department's file clerk can have a lot of responsibility. Each law department typically has procedures in place for requesting files from the file clerk and for filing materials away. It will be important for you to become familiar with these procedures as soon as possible and to get acquainted with the file clerk.

Much like a law firm, a corporate law department may support any number of clerical employees, including messengers, receptionists, and word processing staff.

Advantages and Disadvantages of Working for a Corporate Law Department. Some of the reasons for high job satisfaction among paralegals in corporate law departments are that they typically are offered better pay and benefits than paralegals in many law firms. In addition, paralegals within a corporate law department do not have billing requirements and are not usually required to put in much overtime. Finally, there may be more advancement opportunities for paralegals employed by corporate legal departments. Paralegals may have the opportunity to advance through several levels of paralegal positions within the legal department, and they have the opportunity to learn the workings of the business of the corporation and advance into other departments, such as compliance, marketing, or personnel.

Even with all the advantages offered by corporations, many paralegals would not give up the fast pace and excitement unique to law firms. Paralegals within corporate law departments may be expected to perform administrative functions not required of paralegals within law firms and may be more prone to frustrations caused by working within a large bureaucracy (Figure 2–11).

NONPROFIT CORPORATIONS

A growing number of paralegals are finding employment with nonprofit corporations. Nonprofit corporations are a type of corporation formed for

FIGURE 2–11
Advantages and disadvantages of working for a corporate law department

ADVANTAGES	DISADVANTAGES
• No billing requirements • Better pay than most law firms • Better benefits than most law firms • Less overtime required than most law firms • More advancement opportunities	• Work may be more specialized and less interesting • May have more duties of an administrative nature • May suffer frustrations from working for a large bureaucracy

specific reasons, such as charitable, civic, educational, and religious purposes. The work of paralegals who work for nonprofit corporations closely resembles the work of paralegals who work for ordinary business corporations, with a couple of exceptions. Many paralegals who work for nonprofit corporations must be familiar with state and federal requirements specifically for nonprofit corporations, and they must be familiar with procedures for applying for and retaining tax exempt status.

In many nonprofit corporations, the atmosphere is more relaxed and informal. There may also be more of an emphasis on cost containment, and paralegal salaries may not be as high. Regardless, many paralegals who work for charitable nonprofit organizations report that they find their work very rewarding.

GOVERNMENT EMPLOYERS

Thousands of paralegals are employed in all levels of government, including federal, state, and local. These paralegals work for agencies that represent the public. Their clients are the citizens in their jurisdiction.

FEDERAL GOVERNMENT

In a recent survey by the National Federation of Paralegal Associations, only 1 percent of the respondents indicated that they work for the federal government.[8] However, individuals with a paralegal education or background may be hired for several law-related positions with titles other than paralegal. The federal government reports that it has more than 300,000 law-related positions for which paralegals may be qualified and that the number of paralegals in the federal government has increased more than 30 percent since 1986. The following are some of the reasons for the strong growth of the number of paralegals in the federal government:[9]

- The expanding professionalism in the field, due to more exacting and standardized educational and credentialing requirements
- The explosion of law-related concerns and responsibilities at all levels of the workplace and throughout society

- The need for individuals with legal or quasi-legal training and expertise to handle these responsibilities
- Increasing employer awareness that paralegals are able to perform many legal tasks at lower costs than lawyers

Paralegals who work for the federal government generally are well paid and have great benefits. For example, new federal employees earn 13 days of vacation each year and four weeks after only three years of service. This is in addition to the 10 paid holidays per year that federal employees receive. Paralegals who work for the federal government also receive low-cost health and life insurance, as well as fantastic pension benefits.

On the down side, many paralegals who work for the federal government find it frustrating to be part of such a huge bureaucracy where simple decisions and minor changes may have to go through several layers of red tape for approval (Figure 2–12).

Paralegals qualify for a number of different types of positions, with varying titles, within the federal government (Figure 2–13). Some of these titles include Environmental Protection Specialist, Foreign Law Specialist, Intelligence Analyst, Civil Rights Analyst, Personnel Management Specialist, Paralegal Specialist, and Legal Clerk and Technician. The positions most closely related to typical paralegal positions are in the Paralegal Specialist Series, which starts at a level GS-9, with a salary range between $30,106 and $39,140. The description of the *0950* Paralegal Specialist Series is as follows.[10]

This series includes positions that involve paralegal work not requiring professional legal competence (not requiring a law degree) where such work is of a type not classifiable in some other series. The work requires discretion and independent judgment in the application of specialized knowledge of particular laws, regulations, precedents or agency practices based thereon. The work includes such activities as (a) legal research; analyzing legal decisions, opinions, rulings, memoranda, and other legal material; selecting principles of law; and preparing digests of the points of law involved; (b) selecting, assembling, summarizing, and compiling substantive information on statutes, treaties, contracts, other legal instruments, and specific legal subjects; (c) case preparation for civil litigation, criminal law proceedings or agency hearings, including the collection, analysis, and evaluation of evidence, such as fraud and fraudulent, and other irregular activities or violations of laws; (d) analyzing facts and legal questions represented by personnel administering specific federal laws, answering the questions where they have been settled by interpretations of applicable legal provisions, regulations, precedents, and agency policy, and in some instances preparing informative and instructional material for general use; (e) adjudicating applications or cases on the basis of pertinent laws, regulations, policies and precedent decisions; or (f) performing other paralegal duties. Work in this series may or may not be performed under the direction of a lawyer.

PROS

Good Pay. Federal salaries for paralegal professions are competitive with any other employer. In fact, they are superior to the salaries offered by state and local governments and are better than many private sector employers. According to the latest U.S. Government statistics, the average annual salary for paralegals who worked for the federal government was almost 25 percent higher than the average annual salary in the private sector. One of the chief reasons for this is that private industry often employs paralegal professionals in a quasi-clerical capacity. The U.S. Government does not. Paralegals in the U.S. Government do paralegal work, period.

Recognition of Professional Credentials. Since the federal government has established fairly strict hiring criteria for paralegals, there is never any question about professional status, in contrast to what often happens in the private sector. Federal paralegal employees are always treated as professionals, never as clerical help.

Excellent Fringe Benefits. New federal employees earn 13 days of paid vacation (called annual leave) each year and four weeks after only three years of service. In addition, there are 10 paid federal holidays each year. Federal employees and their families are able to select from a variety of low-cost health insurance and life insurance policies, and are allowed to change health coverage during an annual "open season" without any penalties, such as pre-existing condition exclusions, that are common in the private sector. Federal pensions are quite high in comparison to private sector plans, and vesting usually occurs in a shorter period of time. In addition, the U.S. Government is in the forefront of employers who provide child care facilities for employees. Many federal offices now offer such facilities on site.

Job Security. There is no more permanent organization than the U.S. Government. It will not go out of business. While job security in specific agencies or with respect to specific functions is not as certain as it was several years ago, it is still better than in many parts of the private sector. When there is a layoff (called a reduction-in-force), the government generally seeks to locate other positions within the federal service for its threatened workers. However, this rarely happens with a growth occupation such as the paralegal profession.

Civil Service Protection. A variety of rigorously enforced laws and regulations ensure equal opportunity for all individuals seeking federal employment and require fair, nondiscriminatory treatment for each member of the federal workforce. No other employees are covered by anything approaching the matrix of legal protections surrounding career civil servants. As a result, there are superior job opportunities for women, minorities, and disabled job applicants, as well as superior protective mechanisms available should you be threatened with a job loss for any reason.

Job Mobility. Because the federal government is so large and far-flung, there are vast opportunities to move from position –to position, agency –to agency and place –to place. According to statistics compiled by the U.S. Office of Personnel Management, federal paralegal employment is becoming more decentralized. Now almost 60 percent of the paralegals employed by the U.S. Government work in federal facilities outside of the Washington, D.C. metropolitan area. Moreover, a federal employee can make such moves without losing seniority or benefits.

The Nature of the Work. Job satisfaction for paralegal professions is high in the U.S. Government. The level of responsibility is often substantial and many of the legal issues addressed are of national significance.

FIGURE 2–12
Pros and cons of federal employment (Adapted from *The Paralegal's Guide to U.S. Government Jobs, Seventh Ed.*, published by Federal Reports, Inc., 800-296-9611, www.attorneyjobs.com.)

FIGURE 2–12
—*Continued*

CONS

The Application Process. It is a little more complicated to apply for a federal position than to apply for one in private industry. It may also take a little longer. However, if you follow the advice in this book, you can succeed and gain all the rewards outlined above.

The Bureaucracy. It takes a long time to get anything done in a large organization such as the federal government. In some agencies, your work may be reviewed by more levels of authority than you can imagine. This can be frustrating to some people. Red tape is prevalent in many aspects of the federal workplace, but if you take the time at the beginning to learn about the key regulations that apply to you and your office, you can avoid a lot of delay

Being a "Scapegoat." Federal employees make easy targets for politicians and the media. Unlike almost any other group in society, they are prohibited by law from talking back! Consequently, the newspapers and evening news programs are full of frontal attacks on the federal bureaucracy. You have to grow accustomed to having your agency and perhaps your program or project discussed in the national media.

FIGURE 2–13
*Top ten paralegal
employers among
federal agencies*

1. Department of Justice
2. Social Security Administration
3. U.S. Court System (nationwide)
4. Department of Treasury
5. Department of the Army
6. Department of Transportation
7. Department of the Navy
8. Department of Labor
9. National Labor Relations Board
10. Department of State

NOTE: some positions in this series may be designated *Legal Research and Analyst; Legal Researcher and Analyst-Criminal; Legal Researcher and Analyst-Energy/Natural Resources; Legal Researcher and Analyst-Copyright/ Patent/Trademark; Legal Researcher and Analyst-Environment; Legal Researcher and Analyst-Duties/Tariffs/ Customs; or Fines, Penalties, and Forfeiture Officer.*

Application for employment with the federal government is made either through the U. S. Office of Personnel Management or directly to the hiring agency. Additional information concerning federal jobs for paralegals can be found in The Paralegal's Guide to U.S. Government Jobs, available from Federal Reports, 1010 Vermont Avenue NW, Suite 408, Washington, DC 20005; (202) 393-3311. You can learn about current job openings with the federal government by calling their Career America Connection telephone line. This is a 24-hour-a-day automated phone system that provides information about current job openings with the federal government. Following is a list of local phone numbers to access the Career America Connection. If there is no local number in your area, call 912-757-3000.

Alabama, Huntsville: 205-837-0894
California, San Francisco: 415-744-5627
Colorado, Denver: 303-969-7050
District of Columbia, Washington: 202-606-2700
Georgia, Atlanta: 404-331-4315
Hawaii, Honolulu: 808-541-2791
Illinois, Chicago: 312-353-6192
Michigan, Detroit: 313-226-6950
Minnesota, Twin Cities: 612-725-3430
Missouri, Kansas City: 816-426-5702
North Carolina, Raleigh: 919-790-2822
Ohio, Dayton: 513-225-2720
Pennsylvania, Philadelphia: 215-597-7440
Texas, San Antonio: 210-805-2402
Virginia, Norfolk: 804-441-3355
Washington, Seattle: 206-553-0888

You can also research available positions with the federal government at the *Federal Jobs Digest* Web site at **http://www.jobsfed.com.** This site lists all currently available positions with the federal government and gives you the opportunity to post your resume for prospective federal employers.

STATE GOVERNMENT AND LOCAL GOVERNMENTS

In addition to the federal government, state and local governments are a significant employer of paralegals. In a recent survey by the National Federation of Paralegal Associations (NFPA), more than two percent of the respondents indicated that they worked for a state government.[11] Nearly every state in the country employs paralegals, although the titles and job descriptions of those individuals vary from state to state. Paralegals who work for state governments may work for any branch of the state government. The state attorney general's office, district attorney's office, state legislatures, and state courts all employ paralegals. Paralegals may also work for state-funded agencies designed to help the poor or elderly.

Figure 2–14 is a list of the state government agencies where questions concerning paralegal employment may be directed.

Any local government that employs attorneys may also employ paralegals. Larger metropolitan areas usually employ a significant number of paralegals in their city attorneys' offices. Paralegals may also work for legal aid clinics or other agencies funded by cities, counties, or other local governments.

Many paralegals who work for state and local governments, especially those who work with agencies who help those in need, find their work very challenging and fulfilling. Paralegals may be in a position to help their clients through the maze of government bureaucracies to find the help they need with food, shelter, and other necessities. Paralegals who work for state

Alabama
Personnel Department
64 N. Union Street
Montgomery, AL 36130
334-2442-3389
http://www.personnel.state.al.us

Alaska
Department of Administration
Division of Personnel
P.O. Box 110201
Juneau, AK 99811-0201
907-465-4430
http://www.state.ak.us

Arizona
Department of Administration
Human Resources Division
1831 West Jefferson Street
Phoenix, AZ 85007
602-542-4966
http://www.hr.state.az.us

Arkansas
Office of Personnel Management
1509 West 7th Street
Little Rock, AR 72201
501-682-1823
http://arstatejobs.com

California
State Personnel Board
801 Capitol Mall
P.O. Box 944201
Sacramento, CA 94244-2010
916-445-5291
http://www.ca.gov/s/working/employ.html

Colorado
Department of Personnel
State Centennial Building
1313 Sherman Street
Denver, CO 80203
303-866-2321
http://www.state.co.us

Connecticut
Personnel Division
Department of Administration Services
165 Capitol Avenue
Hartford, CT 06106-1658
860-713-5025
http://www.das.state.ct.us

Delaware
State Personnel Office
Townsend Building
401 Federal Street
Dover, DE 19901
302-739-5458
http://www.state.de.us/spo/empsvc.htm

District of Columbia
D.C. Personnel Office
441 4th Street, NW
Washington, D.C. 20001
202-442-9700
http://www.dcop.dcgov.org

Florida
Department of Labor & Employment
Security
Hartman Building, Room 209
2012 Capitol Circle SE
Tallahassee, FL 32399
850-488-5627
http://jobsdirect.state.fl.us

Georgia
State Merit System of Personnel
Administration
200 Piedmont Avenue
Atlanta, GA 30334
404-656-6667
http://www.state.ga.us

Hawaii
Department of Human Resources
Development
State Recruiting Office
235 S. Beretania St., Room 1100
Honolulu, HI 96813
808-587-0977
http://www.state.hi.us

Idaho
Personnel Commission
700 West State
Boise, ID 83720
208-334-2263
http://www.ipc.state.id.us

Illinois
Dept. of Central Management Services
Bureau of Personnel
505 Stratton Office Building
Springfield, IL 62706
217-524-1321
312-814-2398 (Chicago)
http://www.state.il.us/cms

FIGURE 2–14
*State government
agencies*

Indiana
State Personnel Department
402 W. Washington
Government Center South, Room W161
Indianapolis, IN 46204
317-233-0800
http://www.state.in.us/jobs

Iowa
Department of Personnel
Grimes State Office Building
E. 14th Street & Grand Avenue
Des Moines, IA 50319
515-281-3087
http://www.state.ia.us/jobs

Kansas
Department of Administration
Division of Personnel Services
Landon State Office Building
900 SW Jackson Street
Topeka, KS 66612-1251
785-296-5930
http://da.state.ks.us/ps/aaa/recruitment/

Kentucky
Department of Personnel
200 Fair Oaks Lane, 5th Floor
Frankfort, KY 40601
502-564-8030
http://www.state.ky.us/agencies/personnel/
pershome.htm

Louisiana
Department of Civil Service
P.O. Box 94111
Capitol Station
Baton Rouge, LA 70804-9111
225-342-8285
http://www.dscs.state.la.us

Maine
Bureau of Human Resources
State Office Building
State House Station 4
Augusta, ME 04333
207-287-3761
http://janus.state.me.us/employee/jobs

Maryland
Department of Personnel
State Office Building #1
301 W. Preston Street
Baltimore, MD 21201
800-705-3493
http://dop.state.md.us

Massachusetts
Department of Personnel Administration
One Ashburton Place
Boston, MA 02108
617-727-3777
http://www.state.ma.us/hrd

Michigan
Department of Civil Service
Capitol Commons Center
400 South Pine Street
P.O. Box 30002
Lansing, MI 48909
517-373-3030
http://www.state.mi.us/mdcs/index.htm

Minnesota
Department of Employee Relations
200 Centennial Office Building
658 Cedar Street
St. Paul, MN 55101
651-296-2616
http://www.doer.state.mn.us

Mississippi
State Personnel Board
301 N. Lamar Street
Jackson, MS 39201
601-359-2348
http://www.spb.state.ms.us

Missouri
Office of Administration
Division of Personnel
P.O. Box 388
Jefferson City, MO 65102
573-751-4162
http://www.state.mo.us

Montana
Department of Administration
Personnel Division
Mitchell Building, Room 130
125 S. Roberts
Helena, MT 59620
406-444-3871
http://www.state.mt.us/doa/spd/spdmain.
htm

Nebraska
Department of Personnel
Box 94905
Lincoln, NE 68509-4905
402-471-2075
http:www.wrk4neb.org

FIGURE 2–14—
Continued

Nevada
Department of Personnel
209 E. Musser Street, Room 101
Capitol Complex
Carson City, NV 89710
775-684-0160
http://www.state.nv.us/personnel/index.html

New Hampshire
Division of Personnel
State House Annex
25 Capitol Street, Room 1
Concord, NH 03301
603-271-3261
http:www.state.nh.us/das/personnel

New Jersey
Department of Personnel
Station Plaza, Building 4
Trenton, NJ 08625
609-292-8668
http://www.state.nj.us/personnel

New Mexico
State Personnel Office
2600 Cerillos Road
P.O. Box 26127
Santa Fe, NM 87505
505-476-7777
http://www.state.nm.us/spo/recruit.htm

New York
Department of Civil Service
State Office Building
Campus
Albany, NY 12239
518-457-6216
http://www.cs.state.ny.us

North Carolina
Office of State Personnel
116 West Jones Street
Raleigh, NC 27603-8004
888-926-8677
http:www.osp.state.nc.us

North Dakota
Central Personnel Division
Office of Management & Budget
State Capitol, 14th Floor
Bismarck, ND 58505
701-328-3293
http://www.state.nd.us

Ohio
Department of Administrative Services
Human Resources Division
30 E. Broad Street, 28th Floor
Columbus, OH 43266
614-466-3455
http://www.state.oh.us/das/dhr/index.htm

Oklahoma
Office of Personnel Management
2101 North Lincoln Boulevard
Oklahoma City, OK 73105
405-521-2177
http://www.state.ok.us/~opm/index.html

Oregon
Department of Administrative Services
Human Resources Services Division
155 Cottage Street N.E.
Salem, OR 97310
503-378-8344
http://www.dashr.state.or.us/jobs/

Pennsylvania
Bureau of State Employment
110 Finance Building
Harrisburg, PA 17120
717-787-5703
http://www.bse.state.pa.us

Rhode Island
Office of Personnel Administration
289 Promenade Street
Providence, RI 02908
401-277-2160
http://www.info.state.ri.us

South Carolina
Employment Security Commission
1550 Gadsen Street
P.O. Box 995
Columbia, SC 29202
803-737-2400
http://www.sces.org

South Dakota
Bureau of Personnel
500 E. Capitol
Pierre, SD 57501-5070
605-773-3148
http://www.state.sd.us/bop/bop.htm

FIGURE 2–14—
Continued

Tennessee
Department of Personnel
505 Deaderick Street
Nashville, TN 37243-0635
615-741-4148
http://www.state.tn.us/personnel/
employ.htm

Texas
State Auditor's Office
P.O. Box 12067
419 Reagan State Office Building
Austin, TX 78711-2067
512-463-5788
http://www.state.tx.us/Employment

Utah
Department of Human Resource
Management
State Office Building, Room 2120
Salt Lake City, UT 84114
801-538-3062
http://www.dhrm.state.ut.us/

Vermont
Department of Personnel
110 State Street, Drawer 20
Montpelier, VT 05620
802-828-3483
http://www.state.vt.us/pers

Virginia
Human Resources Management Services
Room 101, P.O. Box 1358
Richmond, VA 23218
804-371-8050
http://www.careerconnect.state.va.us/
index.htm

Washington
Department of Personnel
600 S. Franklin
P.O. Box 1789
Olympia, WA 98504
360-664-1960
http://access.wa.gov

West Virginia
Division of Personnel
Building 6, Room 420
1900 Kannawha Blvd. E.
Charleston, WV 25305
304-558-3950
http:www.state.wv.us/admin/personel/jobs

Wisconsin
Division of Employment Relations
149 East Wilson Street
P.O. Box 7855
Madison, WI 53707
608-266-1731
http://jobs.der.state.wi.us.static

Wyoming
Department of Employment
122 West 25th Street
Cheyenne, WY 82002
307-777-7672
http://wydoe.state.wy.us

FIGURE 2–14—
Continued

and local governments are not required to bill their time, and few positions require overtime. They report that the atmosphere is generally more relaxed and congenial than that of a law firm.

On the down side, paralegals employed by state and local governments rank among the lowest on the pay scale. Respondents to a recent survey who work for state governments reported an average base salary of $30,666, compared with the average base salary of $33,580 reported by paralegals working for law firms and $36,738 reported by paralegals working for the federal government.[12] State and local governments are often under budgetary constraints that prohibit them from paying premium salaries to their employees, and certain agencies are always in danger of losing their funding. Budgetary considerations may also mean that resources, such as office space and clerical help, may be fewer than those available to paralegals who work in the private sector (Figure 2–15).

ADVANTAGES	DISADVANTAGES
• Many paralegals find their work in state and local governments to be fulfilling work. • Paralegals who work for state and local governments usually have no billable hour requirements. • Many state and local government positions offer less stressful environments and less required overtime than law firms. • Many state and local governments offer excellent benefits.	• Paralegal salaries in state and local government tend to be lower than the salaries of those in the federal government or private sector. • Budgetary considerations often mean scarce resources for paralegals who work in state or local governments.

FIGURE 2–15
Advantages and disadvantages to working for state and local governments

SELF-EMPLOYED AND TEMPORARY PARALEGALS

Paralegals may choose to be self-employed or work on a temporary basis for a variety of reasons. Some paralegals enjoy the flexibility of being able to accept or turn down assignments and work only as much as they choose. You may choose to work on a temporary basis while you are looking for a permanent position. Working on a temporary basis allows you to try several different types of positions to determine what specialty and type of environment you prefer. Self-employed paralegals who work on a temporary or contract basis, referred to as *freelance paralegals*, rely on their own marketing skills and contacts. Other temporary paralegals work for agencies that provide them with temporary positions for a fee—usually a percentage of their pay as temporary paralegals.

Both law firms and corporate law departments utilize the services of freelance paralegals and temporary paralegal agencies. Some law firms depend on the assistance of temporary paralegals to meet the challenges they face with wildly fluctuating workflow. Often a firm will require several additional paralegals to assist with a large court case. Corporate law departments also face challenges with fluctuating workflow. In addition, corporations are always being challenged by management to keep the costs of the law department down, while providing quality legal services throughout the company. The aim of many legal departments is to maintain an experienced group of *core* employees and hire temporary personnel on an *as needed* basis.

Both law firms and corporations benefit from hiring temporary paralegals who do not require vacation pay, sick pay, or other benefits that must be provided to permanent employees.

SELF-EMPLOYED PARALEGALS

Self-employed, or *freelance* paralegals offer their services to law firms, corporate law departments, and the public. Successful freelance paralegals usually have extensive and specialized experience and several contacts in the legal community. Paralegals who sell their services directly to the public are often referred to as legal technicians or independent paralegals.

Self-employed paralegals enjoy versatility and a certain amount of independence in their work. However, self-employment does have its drawbacks. Success as a self-employed paralegal often depends on the paralegal's experience, technical skills, marketing skills, contacts and the market for the services. Self-employed paralegals usually are specialists in one or more area of law; commonly, self-employed paralegals specialize in complex litigation, probate, or corporate law.

Legal technicians and independent paralegals are restricted in the types of services they can provide by statutes concerning the unauthorized practice of law and by ethical considerations. Whereas paralegals who work under the supervision of an attorney on a freelance or contract basis usually need not concern themselves with the unauthorized practice of law, it is a major concern for any legal technician or independent paralegal.

Statistics on salaries of temporary and self-employed paralegals are hard to come by. It is difficult to compare the salaries of traditional paralegals with salaries of temporary and freelance paralegals because the latter group of individuals may work fewer hours than traditional paralegals. However, an experienced self-employed paralegal has the potential to earn a much higher than average income. For example, suppose that you are a paralegal who has a specialized expertise in probate in the state in which you live. There may be small- or medium-sized law firms in your area that do little probate work but like to have the capability to assist their clients when necessary. They may hire you to come in to the office on an as-needed basis to assist with their attorney's probate work, such as collecting the necessary information from the client and other sources and completing the forms that are required by the probate courts. You may charge your time at $50 per hour and the law firm could bill their clients $80 per hour for your time. Here is how both you and your law firm clients benefit from this scenario.

From your perspective: You can receive $50 per hour and have a variety of work. You can set your own hours (within reason) and turn down work when necessary. If you wish to work 40 hours per week (and can find that much work), you can earn as much as $100,000 per year with two weeks vacation.

From the law firm's (your client's) perspective: Their client's work gets done without having to hire any new employees. There is little overhead associated with your work. They do not have to offer you the benefits they have to provide for their traditional employees, such as federal and state income taxes, health insurance, life insurance, and so forth. In addition, because they only pay you for your billable hours, the firm earns $30 for every hour you work (the firm's $80 per hour billed to the client, minus your $50 per hour fee).

However, before you start spending that $100,000 per year, here are a few things to consider. This scenario would apply to other areas of law besides probate but would only work for paralegals who have specific expertise and enough experience to work with little attorney supervision. You may have trouble finding work unless you have a lot of contacts in the field. Your overhead may cut deeply into your profits and would probably include marketing and computer equipment. Additionally, you would have to pay income tax on all your earnings, including self-employment tax. You would also have to furnish your own health insurance and any other insurance or employee benefits you require. If you are successful, you may actually end up working more hours than you would like to. While you can charge $50 per hour for all of your billable time, you may find that you spend a significant amount of non-billable time maintaining your business. It is also hard to turn down assignments when you get too busy. Attorneys will be hesitant to call again if they do not feel they can count on your services when they need them.

PARALEGAL AGENCIES

If you wish to work as a temporary paralegal but have limited experience and few contacts in the legal field, a temporary legal placement agency could be the answer. There are numerous temporary agencies in major metropolitan areas, and there are major differences between them. Here are a few things to look for if you are considering working through a temporary employment agency.

1. Choose an agency that specializes in legal placement. These agencies will have the "ins" with the major law firms and corporate law departments where you will want to work.
2. Choose an agency that places paralegals, lawyers, and legal administrators. Many services that specialize in placing legal secretaries and law firm support staff also place paralegals, but the positions they fill may be of a more clerical nature.
3. Find out about benefits. If you are considered an employee of the temporary placement service, you may be entitled to benefits. If, however, the agency simply places you at a law firm or legal department that takes over as your employer, you may not be entitled to benefits from your employer as a temporary employee.
4. Talk with representatives of several agencies and be specific with regard to what type of work you want to do, where you want to work, and what your salary requirements are. If one agency cannot find what you are looking for, perhaps another agency can.

Focus on Ethics: *Client Confidentiality*

As a paralegal, you will be in a position to learn some very personal, private, and interesting information about your law firm's clients. You will learn details concerning their cases and their personal lives. If you work in a corporate law department, you may be in a position to learn some very sensitive information concerning the corporation, including personal information about employees or information that could affect the price of the corporation's stock.

Whatever the secrets you learn, it is always important that you follow the rules of ethics concerning client confidentiality. With certain exceptions, paralegals have an ethical duty to keep all information learned from clients confidential. The client-lawyer relationship is based on loyalty and requires that the lawyer, and any paralegals involved, maintain confidentiality of information relating to the representation. The confidential relationship between the client and attorney encourages the client to communicate fully and frankly with the attorney, even with regard to matters that may be damaging or embarrassing to the client.

With some exceptions, information imparted to attorneys and paralegals in the course of representing the client must be kept confidential and may not be discussed with others outside of the office. The exact rule of confidentiality and the exceptions to the rule vary from state to state. It is important that the pertinent state code of ethics be consulted whenever a question arises.

In addition to understanding the rules concerning client confidentiality, you will need your common sense and an understanding of the practical issues you will face to avoid inadvertent disclosures. Following are some practical suggestions for maintaining client confidentiality:

- Keep office conversations concerning confidential client information to a minimum and avoid gossip.
- Meet with clients at a location in your office where your conversation cannot be overheard and use extra caution that no confidential information can be overheard when meeting outside the office, such as at a business lunch.
- Keep cellular phone calls with clients at a minimum; advise the client if you are calling from a cellular phone.
- When communicating via e-mail or facsimile, always double-check the telephone number or e-mail address being used. Consider the confidentiality of your message on the receiver's end. Who will pick up the facsimile? Who may read the e-mail?
- Never talk to the press concerning a client or a case without the permission of the supervising attorney.
- Remember that rules of confidentiality apply to all clients, including corporate clients.
- Always keep files and confidential documents in a secure location to prevent loss, theft, or the inadvertent breach of confidential information.
- Never leave confidential information in plain sight on your desk if you meet with clients or others in your office.
- Drafts of confidential documents and other information that is to be disposed of should be shredded whenever possible. Confidential in-

formation should not land in trash baskets that eventually will be emptied into a central location.

- When you are sending information out of the office, you must always double-check to see that nothing is inadvertently included or sent to the wrong person.

There are several exceptions to the rules of confidentiality. For example, confidential client information may be released when requested by the client or when ordered by the court. If you are in doubt as to whether to divulge any information that may be considered confidential, always be sure to ask your supervising attorney or an experienced paralegal first.

SUMMARY

Just a few years ago, law firms and a few government agencies were the only types of employers paralegals had to choose from. Now those choices are numerous, with every expectation that increasing numbers of employers will discover the benefits of hiring paralegals. The type of employer you choose to work for will have a significant impact on your working conditions and your career as a paralegal. Each employer offers its own set of advantages and disadvantages to the paralegals it employs. You will want to choose the employer who most closely fits with your personality, education, skills, and goals.

CAREER TRACK

Who are the prevalent paralegal employers in your area? To find a brief description of the law firms in your area, consult a law firm directory such as *Martindale Hubbell* or *West Legal Directory*. These are both excellent resources that will tell you the names of the law firms and corporate law departments in your area. Listings in these directories include the names of the attorneys in each firm or corporation, as well as their specialties. There are also several directories, such as Directory of Corporate Counsel by Aspen Law, that list corporate counsel exclusively.

Who are the government employers in the city in which you will be working? Call the Career America line in your area for a recorded listing of local paralegal and related positions. Will you be working in or near the state capitol? Contact the state personnel office at the address or telephone number previously listed in this chapter for a description of their paralegal positions and a list of job openings.

For what type of employer would you like to work? To assist you in making this decision, you may want to review the following chart that appears on the next 4 pages. Review the items in the first column to see where your priorities lie, then see how the different employers compare. Which employers meet the most of your expectations and desires? Are you surprised?

Priorities	Law Firm	Corporate Legal Department	Government	Temporary or Freelance
1. It is important for me to earn the highest possible salary.	Larger law firms tend to pay better than medium-sized or smaller law firms.	Corporate legal departments tend to pay better than law firms in general, may be higher than small firms and lower than the largest firms.	Federal government jobs tend to pay well—comparable to larger law firms. Pay at state and local government tends to be among the lowest.	Some temporary positions do not pay very well. Entry level positions tend to be more clerical. Freelance paralegals can demand the highest salary on a per-hour basis, but also have overhead to think of.
2. I do not mind working overtime.	You may be required to work a significant amount of overtime at a large law firm—probably not too much at a smaller firm.	Corporate legal departments generally do not require their paralegals to work a lot of overtime.	Government jobs generally do not require much overtime.	Hours tend to be flexible. Overtime is usually not required.
3. I do not want to have to account for every minute of my work day for billing purposes.	In a law firm you will have to account for your time very closely for billing purposes.	You may have to complete timesheets for budgeting purposes—not as regimented as a law firm.	You may have to complete timesheets for budgeting purposes—not as regimented as a law firm.	You will have to track your time carefully for billing purposes.
4. Benefits are important to me.	Large law firms tend to offer fairly good benefits. Smaller firms tend to offer fewer benefits.	Benefits in a corporate legal department are generally very good and may include profit sharing and stock ownership.	Benefits are very good for federal government employees. Benefits for state and local governments vary.	Temporary paralegals may be offered benefits by the temporary agency for which they work. Freelance paralegals generally provide their own benefits.

Priorities	Law Firm	Corporate Legal Department	Government	Temporary or Freelance
5. I value my free time and want the most vacation possible.	Law firms generally offer the minimum vacation. May be negotiable.	Corporate legal departments tend to offer a little more flexibility and vacation than law firms.	Federal employees probably have the best paid vacation benefits. Paid vacation for state and local employees varies.	Probably no paid vacation, unless you work long term for a temporary agency.
6. I want a lot of variety on the job.	Large law firms generally do not offer as much variety as smaller firms do.	May not be much variety in the larger legal department.	The amount of variety will depend on the agency employer.	Temporary employees and freelance employees generally have the greatest amount of variety in their jobs. Although if they specialize, they may be doing the same tasks on a repetitive basis for different firms.
7. I want to specialize in one area and learn it well.	Large law firms probably offer the best opportunity for specialization. Paralegals in small firms may work in several areas of law.	Paralegals in large corporate legal departments often specialize in one specific area of law.	Paralegals employed in government positions may also specialize.	Successful temporary and freelance paralegals probably specialize in one area of law.
8. I would like to try several different types of specialties and work environments to decide which one I like best.				Working temporary positions is the best way for a paralegal without experience to try several different types of working conditions.

Priorities	Law Firm	Corporate Legal Department	Government	Temporary or Freelance
9. I want to be in a position to help people.	Law firms are in the business of helping people, and there are always pro bono opportunities, but the priority in a law firm is usually profit.	Paralegals in corporate legal departments can participate in pro bono activities outside of work. Otherwise, not much opportunity to help anyone outside of the corporation.	State and local agencies may offer the best opportunity to help others. Federal positions may also offer that opportunity.	Probably not much opportunity to help others except on your own.
10. My work environment is important to me. I want a nice office to work in.	Paralegals in law offices probably have the nicest office space.	Paralegals in corporations usually have private offices, but not always.	Paralegals who work for the government may find themselves without an office if the budget is tight.	Work environment will vary depending on assignment.
11. I like an exciting and fast-paced atmosphere.	Most law firms have an exciting and fast-paced atmosphere.	The atmosphere at a corporate legal department can also be fast paced, but probably more variable.	The atmosphere will depend on the agency. For example, the Attorney General's office may be more fast-paced and exciting than the Social Security Administration.	The atmosphere will vary depending on the assignment.
12. I want to work in the courtroom.	One of your best opportunities to work in a courtroom is with a litigation law firm.	Paralegals who work in a corporate legal department rarely see the inside of a courtroom.	The federal government and state governments offer a variety of non-traditional positions in courtroom settings.	Probably not much chance of assisting in court.

Priorities	Law Firm	Corporate Legal Department	Government	Temporary or Freelance
13. I do not want to work for a large bureaucracy where my actions will require approval by several individuals.	The largest law firms often act as bureaucracies. Decisions may require approval of committees or several individuals. Small firms are the best in this regard.	Corporate law departments are usually subject to most of the procedures imposed on personnel through the corporation.	Federal and state governments are the worst in this regard.	The temporary or freelance paralegal probably need not be too concerned about this.
14. I like to work in a structured environment with a lot of supervision.	Large law firms usually provide a more structured environment.	Corporate legal departments offer a fair amount of structure and supervision. Procedures are in place for most tasks.	Government employees usually find themselves in very structured environments with plenty of supervision.	Temporary and freelance employees generally have the least amount of structure and supervision.

GLOSSARY

Associate An attorney who is an employee of a law firm but does not have an ownership interest.

Billable Hour Hours billed to a client for legal services performed by each attorney, paralegal or other timekeeper.

General Counsel The lead attorney of a corporate law department.

Law Clerk An employee of a law firm or legal department who is in law school studying to become an attorney or who has graduated from law school and is waiting to pass the bar examination.

Law Office Administrator An individual with responsibility for administrative and management functions of the law firm, including personnel, marketing, and budgeting.

Legal Secretary An employee in a law office whose responsibilities include typing legal documents and correspondence, keeping records and files, and performing other duties supportive of the employer's law practice. Legal secretaries usually are more highly skilled, and therefore more highly compensated, than secretaries in general business. *(Black's Law Dictionary, Seventh Edition)*

Partner An owner and a member of a partnership.

Partnership A voluntary association of two or more persons who jointly own and carry on a business for profit. Under the Uniform Partnership Act, a partnership is presumed to exist if the persons agree to share proportionally the business's profits or losses. *(Black's Law Dictionary, Seventh Edition)*

Professional Corporation (PC) A corporation that provides services of a type that requires a professional license. A professional corporation may be made up of architects, accountants, physicians, veterinarians, or the like. *(Black's Law Dictionary, Seventh Edition)*

Professional Limited Liability Company Entity similar to a professional corporation that allows limited liability and partnership taxation status to its members, who must be professionals.

Shareholder One who owns or holds a share or shares in a company, especially a corporation. Also termed *shareowner,* (in a corporation) *stockholder.* *(Black's Law Dictionary, Seventh Edition)*

Sole Practitioner A single attorney who owns and manages his or her own practice of law.

ENDNOTES

[1] *1997 Paralegal Compensation and Benefits Report,* National Federation of Paralegal Associations, Inc., 1997.

[2] Hansen, Mark, "Legal Secretary or Lawyer Lite," *ABA Journal,* January 1999, p. 90.

[3] National Association of Legal Assistants, *1997 National Utilization and Compensation Survey Report,* Table 2.4, 1997.

[4] *Where Profits Start: New Data on 1999 Billing Rates,* Law Office Management and Administration Report, December 1998.

[5] "Billing Rates and Hours Up, But Profits Mainly Flat," *Law Firm Partnership and Benefits Report,* August 1998, citing Altman and Weil 1998 Annual Survey of 483 responding law firms.

[6] *1997 Paralegal Compensation and Benefits Report,* National Federation of Paralegal Associations, Inc., 1997.

[7] "After Years of Stability, Can Law Firms Expect to Increase Billable Hours?," 97-3 *Law Office Management & Administration Report* 1, March 1997.

[8] *1997 Paralegal Compensation and Benefits Report,* National Federation of Paralegal Associations, Inc., 1997.

[9] *The Paralegal's Guide to U.S. Government Jobs, Seventh Edition,* Federal Reports, Inc., 1996.

[10] *The Paralegal's Guide to U.S. Government Jobs, Seventh Edition,* Federal Reports, Inc., 1996.

[11] *1997 Paralegal Compensation and Benefits Report,* National Federation of Paralegal Associations, Inc., 1997.

If you have always thought you would like to go into either medicine or law, now you have an opportunity to do both: Become a legal nurse consultant. Legal nurse consultants are a new type of paralegal (or a new type of nurse) who have training in both medicine and law. Members of the American Association of Legal Nurse Consultants (AALNC) view legal nurse consulting as a specialty practice of the nursing profession. The American Bar Association (ABA) has recognized legal nurse consulting as a paralegal specialty.

Legal nurse consultants bring a unique and valuable expertise to the legal team. They may work as employees of law firms, insurance companies, corporate legal departments, or as independent consultants. Legal nurse consultants may consult on any legal issue that involves injury or illness or where an individual's health is an issue. Most often, legal nurse consultants consult on the following types of cases.

- Personal injury
- Medical malpractice
- Product liability
- Workers' compensation
- Cases involving insurance claims

An important part of any of these cases is the review and evaluation of medical records and a client's condition. Whereas attorneys and paralegals who specialize in areas of law that deal with personal injuries or medical conditions may have some experience in this area, legal nurse consultants bring unique and invaluable expertise. In addition to reviewing medical reports, legal nurse consultants often are responsible for assisting with drafting interrogatories in personal injury and medical malpractice cases. They can be instrumental in assisting attorneys with preparation for questioning opposing clients in depositions and preparation for direct and cross examinations in court. Legal nurse consultants also can perform any other tasks performed by traditional paralegals.

Legal nurse consultants generally have both a nursing license and a paralegal certificate or a degree from a paralegal program. Many schools that offer paralegal training are expanding their programs to include training designed specifically for legal nurse consultants.

The AALNC offers certification to legal nurse consultants who meet certain criteria, including a current nursing license, two years experience as a practicing registered nurse and legal nurse consulting experience. A certificate is not *required* to work as a legal nurse consultant.

In addition to formal training, most independent legal nurse consultants have several years of experience in nursing, as a paralegal, or both. Independent consultants often charge as much as $100 per hour for their professional services. Legal nurse consultants who work for law firms or corporations tend to earn a salary comparable to a highly experienced paralegal.

If you are interested in a career as a legal nurse consultant, you can obtain more information from the AALNC at their Web site at **www.aalnc.org**, or by calling (847) 375-4713. Your school or schools in your area that offer training for legal nurse consulting may also be able to provide you with further information on the legal nurse consulting profession.

Paralegal Specialties

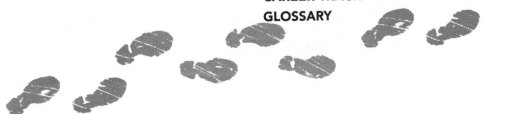

"All jobs are easy to the person who doesn't have to do them."

HOLT'S LAW

INTRODUCTION

Because of the complexity of the practice of modern law, most paralegals specialize in one or a few areas of law (Figure 3–1). Specializing allows you to hone your skills and become an expert in your area. The work of paralegals within different specialties varies greatly, so your choice of specialty will determine the type of work you do. It will also affect what type of employer you work for and how much you earn.

Most paralegals, especially paralegals in smaller law firms, work in more than one area of law. Some paralegals specialize in several areas of law. According to one recent survey, only 16 percent of the paralegals who responded indicated that they worked in only one area of law. The average number of specialty areas selected by paralegals was four. According to the NALA 1997 Paralegal Compensation and Benefits Survey, "Since the first survey in 1986, the findings have consistently reported that legal assistants spend time working in several specialty areas of practice." The following table lists the areas of specialty, in order of selection, in which paralegals indicated they work. The survey had 2286 respondents who answered this question.

There is a correlation between paralegal specialties and paralegal salaries. Naturally, the highest salaries generally are earned by paralegals working in those specialties that are in the greatest demand and that require the greatest amount of education and expertise. On the average, paralegals who specialize in intellectual property, corporate law, environmental law, and litigation currently command the highest salaries. Paralegals who work in family law and criminal law tend to be among the lowest-paid paralegals. More information about salaries earned by paralegals specializing in each area of law is found in Chapter 4 of this text.

From the NALA 1997 Survey*	From the *Legal Assistant Today* 1998-99 Salary Survey†	NFPA 1997 Salary Survey‡
1. Litigation	1. Litigation	1. Litigation
2. Personal Injury	2. Personal Injury	2. Personal Injury
3. Corporate	3. Corporate	3. Trust and Estates
4. Real Estate	4. Insurance Defense	4. Corporate
5. Probate/Estates	5. Estate/Probate	5. Real Estate

*Based on the responses of approximately 2286 paralegals to *The National Association of Legal Assistants 1997 National Utilization and Compensation Survey Report*.

†Based on the responses of approximately 475 paralegals to the *Legal Assistant Today 1998-99 Salary Survey*.

‡Based on the responses of approximately 4000 paralegals to *National Federation of Paralegal Association's 1997 Paralegal Compensation and Benefits Report*.

FIGURE 3–1

The top five specialties

Specialty Area	Number of Respondents Indicating They Work in Specialty Area	Percentage of Respondents Indicating They Work in Specialty Area
Litigation	1387	54%
Personal Injury	964	37%
Corporate	850	33%
Real Estate	826	32%
Probate/Estates	731	28%
Contracts	707	27%
Administrative/ Government/Public	622	24%
Insurance	619	24%
Family Law	613	24%
Office Management	586	22%
Medical Malpractice	573	22%
Bankruptcy	516	20%
Employment	513	20%
Workers' Compensation	477	18%
Criminal	455	17%
Banking/Finance	415	16%
Trust Administration	402	15%
Immigration	376	14%
Tax	364	14%
Intellectual Property	358	14%
Environmental	355	14%
Labor Law	353	14%
Employee Benefits	331	13%
Elder Law	309	12%
Securities/Antitrust	296	11%
Oil & Gas	280	11%
Energy/Utility	261	10%
Admiralty/Maritime	257	10%
Native American/Tribal	233	9%
Entertainment	229	9%

This chapter first will reveal the current top ten list for paralegal specialties and then describe the specialty, the employers of paralegals who specialize in each area of law, and the work performed by paralegals in each specialty. A brief description of the fastest-growing paralegal specialties and other important paralegal specialties then will be given. This chapter concludes with a look at nontraditional paralegal career paths.

Paralegal Profile

PROFILE ON AMY MICHEL

I enjoy the flexibility of my position. I am salaried and have a yearly billable hour requirement. This allows me to take extra vacation time when I am caught up with my work or to leave early on a sunny Friday afternoon. The down side of this, of course, is that when I have a lot of work to do, I am working more than 8 A.M. to 5 P.M.

Name and Location:	Amy Michel, Indianapolis, Indiana
Title:	Paralegal
Specialty:	Litigation
Education:	Bachelor of Arts in Political Science with a minor in Pre-Law from Taylor University, Upland, Indiana. Paralegal Certificate from Indiana University, South Bend.
Experience:	3 Years

Amy Michel has been a paralegal for three years. The majority of her time is spent on files of one of the major clients of the large law firm for which she works. Amy works for a law firm in Indianapolis, Indiana, that employs more than 150 attorneys and 26 paralegals.

Amy is a salaried paralegal who has a billable hour requirement. While this gives her some flexibility in setting her hours, it often requires her to work more than 8 hours per day.

Amy is responsible for as many as 20 to 30 cases at one time—all for the same client. For each case, she gathers relevant documents from the client, drafts discovery requests and responses, reviews medical records, drafts case evaluation letters, and generally manages the progress of the case. She works under the supervision of the responsible attorney on each file.

Amy works independently and she appreciates the responsibility she is given. The attorneys she reports to trust her to know what needs to be done and when it needs to be done. There are only a few situations that require her to "check-in" with her supervising attorney before taking action.

While working on cases for just one client allows Amy to be very familiar with that client, it also means that her work can become monotonous and routine. Amy combats this by trying to make time to work with other attorneys on different types of cases. Doing this also increases her experience in other areas of litigation.

Amy's advice to paralegal students:

My advice would be to talk to as many practicing paralegals as possible to get a good idea of all the various types of paralegal careers available. Learn the educational requirements for each position so you can choose classes and seminars focused on that particular field.

THE TOP TEN PARALEGAL SPECIALTIES

Indisputably, the most common paralegal specialty is *litigation.* More paralegals work in litigation and subspecialties of litigation than any other area of law. Following litigation are several other important specialties (Figures 3–2 and 3–3). The popularity and prominence of these specialties change

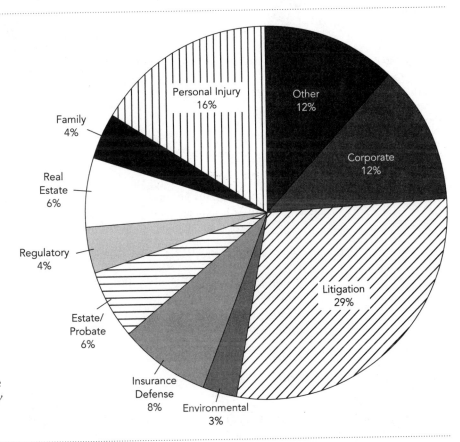

FIGURE 3–2
The most common specialties (From the *Legal Assistant Today* 1998-99 salary survey)

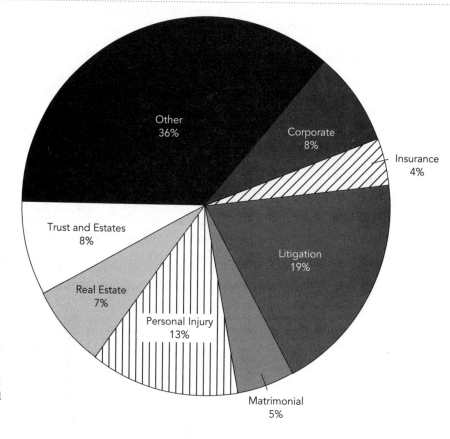

FIGURE 3–2
*The most common specialties (*From the NFPA 1997 paralegal compensation and benefits report)

from time to time, but generally, the top ten most common specialties for paralegals are as follows.

Litigation
Personal injury
Corporate
Real estate
Probate/estates/trusts
Administrative and regulatory law
Insurance law
Intellectual property
Family law
Criminal law

To produce a complete and comprehensive list of tasks performed by paralegals in each specialty would be impossible. The work you do within each specialty will depend on your employer and the attorneys and staff with whom you are working. Every employer has a slightly different method of dividing and assigning the tasks that need to be completed in each area of law. Further, your job description will depend on your level of knowledge and expertise. If you take a position as a litigation paralegal, you will probably not be responsible for interrogatories, depositions, and assisting attorneys at trial in your first year. Likewise, you will probably not be expected to spend an extensive amount of time indexing documents after you have gained extensive experience and knowledge.

The following descriptions and lists of tasks performed by paralegals will give you a general idea of what you may expect throughout a career in each of the following specialties, as well as an idea of some of the tasks most commonly performed.

LITIGATION

The term *litigation* is a broad term that encompasses all lawsuits, legal actions, and proceedings connected to legal actions. *Civil litigation* is the process of resolving disputes between one or more **plaintiffs** and one or more **defendants** through the court system. Unless the parties privately resolve their dispute, the litigation process usually results in a trial or hearing where the parties present their evidence to a judge or jury who decides the dispute.

Litigation paralegals are a diverse group of individuals, and they work in a variety of settings, including law firms of all sizes, corporate law departments, and government agencies. Litigation paralegals are set apart from other paralegals by the fact that they work with lawsuits and other legal actions. Much of their work involves preparation for trial. There are several subspecialties within the litigation specialty, including personal injury, commercial litigation, product liability, class action suits, and medical malpractice.

The duties of litigation paralegals often include the following.

Prelitigation Fact Investigation
1. Interviewing clients and witnesses
2. Obtaining statements from witnesses
3. Gathering and reviewing evidence (police reports, photographs, and so on)
4. Organizing and indexing documentary evidence
5. Researching factual and legal issues

Commencing Litigation
1. Researching the substantive law of cases
2. Drafting pleadings
3. Coordinating service of process
4. Reviewing pleadings from opposing parties
5. Drafting motions
6. Preparing orders after motions

Discovery
1. Drafting written forms of discovery (interrogatories, requests to produce, requests for admissions)

2. Assisting clients in complying with discovery requests
3. Reviewing discovery documents obtained from opposing parties
4. Preparing clients for depositions
5. Digesting and summarizing depositions

Pretrial
1. Researching and recommending possible expert witnesses
2. Attending meetings with the attorneys, clients, and opposing counsel
3. Drafting briefs
4. Assisting with preparation of questions for jury selection
5. Drafting pretrial motions
6. Preparing trial notebooks

Trial
1. Organizing files and evidence for trial
2. Serving witnesses with subpoenas
3. Interviewing witnesses
4. Preparing the client for trial
5. Drafting jury instructions
6. Drafting proposed judgments
7. Assisting with research and preparation of trial briefs
8. Preparing and organizing trial exhibits
9. Preparing trial notebooks for use at trial
10. Assisting attorneys during trial

Posttrial
1. Researching possible posttrial motions
2. Drafting post-trial motions
3. Drafting notices of appeal and requests for transcripts
4. Assisting with research and writing of appellate briefs

Miscellaneous
1. Maintaining firm's calendar system
2. Organizing client files
3. Assisting with computerization of litigation
4. Preparing documents associated with enforcing judgments

Special skills that aid in a successful career as a litigation paralegal include interviewing skills, written and verbal communication skills, and organizational and analytical skills for reviewing and organizing evidence and pleadings. Paralegals who work in litigation must be detail-oriented and able to work under pressure to meet deadlines. Legal research skills and computer proficiency, especially with database programs, are also important to litigation paralegals. Demand is especially high for paralegals with a good background in computers to work on complex, large-scale cases (Figure 3–4).

- Personal injury
- Commercial litigation
- Insurance defense
- Product liability
- Medical malpractice
- Computerized litigation support
- Class action

FIGURE 3–4
*Common litigation
subspecialties*

PERSONAL INJURY

Personal injury is a subspecialty of litigation discussed separately here because so many paralegals specialize exclusively in personal injury. Personal injury is a branch of litigation that deals with actual injury to the person, usually resulting from an automobile accident or some other type of accident due to the negligence of another.

Plaintiff. Paralegals who specialize in plaintiff personal injury work with attorneys to represent individuals who have been injured. Because personal injury matters frequently result in litigation, personal injury paralegals perform many of the same duties as general litigation paralegals. In addition, personal injury paralegals may perform the following duties.

1. Interviewing clients to ascertain the extent of their injuries and to obtain consents for receiving medical information
2. Obtaining medical reports from doctors, hospitals, and other medical facilities
3. Obtaining reports regarding wage loss
4. Collecting other information concerning a client's out-of-pocket expenses stemming from the accident
5. Researching pertinent state laws concerning negligence and personal injury
6. Obtaining insurance information from opposing counsel
7. Preparing settlement demand packages

Skills important to the personal injury paralegal include all those important to the litigation paralegal, plus a knowledge of medical terminology. In addition, the personal injury paralegal may need a special ability to communicate with and interview individuals who have been (sometimes severely) injured.

Defense. Whereas plaintiff personal injury paralegals work with the attorneys representing the injured party, the personal injury paralegal on the defense side works to represent the party who has been accused of the negligence causing the injury. In a personal injury suit, the defendant is often covered by automobile or some other type of insurance, and this coverage usually includes legal defense. Attorneys who represent insurance companies, either in private law firms or as in-house counsel, may employ personal injury defense paralegals. In addition to general litigation duties, personal injury defense paralegals may perform the following tasks.

1. Interviewing clients and witnesses to determine the facts of cases
2. Scheduling medical examinations of plaintiffs by doctors chosen by the defense attorneys
3. Reviewing insurance policies to determine the extent of coverage
4. Reviewing medical information and information concerning a plaintiff's expenses stemming from the accident
5. Reviewing police reports and witness statements

Paralegals working in the personal injury defense area need all the skills required of other litigation and personal injury paralegals.

CORPORATE AND BUSINESS ORGANIZATION LAW

Corporate and business organization law is among the most prevalent of specialties for paralegals. Corporate law paralegals may be employed either in a corporate law department or in a law firm that represents corporations and other businesses. Corporate paralegals are often also specialists in limited liability company law, professional corporation law, nonprofit corporation law, and the law of other business organizations.

Corporate Law. The duties performed by corporate law paralegals often include the following.

1. Drafting all forms of corporate documents
2. Reviewing and updating corporate minute books
3. Drafting corporate resolutions
4. Incorporating and dissolving corporations
5. Preparing foreign qualification documents
6. Assisting with mergers and acquisitions
7. Assisting with compliance with Securities Exchange Commission (SEC) rules and regulations
8. Researching state securities laws
9. Drafting all types of corporate agreements and contracts

The duties performed by a corporate law paralegal who works in a corporate legal department can include all of the above. In addition, the corporate legal department paralegal may be responsible for these duties as well.

1. Subsidiary maintenance
2. Shareholder relations
3. Board of director communications
4. Coordinating with the corporation's stock transfer agent
5. Acting as liaison between the corporation, in-house counsel, and outside counsel

6. Confirming proper service of legal process and opening files for new lawsuits brought against the corporation

Other Forms of Business Organizations. In addition to corporations, state law provides for several other forms of business organizations. Some of the more common types of business organizations include limited liability companies, limited liability partnerships, general partnerships, limited partnerships, nonprofit, and professional corporations. Requirements for these types of business organizations vary by state. The tax structure of these business entities is established by the Internal Revenue Code. Paralegals may work for attorneys who specialize in a particular type of business organization or they may work for attorneys who routinely establish and represent several different types of business organizations. Duties of paralegals specializing in these other types of business organizations may include the following.

1. Researching the law of business organizations, including partnerships, limited liability companies, and nonprofit and professional corporations
2. Drafting documents to form business organizations
3. Drafting resolutions of business organizations
4. Maintaining annual records to formalize business organizations

Successful corporate law paralegals possess a variety of skills, including the ability to draft accurate and concise documents and perform thorough research. They must have the ability to read and understand financial documents. Corporate paralegals must also possess excellent communication skills, including the ability to communicate effectively and professionally in person (Figure 3–5).

REAL ESTATE LAW

Real estate law deals with land and the buildings attached to it, as well as all rights associated with the land. Most real estate law involves the leasing or transfer of real estate from one party to another. Real estate law can also include litigation that may arise due to disputes concerning real estate use and transactions.

FIGURE 3–5
Common corporate subspecialties

- Transactional
- Securities
- Nonprofit corporation law
- Antitrust
- Regulatory
- Mergers and acquisitions
- Contract law

Real estate paralegals work in several different settings. They may work for law firms that specialize in real estate; they may work for title companies, realty companies, property management companies, construction companies, or corporations that invest in real estate. The tasks commonly assigned to real estate paralegals in all of these areas may include the following.

1. Researching zoning ordinances and other laws relating to the transfer and use of real estate
2. Preparing land sale contracts
3. Ordering title work from title companies
4. Reviewing abstracts or certificates of title
5. Preparing maps of property based on the legal description of property
6. Preparing drafts of title opinions
7. Scheduling closings
8. Preparing deeds, notes, and mortgages
9. Reviewing real estate transfer documents prepared by other parties
10. Providing mortgage lenders with necessary documentation
11. Attending closings to assist with document review and execution and the transfer of funds
12. Reviewing title work
13. Disbursing funds
14. Filing the necessary documents after closings

Real estate paralegals must be familiar with real estate law in the communities in which they work. In addition, a successful real estate paralegal must be detail oriented and must have the ability to communicate in writing effectively and precisely. Organizational skills can be equally important to real estate paralegals, who often find themselves working on commercial real estate transactions that involve numerous documents.

ESTATE PLANNING, PROBATE, AND TRUSTS

Estate planning and **probate** are two closely related areas of law. Estate planning concerns planning and preparing for the disposition of an individual's assets after his or her death while taking the individual's wishes and the pertinent tax laws into consideration. Probate concerns the disposition of the assets of someone who has died. Paralegals who specialize in estate planning typically work in law firms for attorneys who prepare estate plans and estate planning instruments for individuals, including wills and a variety of trusts. Paralegals may also assist in transferring assets to trusts and trust administration.

ETHICAL CONSIDERATION
Rules of ethics prohibit paralegals from assuming full responsibility for client trust accounting. Attorneys must retain supervision and responsibility for trust accounting.

Probate paralegals typically work in law firms that assist the families of persons who recently have died to distribute the assets of the deceased's estate pursuant to any will that was left or pursuant to the pertinent state law. Probate paralegals may also work in probate courts, where they perform tasks such as reviewing documents and assisting probate judges, clerks, and individuals seeking the assistance of the probate court.

The work of an estate planning and probate paralegal may include several of the following duties:

Estate Planning

1. Interviewing clients to determine facts relating to their potential estates
2. Reviewing financial information submitted by clients and preparing checklists for attorney review
3. Preparing drafts of wills, trusts, and related documents
4. Obtaining information regarding insurance policies and ensuring that the proper beneficiaries are designated to complement the estate plan
5. Overseeing the proper execution of wills by clients and witnesses
6. Preparing summaries of wills and other documents for clients

Probate

1. Attending client conferences to explain proper procedures following the death of a client or family member
2. Preparing and filing (when necessary) probate forms
3. Assisting with collection and inventory of the assets of the deceased, including contents of safety deposit boxes, bank accounts, and all real and personal property
4. Assisting with the clerical, bookkeeping, and accounting functions relating to estates
5. Preparing estate tax returns
6. Reviewing claims against estates
7. Assisting with the liquidation of assets
8. Maintaining communications with clients to advise them of the progress of settling the estate
9. Preparing documents required for distribution of the assets of the estate

The estate-planning paralegal must have effective interviewing skills to help gather all pertinent information regarding the client's estate. In addition, the estate-planning paralegal must possess the clear and concise writing skills associated with drafting wills, trusts, and other estate-planning documents. As the percentage of elderly citizens in the United States grows throughout the early twenty-first century, transfer of wealth is becoming more important than ever. Demand for paralegals with estate-planning expertise is sure to continue to grow for the foreseeable future.

The paralegal who specializes in probate must be able to communicate effectively with individuals who may be experiencing considerable grief.

The probate process can take several months and sometimes may take years. Because the paralegal is often the probate client's main link to the law firm, it is important that the paralegal communicate frequently and effectively with the client to assure that there are no misunderstandings. The probate paralegal must also have an ability to work with numbers. Paralegals are often responsible for the day-to-day bookkeeping matters concerning the estate, as well as the more complex accounting matters concerning estate tax returns.

ADMINISTRATIVE AND REGULATORY LAW

Administrative law and regulatory law are the areas of law concerning the rules, regulations, and orders created by administrative agencies of the government. Administrative agencies are commissions, corporations, boards, divisions, departments, or other governmental bodies that are charged with administering and implementing particular legislation. Some examples of administrative agencies are the Securities Exchange Commission, Federal Trade Commission, Central Intelligence Agency, Environmental Protection Agency, and the Workers' Compensation Commission. Most administrative agencies are **regulatory agencies.** Regulatory agencies are responsible for proscribing or requiring certain behavior, determining compliance with the law, prosecuting and, occasionally, punishing those who have violated the law. The terms *administrative law a*nd *regulatory law* are sometimes used interchangeably.

Paralegals who work in administrative law work mainly for administrative agencies in federal, state, or local government. In addition, administrative law paralegals may work for private-practice law firms that specialize in the representation of clients in administrative law matters. Paralegals also work in *regulatory* or *compliance* departments, or in the legal department of corporations in regulated industries. Some regulated industries include banking, investments, utilities, healthcare, and insurance companies. Paralegals who work for corporations often assist the in-house counsel or compliance officers in ensuring corporate compliance with regulatory requirements that apply to their industry.

Although under most circumstances it is considered the unauthorized practice of law for a paralegal to represent a client in a court of law, if permitted by federal or state statute, paralegals and other nonlawyers may represent clients at administrative hearings before administrative judges (Figure 3–6).

The work of administrative or regulatory law paralegals is especially diverse because administrative agencies themselves deal with so many different aspects of the law. Some duties typically performed by administrative or regulatory law paralegals include the following.

1. Conducting legal research
2. Collecting information from citizens

Representation is allowed only as permitted by applicable federal statute or regulation by the following agencies:

- Board of Immigration Appeals
- Civil Aeronautics Board
- Comptroller of the Currency
- Consumer Product Safety Commission
- Department of Agriculture
- Department of Health and Human Services
- Department of Justice
- Department of Labor
- Department of Transportation
- Department of Veterans Affairs
- Federal Deposit Insurance Corporation†
- Federal Energy Regulatory Commission
- Federal Maritime Administration‡
- Federal Mine Safety and Health Review Commission
- General Accounting Office
- Internal Revenue Service§
- Interstate Commerce Commissionll
- National Credit Union Administration
- National Mediation Board
- National Transportation Safety Board
- Occupational Safety and Health Review Commission
- Small Business Administration
- U.S. Customs Service
- U.S. Environmental Protection Agency

State Agencies that Permit Nonlawyer Representation

Representation is permitted only as allowed by applicable state statute or regulation by the following state agencies:

Alaska
Human Rights Commission

California
Labor
Unemployment
Workers' Compensation

Illinois
Workers' Compensation

Michigan
Unemployment Compensation

Minnesota
Workers' Compensation

New York
70 percent of state agencies and 63 percent of New York City agencies

Ohio
Workers' Compensation

FIGURE 3–6
Federal Agencies Permitting Nonlawyer Representation (Information compiled by the NFPA's Roles and Responsibilities Committee, Kim Nichols, Coordinator)*

Washington – Seattle (King County)
Nonlawyers are allowed to present ex parte orders that have been agreed on. *Ex Parte* refers to orders that are by and for one party only, without being contested by any person adversely interested.

Washington – Tacoma (Pierce County)
Nonlawyers are allowed to present ex parte orders that have been agreed on. *Ex Parte* refers to orders that are by and for one party only, without being contested by any person adversely interested.

Wisconsin
Workers' Compensation

---

*As reported in the *National Paralegal Reporter,* "Agencies That Allow Nonlawyer Practice," Summer 1999, page 35.
†Only qualified nonlawyers are permitted to represent.
‡Only registered nonlawyers are permitted to appear.
§Nonlawyers must become enrolled agents.
‖Only registered nonlawyers are permitted to practice.

FIGURE 3–6
—Continued

3. Handling complaints and questions from citizens
4. Researching pertinent statutes and administrative rules and regulations
5. Appearing at administrative hearings
6. Drafting numerous types of legal documents
7. Drafting proposed agency regulations

Administrative law paralegals must be proficient at legal research. In addition, they must be able to communicate the results of their research in an effective manner, both verbally and in writing.

The number of paralegals in the administrative or regulatory law area has been growing for several years and will probably continue to do so. As dealing with government agencies becomes more and more complex, the need for paralegals to assist citizens with those dealings and to assist the government with the paperwork will continue to increase.

INSURANCE LAW

Another growing area is insurance law. Insurance paralegals may perform work similar to that of corporate paralegals or litigation and personal injury paralegals. They may work for the legal department of an insurance company on corporate and regulatory matters, or they may work with attorneys who represent insurance companies, either in-house or as outside counsel, in defense of personal injury matters or other matters covered by insurance. The specific tasks performed by these paralegals may include the following.

Corporate and Regulatory
1. Drafting all forms of corporate documents
2. Researching and reviewing state administrative rules and regulations with regard to insurance companies

3. Completing filings with state insurance regulatory authorities
4. Assisting in all aspects of the insurance claims process
5. Preparing foreign qualification documents
6. Assisting with mergers and acquisitions
7. Acting as liaison between the corporation and outside counsel
8. Confirming proper service of legal process and opening files for new lawsuits brought against insurance companies

Insurance Defense Counsel
1. Interviewing clients and witnesses to determine the facts of cases
2. Scheduling medical examinations of plaintiffs by doctors chosen by the defendants' attorneys
3. Reviewing insurance policies to determine the extent of coverage
4. Reviewing medical information and information concerning a plaintiff's expenses stemming from the accident
5. Reviewing police reports and witness statements

INTELLECTUAL PROPERTY LAW

Intellectual property law is becoming one of the more prevalent, and better paying, specialties for paralegals. Fourteen percent of the paralegals responding to the NALA 1997 Salary Survey indicated that they spent more than 40 percent of their time working on intellectual property matters. Paralegals who work in intellectual property deal mainly with **copyrights**, **trademarks**, and **patents**. Much of the work in this area, though rather complex, can be performed by a competent paralegal. Although paralegals cannot give legal advice to intellectual property clients or represent a client in a copyright, trademark, or patent infringement lawsuit, they can perform almost every other duty in that area of law.

Following is a list of some of the tasks typically performed by paralegals who specialize in the area of intellectual property.

Copyrights
1. Assisting with the preparation and filing of copyright applications
2. Researching pertinent copyright laws
3. Researching current copyrights
4. Researching possible copyright infringements
5. Assisting with all aspects of copyright infringement litigation

Trademarks
1. Researching existing trademarks
2. Assisting with the preparation and filing of trademark registration applications
3. Researching pertinent state and federal trademark laws
4. Assisting with all aspects of possible litigation dealing with trademarks
5. Maintaining tickler systems for due dates for renewals of trademarks and other pertinent deadlines

Patents

1. Researching existing patents
2. Assisting with the preparation and filing of patent applications
3. Assisting with any potential patent infringement litigation

Intellectual property law often involves litigation. Paralegals who specialize in this area of law will need the skills of an excellent litigation paralegal who has familiarity with intellectual property and excellent computer skills.

FAMILY LAW

Family law in the United States is concerned with many aspects of the family and the relationship of the family members. Not only does it encompass marriage and divorce, but it also includes child custody, support, adoption, child abuse and neglect, and juvenile delinquency. With more than one million divorces in this country each year, most paralegals who specialize in family law work with attorneys who represent clients going through the divorce process. Family law paralegals assist in attaining a dissolution of the marriage and in reaching a satisfactory arrangement for division of the couple's assets, custody and visitation of any children, and child support and alimony.

Paralegals who specialize in family law work in law firms that specialize in family law or they work for administrative agencies, often serving as advocates for the poor in divorce, custody, and child support matters.

The duties of family law paralegals may include the following.

1. Interviewing clients
2. Completing client questionnaires based on initial interviews
3. Researching family law and procedures
4. Researching and reviewing client's financial information
5. Coordinating service of process
6. Reviewing pleadings received on behalf of clients
7. Drafting correspondence to clients and others associated with case
8. Drafting pleadings and other legal documents, including summonses, petitions, motions, orders, stipulations, and decrees
9. Preparing for and attending depositions
10. Preparing deposition summaries
11. Preparing interrogatories
12. Assisting with preparation of answers to interrogatories
13. Assisting with pretrial preparation
14. Assisting with trial preparation

One new development in family law of particular interest to paralegals is the increasing use of alternative dispute resolution (ADR) to resolve conflicts that arise during marriage dissolution. Because of the heavy backlog in family courts and the adversarial nature of the court system, more and more couples are turning to ADR to resolve their conflicts—often ADR services are recommended by the court (and sometimes even required). Paralegals can serve as an integral part of the ADR team, including acting as mediators.

Excellent interpersonal skills are important to the family law paralegal, who often works with emotional clients. Clients may regard paralegals as more approachable and less intimidating than attorneys, and often they will talk more freely with family law paralegals concerning their cases. Family law paralegals must deal with clients with a mix of empathy, objectivity, and professionalism. In addition to interpersonal skills, paralegals must have excellent organizational skills and the ability to communicate well in writing. Much of the family law paralegal's job involves keeping track of important court dates and other deadlines and drafting documents and correspondence.

CRIMINAL LAW

Criminal law refers to all law dealing with crimes committed by individuals. Paralegals can work on the defense side of criminal law for attorneys who defend those accused of crimes, or they can work on the prosecution side for prosecutors and others who work to prosecute and convict those suspected of crimes.

Criminal Defense Law. Paralegals who specialize in criminal defense law tend to work for small- to medium-size law firms that specialize in criminal law or have a general law practice. Many medium- to large-size law firms either refer all of their criminal matters to another firm or have a small criminal law department to handle minor problems for their clients. Criminal law paralegals may also work for the court systems or for public defenders. Some of the duties typically performed by criminal law defense paralegals include the following.

1. Interviewing clients to determine facts relating to their cases
2. Reviewing police reports and other reports provided by prosecutors
3. Arranging for bail
4. Obtaining statements from witnesses to alleged crimes
5. Assisting with all aspects of discovery
6. Assisting with pretrial and trial procedures
7. Researching legal and factual issues
8. Assisting clients with obtaining information concerning bail
9. Organizing files and evidence for trial
10. Preparing clients for trial
11. Assisting attorneys during trial
12. Researching and drafting post-trial motions
13. Maintaining tickler files to remind attorneys and clients of important court dates and other deadlines.

Skills important to criminal defense law paralegals include the ability to communicate well, both orally and in writing. The criminal law paralegal must have the ability to interview clients and witnesses effectively. The criminal law paralegal must also be able to perform detailed legal research on issues of law. An understanding of the court system and criminal procedures is critical to a criminal law defense paralegal.

In all areas of law, confidentiality is of utmost importance, but in criminal law it is especially so, and the paralegal must accept this responsibility. The criminal law defense paralegal must be able to put aside personal feelings and work *for t*he client.

ETHICAL CONSIDERATION

All confidential information imparted to an attorney or paralegal during the representation of a client must be kept confidential. Under certain circumstances, an attorney may divulge confidential information to prevent the commission of a serious crime.

Criminal Prosecution Law. Criminal law paralegals who work in the prosecution area typically work for state or federal agencies in the office of the prosecutor. The duties usually performed by criminal law paralegals for the prosecution include the following.

1. Interviewing witnesses
2. Conducting criminal investigations
3. Drafting complaints
4. Assisting with pretrial and trial procedures
5. Acting as liaison between prosecutor's office and law enforcement officials
6. Assisting crime victims by giving referrals to appropriate government agencies
7. Preparing crime victims and witnesses for trial
8. Drafting subpoenas
9. Preparing reports required of prosecutor's office
10. Cataloging and preparing exhibits for trial

As with criminal law paralegals who specialize in the defense area, criminal law paralegals for the prosecution must have excellent interviewing, communication, and research skills.

TOP FIVE GROWTH SPECIALTIES FOR THE NEW MILLENNIUM

Several specialties have shown exceptional growth in recent years and show exceptional promise for growth and expansion into the twenty-first century. Some of these specialties are already on the top ten list, such as administrative law, intellectual property law, and insurance law. Other specialties, including elder law, ADR, and Internet specialist, are still in their infancy stage but show great promise due to trends in demographics, changes in the way law is practiced, and improvements in technology. Following are five of the fastest growing specialties for the twenty-first century.

Internet specialist
Elder law
Alternative dispute resolution (ADR)
Employee benefits law
Environmental law

The following sections offer brief descriptions of typical positions in these rapid growth specialties.

INTERNET SPECIALISTS

New technology means new specialties and new opportunities. Paralegals with expertise in computers in general, and the Internet in particular, may find opportunities with both law firms and corporate law departments. Internet specialists can design, implement, and maintain Web sites for their employers. They may also perform both factual and legal research over the Internet. Internet research specialists specialize in finding the answer to any type of question—with remarkable speed. Internet specialists who wish to freelance may find a market for designing and implementing law firm Web sites.

ELDER LAW

Attorneys and paralegals who specialize in elder law deal with issues of special concern to the elderly. Elder law is a rapidly growing specialization, due mainly to the aging population in the United States and complex legal issues that must be faced by the elderly. Twelve percent of the respondents to the 1997 NALA Salary Survey indicated that they worked in the area of elder law at least part of the time. Paralegals were first asked about this specialty in 1997. Some of the issues dealt with by elder law paralegals include estate planning, living wills, social security, Medicare and Medicaid disputes, patient's rights, financial planning, and guardianships.

Paralegals who specialize in elder law may have some of the following specific duties.

1. Researching elder law topics and issues
2. Meeting with elderly clients to explain complex issues to them concerning estate planning, social security, Medicaid, and other elder law issues
3. Making telephone calls to, and corresponding with, social service agencies concerning the rights of the elderly
4. Acting as advocate for the elderly in meetings and hearings with government agencies

5. Assisting with the appointment of guardians and conservators as required
6. Assisting with all aspects of estate planning

Paralegals who work in this area must be familiar with entitlement programs of concern to the elderly and with local, state, and federal regulations dealing with issues of special concern to the elderly. In addition, they must have the communication skills necessary to communicate effectively with the elderly.

ALTERNATIVE DISPUTE RESOLUTION

Alternative dispute resolution (ADR) involves the resolution of disputes through means other than litigation and offers the parties involved in a dispute the chance to settle their differences quickly and fairly, usually at a significantly reduced cost. The two most common means of ADR are arbitration and mediation, although there are several other methods of ADR, including negotiation, neutral evaluation, and mini- and private judging. ADR is becoming an increasingly popular alternative to litigation and is often recommended or coordinated through the court system to help alleviate backlogs in the courts. Paralegals can be involved in virtually every aspect of the ADR process. The activities surrounding ADR processes usually are not considered to be the *practice of law*, so paralegals are not limited in the tasks they may perform. Paralegals can conduct hearings and act as dispute resolution service providers. They may even act as court-appointed mediators. The tasks that ADR paralegals may perform include the following.

1. Interviewing clients and obtaining information concerning the dispute in question
2. Reviewing and evaluating disputes to determine appropriate method for resolution
3. Researching rules governing specific types of ADR proceedings
4. Scheduling ADR proceedings
5. Making physical arrangements for ADR proceedings, including securing a conference room and other facilities and equipment
6. Drafting settlement agreements between parties
7. Drafting findings of the arbitration or mediation board

Paralegals working in the area of ADR must have excellent negotiation and communication skills.

EMPLOYEE BENEFITS LAW

Employers may elect any one of a variety of **employee benefit plans** to compensate their employees in addition to salaries. Some of these plans include pension plans, profit-sharing plans, stock option plans, and employee stock ownership plans. Many of these plans are covered under the Employee

Retirement Income Security Act of 1974 (ERISA) and other federal laws, and they must comply with certain requirements. Paralegals are often involved in drafting, administering, and maintaining compliance of employee benefit plans (Figure 3–7).

Employee-benefits paralegals may work for corporations to draft and maintain the benefit plans for the employees of that corporation, or they may work for law firms that specialize in implementation and compliance of employee benefit plans for several corporate clients. Alternatively, employee-benefits paralegals may work for accounting firms, financial advisors, or other types of businesses that assist clients with the implementation and administration of employee benefit plans.

Some of the specific duties of employee benefits paralegals include the following.

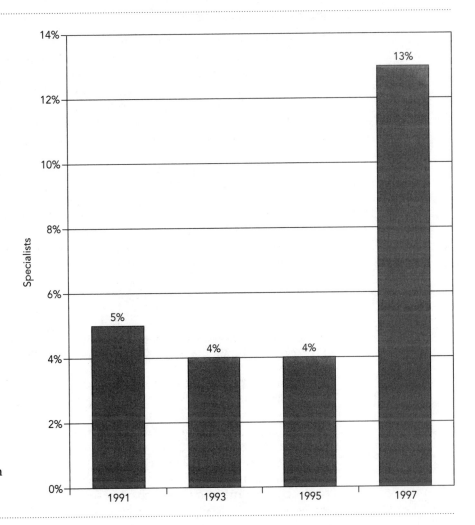

FIGURE 3–7
Growth of the employee benefits law specialty (From the NALA annual salary surveys)

1. Drafting employee benefit plans, including pension, profit sharing, employee stock ownership and stock bonus plans, trust agreements, and life and health insurance plans
2. Drafting summary plan descriptions
3. Submitting employee benefit plans and supplemental documents to the Internal Revenue Service for approval
4. Assisting with the administration of employee benefit plans
5. Drafting notices concerning employee benefit plans
6. Assisting with plan compliance by filing required forms with Internal Revenue Service and Department of Labor

Paralegals who work in the employee benefits area must have excellent writing, research, and organizational skills.

ENVIRONMENTAL LAW

Environmental law deals with implementation and enforcement of laws and regulations concerning environmental issues affecting the use of air, water, and land (Figure 3–8). Paralegals who work in environmental law may work in legal departments of large corporations or law firms with corporate clients to ensure that the corporations are complying with all environmental air, water, and land regulations that may affect them. They may spend time researching the compliance with environmental regulations of target corporations in the event of a possible merger or buy-out. Large real estate development corporations often have their own legal department to assure that all new developments are in compliance with environmental regulations. Other environmental law paralegals work for government agencies, such as the Environmental Protection Agency, that implement or enforce environmental laws and regulations or for lobbyists who represent the interests of groups with concerns related to the environment.

Often, new real estate developments involve environmental law issues and attorneys are called in to help obtain the proper permits. Paralegals may assist with several aspects of new development. Specific duties of environmental law paralegals may include the following.

1. Performing legal research concerning air, water, and land use
2. Reviewing corporate procedures to assure compliance with applicable laws and regulations
3. Drafting memoranda to appropriate corporate personnel regarding compliance with environmental regulations and possible violations
4. Reviewing any notices of violations
5. Maintaining records for correction of violation and payment of penalties of all violations
6. Conducting due diligence searches of actual and potential environmental liability in connection with the purchase of real estate or in connection with the purchase of a new business

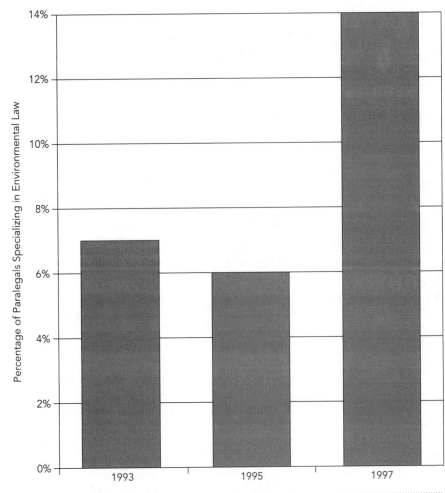

FIGURE 3–8
*Growth of the
environmental law
specialty (*From the
NALA Annual Salary
Surveys)

7. Obtaining or drafting opinions concerning potential environmental liability in connection with the sale or purchase of real estate
8. Monitoring the status of proposed environmental rules and regulations
9. Researching all issues connected with environmental rules and regulations

OTHER IMPORTANT SPECIALTIES

There are numerous other areas of law in which paralegals may specialize; in fact, paralegals may specialize in any area of law that exists (Figure 3–9).

High-Demand Specialties

Corporate Law, including:
- Transactional
- Mergers and acquisition
- Securities
- Contract
- Compliance
- Antitrust
- Corporate finance

Intellectual Property, including:
- Trademarks
- Patents
- Copyrights

Real Estate, including:
- Commercial transactions

Employment Law, including
- Employee benefits/ERISA
- Labor relations

---

*Kay Schroven is the Paralegal Placement Director for The Law Registry in Minneapolis, Minnesota. The Law Registry is a national company specializing in placement of legal professionals.

FIGURE 3–9
Specialties in the highest demand (Courtesy of Kay Schroven)*

Over the years, the practice of law has become more and more specialized with new specialties being introduced all the time. Computer law is one example of an expanding area of practice that did not exist just a few years ago. Some other areas of paralegal specialties include the following.

Admiralty/Maritime. Paralegals who specialize in admiralty/maritime law assist attorneys whose work concerns **maritime law,** the law ruling the carrying of passengers and cargo on navigable waters. Their work often involves litigation concerning personal injuries, vessel collision cases, wrongful death, and other types of actions that can occur on the water.

Advertising Law. Paralegals who specialize in advertising law may work for attorneys who represent businesses to see that the businesses' advertising is in compliance with pertinent laws, or they may work for consumer groups or federal or state agencies to monitor the legality of advertising in that jurisdiction.

Antitrust Law. Antitrust law is a branch of corporate law that concerns compliance with federal and state statutes designed to protect business from unlawful restraints, price discriminations, price fixing, and monopolies. Paralegals who specialize in antitrust law perform federal and state legal research on antitrust law, prepare reports for clients and government agencies, and assist with legal actions brought under the antitrust statutes.

Banking Law. Most paralegals who specialize in banking law work in bank legal departments or trust departments and may work in any aspect of banking law that concerns their employer. Other banking law specialists work for law firms that represent banks or other types of lending institutions.

Bankruptcy Law. Bankruptcy is the system under which a debtor may come into court or be brought into court by creditors. Filing for bankruptcy involves either seeking to have the debtor's assets administered and sold for the benefit of creditors, leaving the debtor discharged from those debts (a straight bankruptcy), or to have those debts reorganized. This is a specialty that flourishes in times of economic adversity when the number of bankruptcies is on the rise. Paralegals who specialize in bankruptcy work for law firms that act as trustees in bankruptcy court or represent the creditors or debtors. Much of their work involves accounting for the debtor's assets and preparing bankruptcy documents.

Civil Rights Law. Civil rights law paralegals most often work for government agencies to help resolve discrimination complaints based on race, age, sex, or religion or they work for private law firms that specialize in civil rights lawsuits.

Collections. Paralegals who work in collections assist clients with the collection of debts owed to them.

Complex Litigation. Complex litigation is a newer subspecialty of litigation that involves large, complex litigation—often product liability and class action suits involving multiple plaintiffs and defendants. Paralegals who work in complex litigation usually work in large law firms. Their work is often specialized and technical, and they may rely heavily on computer technology to organize and assemble research and documents.

Contract Law. Law firms and all types of corporations and organizations are concerned with contract law. Large corporations may have a contracts division of their legal department to negotiate, draft, and review all major contracts the corporation enters into. A paralegal who specializes in contract law may be a member of the team in the contracts division of a legal department, or a contracts paralegal may work for a large law firm that has a contracts department that drafts and reviews contracts for its individual and business clients.

Employment Law. Employment law is the branch of law that concerns the relationship between employers and employees and health and safety issues in the workplace. Paralegals who work in employment law often work for in-house counsel of corporations, for attorneys in law firms who specialize in employment law, or for administrative agencies that deal with employment law issues such as wrongful discharge, discriminatory hiring practices, workers' compensation, and drug and alcohol testing.

Entertainment Law. Paralegals who specialize in entertainment law assist with several types of matters within the entertainment industry, including negotiating, drafting, and reviewing contracts for entertainers and others associated with the entertainment industry. They may work for law firms that represent actors, musicians, or the other individuals in the entertainment industry, or they may work in-house for corporations in the entertainment industry, such as television networks or movie studios.

Ethics and Professional Responsibility. Paralegals who specialize in ethics and professional responsibility most often work for state disciplinary agencies that handle ethics complaints against attorneys.

General Practice. Many attorneys still have general practices that serve clients in a multitude of areas, and they employ many paralegals. Paralegals who work in general practice law firms perform several of the duties performed by paralegals who specialize in family law, estate planning and probate, real estate, bankruptcy, and criminal law.

Health Law. Health law is the area of law that concerns the interests of healthcare providers and health-related businesses, including business structuring, handling transactions, and regulatory concerns. Health law may also include litigation concerning healthcare providers. Paralegals who specialize in health law may work in-house for healthcare provider corporations, or they may work for attorneys in law firms who specialize in representation of healthcare providers.

Immigration Law. Most paralegals who work in **immigration** law work to assist clients with their legal immigration to the United States. They help clients through the required paperwork, meetings, and hearings with immigration officials. Immigration law paralegals work for state or federal agencies or for law firms that specialize in immigration law.

Investigations. Because of their knowledge of the law and attention to detail, paralegals often work as investigators either for law firms or private investigation firms. Law firms often use the services of an investigator to obtain the facts surrounding cases they handle, especially those involving personal injury.

Labor Law. Paralegals who work in labor law usually work for corporate legal departments, or for law firms that specialize in representation of businesses or individuals with labor law matters, including union contracts and negotiations.

Landlord and Tenant Law. Paralegals who specialize in this area of law assist attorneys representing either the landlord or tenant in disputes concerning either commercial or residential leases.

Legal Nurse Consultant. Legal nurse consultants are paralegals who have both medical and legal training. Legal nurse consultants have been trained as nurses and have completed paralegal studies as well. Legal nurse consultants often use their expertise to assist in the personal injury litigation process. They may work for plaintiff or defense personal injury law firms or for insurance companies. For more information on legal nurse consultants, see the feature preceding this chapter.

Medical Malpractice. Paralegals who specialize in medical malpractice may work for law firms that specialize in bringing suits against doctors and medical institutions for malpractice, or they may work for defense firms that represent insurance carriers handling medical malpractice insurance.

Military Law. Paralegals within the military assist attorneys with all types of military proceedings.

Municipal Bonds. Municipal bond paralegals must have a background in finance. They most often work for cities or for large law firms that represent cities to raise funds for special projects.

Native American/Tribal. Paralegals who work in the Native American or tribal area of law work with attorneys on Indian reservations to represent individuals in tribal court. Paralegals usually are allowed to represent clients in tribal court.

Nonprofit Corporations. The work of paralegals who specialize in nonprofit corporate law, a subspecialty of corporate law, closely resembles the work of corporate paralegals, with a few additions. Nonprofit corporate paralegals often assist with the formation of nonprofit corporations, applying for tax-exempt status and on-going filings and maintenance of the nonprofit corporation.

Oil and Gas. Oil and gas paralegals work mainly on leases for exploration and drilling and disputes over oil and gas ownership rights.

Securities Law. Securities law is a branch of corporate law that concerns compliance with federal and state securities laws, including filing registration statements and annual statements with the SEC and state securities agencies. Paralegals specializing in this area must have a good knowledge of corporate law and securities regulations.

Sports Law. Sports law paralegals usually work for attorneys who represent sports figures and others associated with major league sports. Their work often involves drafting and reviewing contracts and litigation concerning contract disputes.

Tax Law. Tax law paralegals help to prepare complicated tax returns and research complex tax issues for clients.

Workers' Compensation. The work of paralegals who specialize in **workers' compensation** matters resembles the work of personal injury paralegals in many respects because workers' compensation involves personal injury. However, workers' compensation matters are not heard within the court system. Instead, they are heard by the Workers' Compensation Appeals Board, which has its own rules and regulations. Like other administrative agencies, in many states the Workers' Compensation Appeals Board allows paralegals to appear before it on behalf of clients, so long as the clients agree.

NONTRADITIONAL PARALEGAL CAREER PATHS

You may begin your career in a traditional paralegal position, stick to your chosen path, and advance to new paralegal positions with more responsibility. You may add or switch specialties or become a highly specialized expert in one or two areas of law. In addition to the traditional paralegal role, working for an attorney in a traditional specialty, there are several other options available to you. You can expand your career possibilities by following a nontraditional career path.

Changes in your career may move you up the ladder and promote you to an advanced paralegal or paralegal management position. Paralegals with management experience or ability often make excellent paralegal managers because they have a unique understanding of the challenges faced by paralegals.

You may move to other nonparalegal legal positions, such as human resources, marketing, public relations, systems manager, or other positions required to run a law firm or legal department. Currently, there is a high demand for computerized litigation support. Paralegals who are proficient with database software and trial presentation software can provide a useful service in streamlining the litigation process. Your paralegal training and experience will provide you with relevant qualifications for such a position. You already will be familiar with legal terms and procedures, as well as with law firm or legal department politics.

Many paralegals find that the skills they acquire through their work translate well to other careers. Abilities such as research, writing, communications, attention to detail, and interpersonal skills can prepare you for several different types of careers. Employers other than the traditional paralegal employers will appreciate these skills. Your paralegal training can be useful in a business career in management, marketing, sales, lobbying, contract administration, or human resources—just to name a few. Many paralegals have left law firms to work for vendors they have met and worked with throughout their careers, including law book publishers, law office equipment vendors, or any other vendors that serve law firms.

Eventually, you may want to leave the traditional workforce to strike out on your own as an entrepreneur. Many paralegals have done this by making use of the contacts they have made throughout their paralegal careers and beginning businesses that offer services to law firms such as temporary employment services, court reporting services, or law firm billing and collection services.

Teaching is another course many paralegals choose to follow. Throughout your education, many of your instructors will probably be paralegals or former paralegals. Often school administrators value the hands-on experience of paralegal instructors. Although some paralegal programs make it a policy to hire only attorney instructors, in most universities a bachelor's or master's degree will qualify you as a candidate for teaching paralegal courses. Some community colleges will consider paralegal instructors who have an associates degree—if they are experienced and knowledgeable and have excellent communication skills.

Your paralegal career may also motivate you to further your education. You may find that after assisting with the practice of law you would like to attend law school and practice on your own. Many paralegals also continue their education by obtaining advanced degrees in related areas, such as a master's degree in business, library science, or public administration.

Focus on Ethics: *Conflicts of Interest*

Attorneys and their paralegals owe a duty of loyalty to their clients. During your paralegal career, you must be aware of any personal interests you may have that conflict with the interests of any clients you work to represent. What if your law firm's new client is suing your brother's business? In addition, you must be aware of any conflicts between clients you have helped to represent—both currently and in the past. What if the law firm that has just hired you represents a client who is suing a client of the firm you just left?

When the interests of a client conflict with the personal interests of an attorney, another client of the attorney, or a past client of the attorney, the attorney has a potential conflict of interest. If the representation of a new client presents a possible conflict of interest, the attorney must turn down the new representation or obtain consent of both parties. Paralegals must be aware of and abide by the ethical rules concerning conflicts of interest that govern attorneys. The paralegal's personal interests must not conflict with those of a client of an attorney the paralegal is assisting. In addition, the paralegal must not be in a position to assist a client who has an interest adverse to a current or former client. Specific rules concerning conflicts of interest are included in the rules of ethics for attorneys in every state, as well as in the model rules of ethics of the NFPA and the NALA.

PRACTICAL CONSIDERATIONS

The consequences of an undisclosed conflict of interest involving a paralegal and a client of the firm or organization employer can have devastating affects for the client, the supervising attorney, the law firm, and the paralegal. If, as a paralegal, you have any question concerning a possible conflict of interest you may be involved in, you must report it to your supervising attorney immediately.

Here are some steps you can take to be certain that you are not involved improperly in a conflict of interest situation.

1. Keep a current list of client names and matters related to all files on which you work. This may be as simple as keeping copies of your billing reports.
2. When you leave your position in a law firm, take a list of the clients on whose files you have worked and the related matters to compare with any files you may be assigned to in the future. This list should be kept confidential. The only information to be disclosed from this list would be the name of a former client (or opposing party) whose file you have worked on if a conflict of interest arises.
3. Keep current with your firm's conflict of interest procedures. Law firms commonly circulate weekly lists of new clients and new matters

that the firm is representing. This list should be checked against your current list of clients and any lists from previous employers.

4. If your firm takes on a client with whom you have a personal interest, either a financial interest or a personal relationship, that information should be reported to the supervising attorney as soon as possible.

5. If you ever even suspect that you may be involved in a conflict of interest situation, report it to your supervising attorney or other appropriate individual in your law firm or law department immediately.

Above all, if you have any questions concerning conflicts of interest, consult the rules of your paralegal association and the rules applicable to attorneys in your jurisdiction.

SUMMARY

It is not possible to cover in one chapter all of the possible paralegal specialties available to individuals who have paralegal training and experience. As a paralegal, you may specialize in virtually every area of law that exists—and new areas are constantly being created. With the increasing complexity of the practice of law and the possibilities that exist with current technology, paralegals can become an integral part of any legal service team. With the right training and experience, you can choose an employer and a specialty that will suit your personality and needs.

CAREER TRACK

The type of specialty you choose will be important to your career.

What type of specialty do you think you would enjoy? Is it a specialty that is common in the city or area in which you plan to work? Is it a specialty that offers the salary, benefits, and work environment you would enjoy?

If there are one or a few specialties that are of particular interest to you, you will want to be sure to plan your education accordingly.

It is important to remember that most paralegals specialize or work in more than one area of law. You will be better prepared to face the workforce if you have expertise and some experience or exposure to several complementary areas of law. For example, if you have taken courses in administrative law and worked with the elderly, you may find yourself marketable to government agencies that assist the elderly. A background in corporate law combined with extensive coursework in litigation could make you valuable to a corporate legal department or a law firm that specializes in commercial litigation.

If you feel you need more information on specialties, your state or local paralegal association, or the state bar association in your area may be of assistance. The current NFPA Compensation Report and the *Paralegal*

Responsibilities booklet published by the NFPA both provide useful information on paralegal specialties. These documents may be obtained by contacting the National Federation of Paralegal Associations at P.O. Box 33108, Kansas City, MO 64114-0108, or on the Internet at **www.paralegals.org**. The NALA Survey Report referred to in this chapter may be obtained by contacting the National Association of Legal Assistants at 1516 S. Boston #200, Tulsa, OK 74119, calling 918-587-6828, or from the NALA Web site at **www.nala.org**.

Also, check in from time to time on the companion Web site to this text at **www.westlegalstudies.com**, where you will find updated statistics on the hottest specialties for paralegals and helpful links to several sites for more information.

GLOSSARY

Administrative Law Law, including rules, regulations, orders, and decisions, to carry out regulatory powers and duties of administrative agencies.

Bankruptcy The system under which a debtor may come into court, or be brought into court by his or her creditors, either seeking to have his or her assets administered and sold for the benefit of creditors and to be discharged from his or her debts, or to have his or her debts reorganized.

Copyright A property right in an original work of authorship (such as a literary, musical, artistic, photographic, or film work) fixed in any tangible medium of expression, giving the holder the exclusive right to produce, adapt, distribute, perform, and display the work. *(Black's Law Dictionary, Seventh Edition)*

Defendant A person sued in a civil proceeding or accused in a criminal proceeding. *(Black's Law Dictionary, Seventh Edition)*

Employee Benefits Law Area of law dealing with the drafting, implementation, maintenance and compliance of all types of employee benefit plans, including pension plans, profit-sharing plans, and welfare benefit plans.

Environmental Law Area of law dealing with implementation and enforcement of laws and regulations concerning environmental issues affecting the use of air, water, and land.

Estate Planning The preparation for the distribution and management of a person's estate at death through the use of wills, trusts, insurance policies, and other arrangements, especially to reduce estate-tax liability. *(Black's Law Dictionary, Seventh Edition)*

Immigration The act of entering a country with the intention of settling there permanently. *(Black's Law Dictionary, Seventh Edition)*

Intellectual Property Law The law governing copyrights, patents, trademarks, and trade names.

Maritime Law The body of law governing marine commerce and navigation, the transportation at sea of persons and property, and marine affairs in general; the rules governing contract, tort, and workers' compensation claims arising out of commerce on or over water. Also termed *admiralty; admiralty law. (Black's Law Dictionary, Seventh Edition)*

Patent The governmental grant of a right, privilege, or authority. The official document so granting. *(Black's Law Dictionary, Seventh Edition)*

Personal Injury In a negligence action, any harm caused to a person, such as broken bone, a cut, or a bruise; bodily injury. Any invasion of a personal right, including mental suffering and false imprisonment. For purposes of workers' compensation, any harm (including worsened preexisting condition) that arises in the scope of employment. *(Black's Law Dictionary, Seventh Edition)*

Plaintiff The party who brings a civil suit in a court of law. Abbr. Pltf. *(Black's Law Dictionary, Seventh Edition)*

Probate To admit a will to proof. To administer a decedent's estate. *(Black's Law Dictionary, Seventh Edition)*

Regulatory Agency Agency that receives its power from the legislative branch of the government to oversee and regulate certain industries and professions.

Securities Instruments such as stocks, bonds, notes, convertible debentures, warrants, or other documents that represent a share in a company or a debt owed by a company or government entity.

Trademark A word, phrase, logo, or other graphic symbol used by a manufacturer or seller to distinguish its product or products from those of others. *(Black's Law Dictionary, Seventh Edition)*

Workers' Compensation A system of providing benefits to an employee for injuries occurring in the scope of employment. Most workers' compensation statutes both hold the employer strictly liable and bar the employee from suing in tort. Also termed *workmen's compensation; employers' liability.* *(Black's Law Dictionary, Seventh Edition)*

Feature   The Question of Overtime

Whether paralegals should receive overtime pay is a question that has been surrounded by controversy almost since the inception of the paralegal profession. The proponents for paying overtime to paralegals feel that the Fair Labor Standards Act, which requires the payment of overtime compensation to employees, should apply to paralegals. Those opposed to overtime for paralegals feel that paralegals are exempt from the Fair Labor Standards Act under one or more specific categories and are therefore not entitled to additional pay in the form of overtime compensation. Both sides present convincing arguments.

The Fair Labor Standards Act (FLSA) entitles employees to compensation equal to 1½ times their hourly wage for each hour they work in excess of 40 per week. This Act applies to all workers, unless they are considered exempt based on the type of position they hold. All nonexempt employees are entitled to overtime pay under the FLSA. Paralegals may be considered exempt employees if their work falls under an exempt category as defined in Title 29 of the Code of Federal Regulations. The exempt categories, which are defined by duties and responsibilities, most often used to exempt paralegals from the FLSA include executive, professional, and administrative.

State labor law also provides for overtime pay to employees who are nonexempt. However, the state's definition of nonexempt may be different than that of the Department of Labor.

In a 1994 case in Texas that dealt specifically with overtime compensation for paralegals, the jury found that legal assistants were administratively exempt from the overtime provisions of the FLSA.[i] The jury found that the primary duties of the legal assistants employed at the defendant law firm fell within the administrative category of exemptions. However, in a 1996 opinion by the U.S. Department of Labor, Wage and Hour Division, the Department concluded that the paralegal who was the subject of the inquiry was engaged in the "production of work" for his or her employer and that the paralegal did not qualify for exemption as a bona fide administrative employee as defined in the regulations.

The 1997 Survey of the NFPA gathered information regarding salary, benefits, and overtime from over 4000 paralegals nationwide. Responses to that survey indicated that almost 40 percent of paralegals work in excess of 40 hours per week,[ii] and about half of those paralegals

---

[i] *Reich v. Page & Addison, P.C.*, No. 91-CV-2655-P (N.D. Tex., 1994).

[ii] National Federation of Paralegal Associations, Inc. Paralegal Compensation and Benefits Report (1997).

consider themselves to be nonexempt and are not entitled by law to overtime compensation.[iii]

The average salary paid to exempt paralegals is somewhat higher than that paid to nonexempt paralegals. Exempt paralegals report an average salary of $33,585 compared with $31,229 reported by nonexempt paralegals.[iv] Almost 32 percent of the paralegals responding to the 1997 NFPA survey indicated that they received overtime compensation in the form of pay. Roughly 29 percent indicated that they received compensation time or a combination of compensation time and cash for hours worked in excess of the normal work week. Nearly one third of the paralegals responding to the survey indicated that they received no overtime compensation.

Paralegals are surprisingly divided on the issue of overtime pay. About half of all working paralegals feel they should be seen as exempt employees not entitled to overtime compensation. They feel that in order to be perceived as true professionals and not part of the law firm's support staff, they should be considered exempt. In contrast, some paralegals feel that they should be fairly compensated for overtime with additional pay. Although they consider themselves to be professionals, they recognize that the attorneys in the office who are considered professionals earn considerably more than paralegals.

Some law firms compensate their paralegals for overtime even if they consider them to be exempt. They may compensate them by granting them compensation time—time off they can schedule at their pleasure. Other firms handle the overtime compensation issue by awarding year-end bonuses to paralegals, which reflects in some way the overtime worked by the paralegal. However, neither of these solutions meet the federal guidelines for nonexempt employees.

The attorneys at many law firms do not even consider the possibility that their paralegals may be considered nonexempt employees. They see their paralegals as salaried professionals and treat them that way. They are not considered clerical workers.

Several factors will determine whether you are paid overtime for your work as a paralegal, including the following.

(1) The applicability of the Department of Labor's definitions of nonexempt to your job description
(2) The applicability of your state's definitions of nonexempt to your job description
(3) The general trend followed by law firms and other paralegal employers in the metropolitan area in which you work
(4) The policy of your employer

[iii] National Federation of Paralegal Associations, Inc. Paralegal Compensation and Benefits Report (1997).
[iv] Ibid.

Paralegal Salaries and Benefits

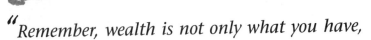

"Remember, wealth is not only what you have,

but also what you are."

GARY JENKINS

INTRODUCTION

As you contemplate your future as a paralegal, you are probably very interested in the salary and benefits you can expect to receive throughout your career. As with any profession, paralegal salaries are based on market conditions, including the supply and demand for workers in the field, as well as the geographic location of the job. Several other factors will contribute to your paralegal salary and benefits, including your experience, education, type of employer and, to a lesser extent, your specialty, billable hour requirements, and paralegal credentials. The demand for paralegals is increasing at a rapid rate, while the supply of new paralegals (the number of individuals completing paralegal education programs) seems to be increasing at a somewhat slower pace. This can be good news for you if you choose a career as a paralegal.

Information concerning paralegal salaries and benefits can be derived from several sources, each of which collects slightly different data and offers slightly different figures. This chapter examines information from several sources concerning paralegal salaries and benefits and then looks to the factors that will determine your salary as a paralegal, including your geographic location, your experience, your education, and your employer. This chapter then examines the possible impact on your salary of your chosen specialty, and your billable hour requirements. This chapter concludes with a look at paralegal bonuses and benefits.

Paralegal Profile

PROFILE ON JILL E. STIEG

Do not be afraid to stumble along the way. You will learn from your mistakes. Mistakes are humbling; they will make you a great paralegal.

Name and Location:	Jill E. Stieg, Appleton, Wisconsin
Title:	Paralegal
Specialty:	Family Law
Education:	Bachelors Degree in Criminal Justice from University of Wisconsin, Oshkosh. Paralegal Certificate from American Institute for Paralegal Studies.
Experience:	9½ Years

Jill Stieg is an experienced family law paralegal who works for a small law firm in Appleton, Wisconsin. She is the Fox Valley Chapter Director of the Paralegal Association of Wisconsin, Inc.

The law firm Jill works for employs fourteen attorneys and eight paralegals. She is responsible for assisting with the family law services provided to the firm's clients. Some of the tasks she performs on a regular basis include meeting with clients to review and sign divorce papers, gathering financial records, interviewing potential witnesses in custody disputes, drafting several types of legal documents associated with family law, limited legal research, and training new attorneys and paralegals in family law procedures.

Some of the family law matters Jill works on can be both interesting and complex, especially when second and third marriages and several million dollars are involved. Jill recently worked on a file where she was required to spend 10 hours meeting with a financial planner to trace the assets of a divorcing couple.

Jill enjoys a great deal of client contact and a high level of responsibility. She also enjoys the people with whom she works and says that the staff and attorneys "are good people and fun to be around." On the downside, she reports that the stress level in family law can be tremendous at times.

Jill's advice to paralegal students?

Be computer literate. If you have an opportunity to intern as a paralegal, do that. You never know if it will lead to a job. Be well organized and have good communication skills. You will need to speak effectively with other professionals.

Be assertive with your boss. Remember you are educated as a paralegal and should be used in that capacity.

SOURCES OF INFORMATION

New statistics on paralegal salaries are being constantly released. The national paralegal associations, *Legal Assistant Today* magazine, and the federal government provide the most extensive and consistent information. Several national associations, legal consulting firms, and most state and local paralegal associations also conduct periodic salary surveys. Although not as comprehensive as the national surveys, the results of surveys done by your local association can be even more meaningful to you.

The information in this chapter is based on the most current surveys available in late 1999. Although figures change from year to year, most of the general conclusions that can be drawn and most of the trends that can be detected remain constant for several years. Up-to-date figures from each of these sources can be found at **www.westlegalstudies.com**, the companion Web site to this text. The Web site is updated quarterly.

THE NATIONAL FEDERATION OF PARALEGAL ASSOCIATIONS, INC. PARALEGAL COMPENSATION AND BENEFITS REPORT

Biannually, the NFPA mails questionnaires to several thousand paralegals across the United States, including NFPA members. The NFPA Paralegal Compensation and Benefits Report is based on the responses to that questionnaire received by the NFPA, which include some responses received via the NFPA's Internet home page. The most recent Compensation and Benefits Report is based on the responses of more than 4,000 paralegals.[1] Up-to-date information about the most current Compensation and Benefits Report can be found at the NFPA home page at **www.paralegals.org** or the companion Web site to this text.

To better understand the results of the NFPA surveys, it is important to understand who the respondents are. The *average* paralegal who responded to the 1997 NFPA salary survey is a 38-year-old white female with a bachelors degree who has completed an ABA-approved program for paralegal studies. She has worked for 7 to 10 years and has a billing rate of $41 to $80 per hour. Her salary is $34,514, with a $2,094 annual bonus. She is the most satisfied with the attorney contact on her job and her level of responsibility. She is the least satisfied with her bonus, salary, and secretary support.

Characteristic	Average Response	Percentage of Average Population with Characteristic
Gender	Female	92%
Race	Caucasian	91%
Age	National average	38
Education – College	Bachelors degree	53%
Education – Paralegal	Paralegal studies	85%
	ABA-approved	64%
Employer Type	Law firm	71%
Time Employed as a Paralegal	National average	7–10 years
Billing Rate	$41–$80/hour	66%

Salary	National average	$34,514
Bonus	National average bonus	$2,094
	Percent receiving a bonus	64%
Areas of Greatest	Attorney contact	33%
Satisfaction	Responsibility	34%
Areas of Least	Bonus	45%
Satisfaction	Salary	29%
	Secretary support	36%

THE NATIONAL ASSOCIATION OF LEGAL ASSISTANTS NATIONAL UTILIZATION AND COMPENSATION SURVEY REPORT

The NALA has conducted a biannual Utilization and Compensation Survey since 1986. The most recent Survey Report was based on nearly 3,000 responses to the NALA Survey.[2] Information on the most current NALA Utilization and Compensation Survey can be found on the NALA Website at www.NALA.org. Aside from the fact that a majority of the respondents to the 1997 NALA survey were members of NALA, the profile of the average respondent to this survey is very similar to that of the average 1997 NFPA survey respondent. The table below represents a profile of the average respondent to the 1997 NALA survey.

Characteristic	Average Response	Percentage of Average Population with Characteristic
Gender	Female	96%
Age	National average	42
Education – College	Bachelors degree	41%
Employer Type	Law firm	75%
Time Employed with Current Employer	National average	7 years
Professional Association and Credentials	Members of NALA	56%
	Certified Legal Assistant	44%
Salary	National average	$33,949
Bonus	National average	$2,062

LEGAL ASSISTANT TODAY ANNUAL SALARY SURVEY

The *Legal Assistant Today* Annual Surveys are another important source for information on paralegal salaries. Although the sample sizes of the surveys are significantly smaller than those of either the NFPA or NALA surveys,[3] the *Legal Assistant Today* surveys have two advantages over either of those surveys. First, the *Legal Assistant Today* surveys measure responses from the readers of *Legal Assistant Today,* rather than one of the associations. Readers of *Legal Assistant Today* may be members of either national association or members of no paralegal association. Second, the *Legal Assistant Today* survey is published annually instead of biannually, which makes the survey results the most current available every other year.

OTHER SOURCES

Although the national paralegal associations and *Legal Assistant Today* provide the most comprehensive paralegal salary information, they are not the only sources of information on the subject. Other national associations, such as the Legal Assistant Management Association, conduct surveys of law office personnel that include information on paralegal salaries. These surveys usually are available to members, and to nonmembers for a fee. Other sources to consult for information on paralegal salaries and benefits include publications aimed at attorneys, the federal government, and state and local paralegal associations.

Several federal government agencies gather information and compile statistics concerning employment in the United States. The Bureau of Labor

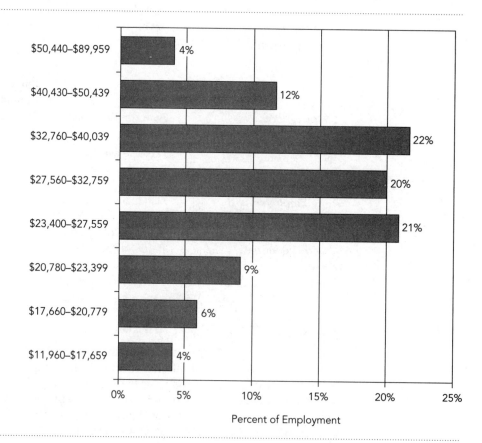

FIGURE 4–1
1997 National ccupational employment and wage data: Wage range of paralegal personnel

Statistics publishes annual occupational employment and wage data. See Figure 4–1.

Here is a summary of the current overall average salaries reported by several of the avaliable sources.

Source	Overall Average Paralegal Salary Reported
National Federation of Paralegal Associations	$34,514
National Association of Legal Assistants	$33,949
Legal Assistant Today	$35,115
Bureau of Labor and Statistics	Between $32,760 and $40,039

When considering the results of any survey, you must consider who the survey participants are and how they may differ from the average population. You must also consider the differences between your situation and that of the respondents. Again, the respondents to the national surveys tend to be a very experienced group of paralegals. Because you can generally expect your salary to increase with your experience, the reported salaries will be higher than salaries of paralegals with little or no experience.

HOW THE GEOGRAPHIC LOCATION OF YOUR WORK AFFECTS YOUR SALARY

Paralegal salaries, like salaries in most professions, are greatly affected by the location of the work. Salaries paid on both the East and West Coasts, where the cost of living is generally higher than the midsection of the country, tend to be the highest. This may also be due to the fact that most of the larger cities in the country are located on either coast. Paralegal salaries in large metropolitan areas tend to be much higher than salaries offered in smaller towns and rural areas. The highest paralegal salaries are paid in large cities on the West Coast.

BY METROPOLITAN AREA

According to the 1997 NFPA study, the highest reported average salary by city was in San Francisco, where average paralegal salaries exceed $46,000.[4] This is not too surprising considering that the cost of living in San Francisco is 174.2 percent of the national average, and the median price of a home (3-bedroom) in San Francisco is $356,435.[5] In Indianapolis, Indiana, where the cost of living is approximately 5 percent below the national average, and the median price of a home (4-bedroom) is $158,900,[6] the average paralegal salary is $31,042.[7]

Paralegal salaries tend to be higher in large metropolitan areas for several reasons, including the following.

- Paralegals are in higher demand in large metropolitan areas.
- The largest law firms are located in large metropolitan areas.
- The cost of living tends to be higher in large metropolitan areas.

See Figure 4–2.

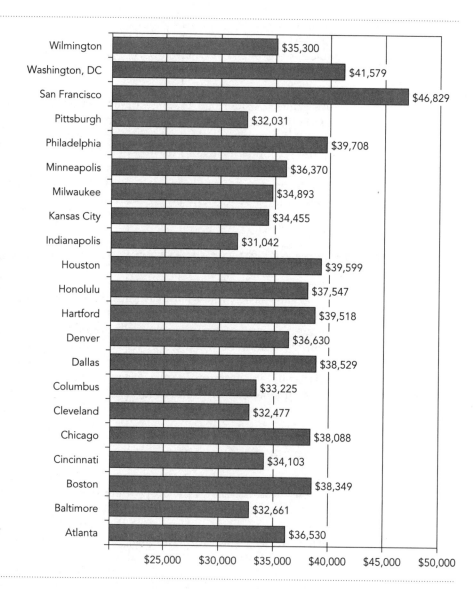

FIGURE 4–2
NFPA 1997 survey results: Average base paralegal salary by metropolitan area

BY GEOGRAPHIC REGION

In addition to the size of the city in which you work, the geographic region of the country will have a significant impact on your paralegal salary. In general, the highest salaries are paid on the West Coast, followed by the eastern region of the United States. Although different measures are used by the various studies conducted, in each case, the West Coast, including the state of California and its large metropolitan areas, has reported the highest salaries. Regions of the country that are the least densely populated generally report the lowest salaries. The states reporting the highest salaries are California, Massachusetts, and Florida. Again, these are all states where the cost of living tends to be quite high.

In addition to the cost of living in each region, other factors that may affect paralegal salaries by region include the following.

- The demand for paralegals in the region
- The availability of a quality paralegal education in the region
- Utilization of paralegals in the region
- Recognition of the paralegal profession within the region

The NFPA Survey Results. The NFPA has divided the respondents to its survey into twelve geographical regions. The highest average base salary of the most recent survey ($40,456) was reported by Region 12, which includes the states of California and Hawaii. Included in Region 12 are some very large metropolitan areas, including Los Angeles and San Francisco, where the highest incomes generally are reported. The average salary in Region 5 ($29,160) was the lowest. Region 5 includes Alabama, Kentucky, and Tennessee. It is an area of the country where salaries in general tend to be lower, as does the cost of living. See Figure 4–3.

The NALA Survey Results. Although the information gathered from the NALA surveys is somewhat different than that gathered by the NFPA survey, the results of the two surveys generally agree. The respondents to the 1997 NALA survey represent all fifty states and the Virgin Islands. The survey participants were categorized into seven geographical regions.

As with the NFPA survey, the highest salaries reported in the most recent NALA survey were in Region 7, which includes the West Coast and the large metropolitan areas in California. The lowest reported average income from the NALA survey was reported in Region 6, the Rocky Mountains, which includes more rural areas and fewer large metropolitan areas. See Figure 4–4.

The *Legal Assistant Today* Survey Results. The *Legal Assistant Today* surveys measure average paralegal salaries by state and by four geographic regions. The states reporting the highest salaries in the 1998–99 survey were Massachusetts ($43,200), California ($41,146), and Florida ($40,229). The states reporting the lowest average paralegal salaries were Nebraska ($24,440), New Mexico ($25,307), and Wyoming ($25,875). The average

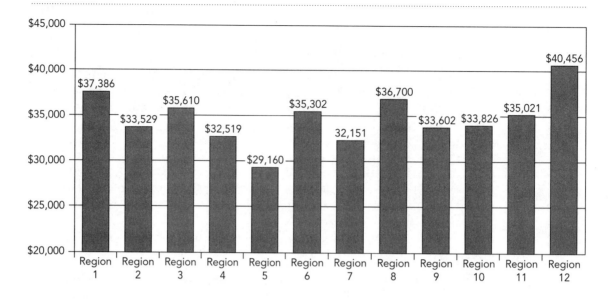

FIGURE 4–3

NFPA 1997 survey results: Average base salary by region

Region 1 (8% of total participants): CT, MA, ME, NH, RI, VT; Region 2 (10%): NJ, NY, PA; Region 3 (7%): DE, MD, VA, DC, WV; Region 4 (9%): FL, GA, NC, SC; Region 5 (3%): AL, KY, TN; Region 6 (12%): AR, LA, MS, OK, TX; Region 7 (12%): IN, MI, OH; Region 8 (11%): IA, MN, ND, SC, WI; Region 9 (8%): IL, KS, MO, NE; Region 10 (5%): AK, ID, MT, OR, WA; Region 11 (7%): AZ, CO, NM, NV, UT, WY; Region 12 (7%): CA, HI.

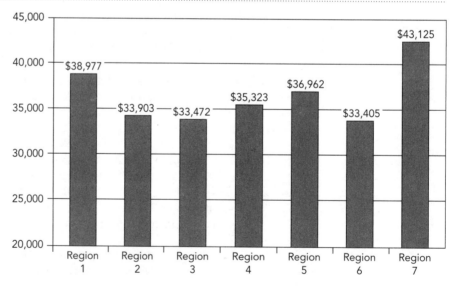

FIGURE 4–4

NALA 1997 survey results: Average compensation by region

Region 1 (130 participants, 6% of total): CT, ME, MA, MD, NH, NJ, NY, PA, RI; Region 2 (161 Participants, 7%): IL, IN, MI, OH, WI; Region 3 (211 participants, 10%): IA, KS, MN, MO, NE, ND, SD; Region 4 (832 participants, 38%): AL, AR, FL, GA, KY, LA, MS, NC, TN, VA, WV; Region 5 (529 participants, 6%): AZ, NM, OK, TX; Region 6 (108 participants, 5%): CO, ID, MT, UT, WY; Region 7 (193 participants, 9%): AK, CA, HI, NV, OR, WA.

salary figures from the states on the lower end, however, may be less meaningful because there were fewer than ten verifiable submissions from each of those states. The regional information from this survey is not particularly helpful because the regions used are large and include a diverse group of states and metropolitan areas. For example, the West Region includes average salaries from paralegals working in both California and Wyoming. The salary for this region is not indicative of either the high salaries earned in the West Coast metropolitan areas or the low salaries earned in Western rural areas. For more detailed information by state, see the current January/February issue of *Legal Assistant Today* magazine or the companion Web site to this text at **www.westlegalstudies.com**.

HOW YOUR EXPERIENCE AFFECTS YOUR SALARY

Paralegal employers value the experience of their paralegals. Paralegals with a high level of experience can generally command a much higher salary than paralegals with little or no experience.

The respondents to the NFPA and the NALA surveys tend to represent a large group of experienced paralegals. The average years of experience of respondents to the 1997 NFPA survey was 7 to 10 years. The average years of experience of legal assistants responding to the 1997 NALA survey was 13 years and the median number of years was 12. As you would expect, all survey results demonstrate the value placed on paralegal experience. Paralegals with up to three years of experience reported salaries in the $29,000 to $31,000 range, although starting salaries for paralegals were reported in the $22,000 to $25,000 range. On the other end of the scale are paralegals with more than 20 years of experience whose salaries averaged in the low- to mid-$40,000 range.

THE NFPA SURVEY RESULTS

According to the results of the 1997 NFPA survey, the average salary by years of experience ranged from $30,662 for paralegals with less than one year experience to $46,288 for paralegals with more than 20 years' experience. See Figure 4–5.

THE NALA SURVEY RESULTS

Similar to the results of the NFPA survey, the results of the 1997 NALA survey indicated that the average salary of paralegals increased incrementally with the paralegals' years of experience. The NALA survey measured both average salary and average compensation. The figures for average compensation take bonuses into account. See Figure 4–6.

The NALA survey indicated there was little difference in earnings between the paralegals with 16 to 20 years, 21 to 25 years, and over 26 years

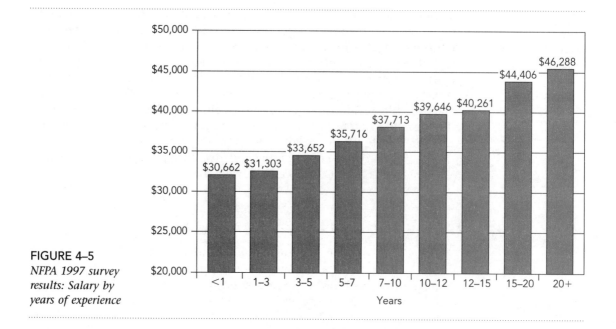

FIGURE 4–5
NFPA 1997 survey results: Salary by years of experience

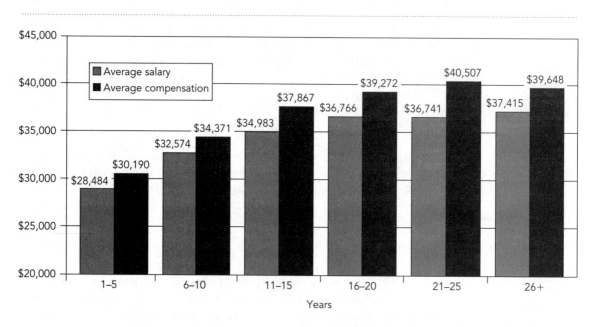

FIGURE 4–6
NALA 1997 survey results: Salary and compensation by years of experience

of experience. In fact, paralegals with 21 to 25 years experience actually earned more than the paralegals with over 26 years of experience. One explanation for this is the general trend for paralegal salaries to level off after paralegals have been on the job for several years and have hit the pay ceiling for their position. There is a certain amount of pressure within law firms to keep the pay of paralegals below that of the associate attorneys in the firm who feel they should earn more because of their education and because, unlike paralegals, they are authorized to practice law.

THE *LEGAL ASSISTANT TODAY* SURVEY RESULTS

The *Legal Assistant Today* 1998-99 survey results support the findings of both the NFPA and the NALA surveys. Paralegals responding to the *Legal Assistant Today* survey with more than 20 years of experience reported a promising average salary of $48,246. See Figure 4–7.

STARTING SALARIES

Starting salaries, the salary you may expect as you begin your career, are measured by the biannual NFPA surveys. The highest percentage of new paralegals responding to the 1997 survey reported that their starting salary was between $22,001 and $25,000. Your salary may vary from this average based on any combination of the factors discussed within this chapter. In addition, your first paralegal employer may take your other work experience into consideration. Even if you have never worked as a paralegal before,

FIGURE 4–7
Legal Assistant Today *1998-99 salary survey results: Salary based on years of experience*

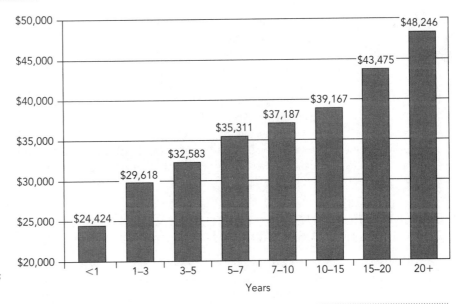

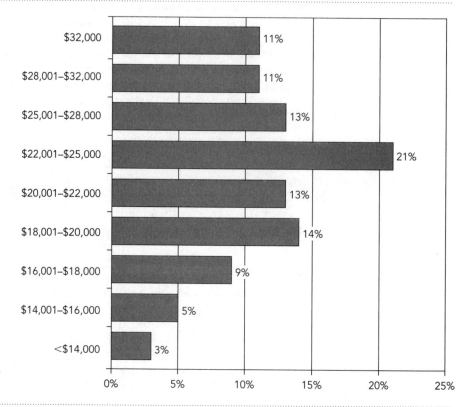

FIGURE 4–8
NFPA 1997 salary survey results: Starting base salaries for new paralegals

your related work experience may be of significant value and may earn you a higher-than-average starting salary.

Having a unique set of skills or possessing skills that are in high demand may also allow you to command a higher-than-average salary. For example, if you speak a foreign language or are highly proficient with computers, a potential employer may be willing to pay a higher starting salary to hire you. According to the 1998-99 *Legal Assistant Today* survey, paralegals who considered themselves as having above average technical expertise reported an average salary of $35,897, compared with paralegals who possessed average technical expertise ($34,492) or below average expertise ($32,700). See Figure 4–8.

HOW YOUR EDUCATION, TRAINING, AND CREDENTIALS AFFECT YOUR SALARY

Paralegals have a wide variety of educational backgrounds. Some of the options for paralegal education include the following.

- A four-year degree in paralegal studies
- A four-year degree in any major with a paralegal certificate

- A two-year paralegal degree
- A two-year degree in any major with a paralegal certificate
- A paralegal certificate
- A masters degree in paralegal studies
- A masters degree in any major with a paralegal certificate
- Some college credits and on-the-job training
- A high school diploma and on-the-job training.

At this time, there are no national or statewide requirements for a paralegal education. Some paralegal employers require their paralegals to have a four-year degree. See Figure 4–9. More information on paralegal education options can be found in Appendix B to this text.

There is a direct correlation between the level of education and average paralegal salaries. All of the major surveys indicate that those paralegals holding a graduate degree earn more than those holding a bachelors degree, and that both of those groups tend to earn more than paralegals holding an associate degree. The correlation between salary and paralegals with other educational backgrounds is somewhat looser. The effect of your level of education on your salary can vary by location. For example, if you work in a city that has a college with a two-year paralegal program that is approved by the ABA and has an excellent reputation, local employers may offer graduates of that program a salary that equals that of paralegals who have a four-year degree.

One surprise with regard to education and average salaries is the high average salary of paralegals with only a high school education. Respondents

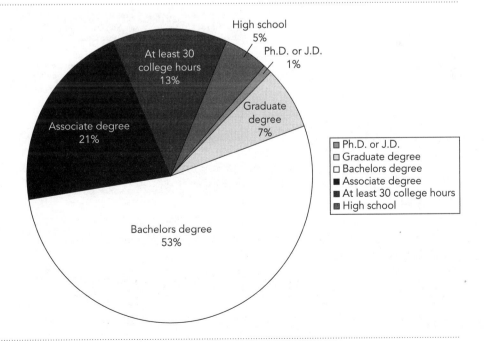

FIGURE 4–9

NFPA 1997 survey results paralegal education

to the 1997 NFPA salary survey with only a high school diploma reported an average salary of $34,730, compared with the $32,290 average salary reported by individuals with an associate degree. A possible explanation for this is that these individuals with only a high school diploma may have been at their current positions for several years and received much of their training on the job. Almost without exception, paralegal employers currently require at least some college for the paralegals they hire.

The results of both the NALA survey and the *Legal Assistant Today Survey* agree with the NFPA survey in this regard. In both of those surveys the highest average salaries were among those with advanced degrees, followed by those holding bachelor degrees, high school diplomas, and associate degrees. See Figure 4–10.

SALARY BY CLA AND RP DESIGNATION

In addition to measuring the average salary and compensation by education, the NALA surveys measure the average salary for NALA members, NALA nonmembers, and those paralegals who have passed the Certified Legal Assistant examination. The Certified Legal Assistant examination is offered by NALA as part of its voluntary certification program for legal as-

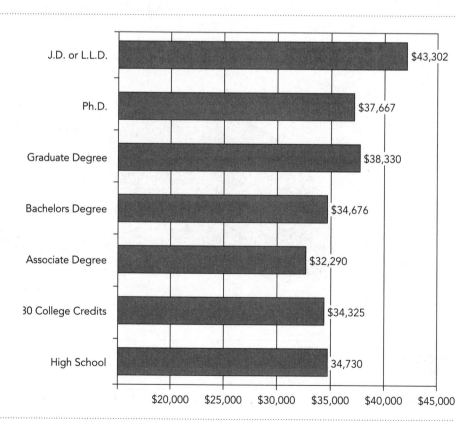

FIGURE 4–10
NFPA 1997 survey results: Average base salary by education

sistants who meet with certain established criteria. Those who meet with the established requirements and pass the Certified Legal Assistant examination earn the CLA credentials. The CLA Specialist credentials are offered to legal assistants who pass the CLA examination and additional specialty examinations. The results of the 1997 NALA salary survey indicate that paralegals who are members of NALA and who have a CLA designation or a CLA specialist designation earned an average salary higher than the national average. Those with a CLA Specialist designation earned the highest average salary ($36,678) compared with the national average for paralegals ($33,949). See Figure 4–11.

According to the *Legal Assistant Today* survey, the average salary earned by paralegals with a CLA designation was $38,532, compared with those paralegals without a CLA designation who earned an average of $34,318.

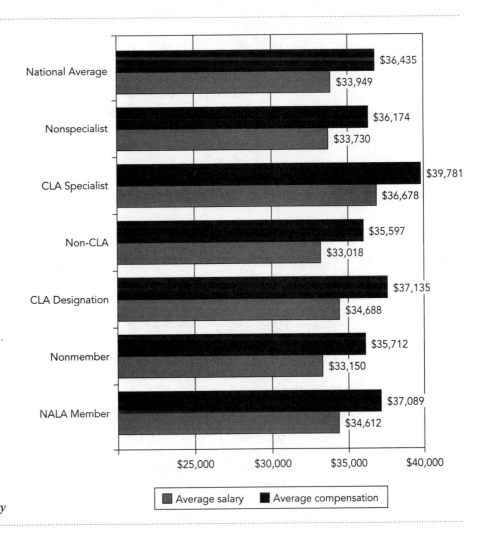

FIGURE 4–11
NALA 1997 survey results: Average salary and compensation by professional activity

The average salary earned by respondents to that survey who have passed the NFPA's Paralegal Advanced Competency Examination (PACE) and earned the Registered Paralegal credential was $43,374 while the average salary of those who have not earned the Registered Paralegal designation was $36,473. This figure may have little real significance, however, because the PACE is still relatively new and few of the respondents to the survey (1 percent) had taken the test.

More information about both the CLA exam and PACE is found in Chapter 5 of this text.

HOW YOUR EMPLOYER AFFECTS YOUR SALARY

As discussed in Chapter Two of this text, the type of employer you work for will affect your work responsibilities, your work environment, and your salary and benefits. Overall, large law firms, corporate legal departments, and the federal government tend to offer the highest pay and best benefits. Smaller law firms and local government agencies generally offer the lowest pay and the fewest benefits.

ETHICAL CONSIDERATION

It is considered unethical for attorneys to split their fees with nonlawyers, including paralegals. Your paralegal compensation cannot be based on a percentage of fees you help to generate.

THE NFPA SURVEY RESULTS

Most (72 percent) of the respondents to the 1997 NFPA salary survey were employed by law firms. The next largest group (21 percent) of the respondents work for corporations. Paralegals who work for nonprofit corporations, state governments, the federal government, freelance, and other employers were also represented; however, none of these groups accounted for more than 2 percent of the total respondents to the survey. Because of the low numbers in these groups, the reported average salaries may not be accurate.

The paralegals who reported the highest salary in the NFPA survey were the self-employed legal technicians and freelance paralegals. However, the respondents in this category were very few, and the NFPA cautions against over-analysis of the reported figures. The next highest reported salaries were reported by paralegals working for corporations. They reported an average base salary of $38,328. Paralegals working for the federal government reported average salaries of $36,738, followed by $33,580 reported by paralegals working for law firms. This portion of the survey does not distinguish by size of the law firm or legal department, a factor which may determine the salary received. See Figure 4–12.

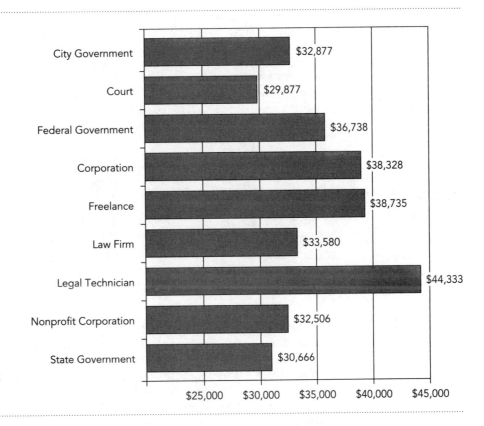

FIGURE 4–12
NFPA 1997 salary survey results: Average paralegal salaries by type of employer

THE *LEGAL ASSISTANT TODAY* SURVEY RESULTS

The *Legal Assistant Today* survey also measured the average salary of respondents according to the employer for whom they work. Again, there are no surprises. Corporate paralegals earned the highest salary, followed by paralegals in law firms, and paralegals who work for the government. You must keep in mind that the vast majority of paralegals responding to this survey (67 percent) indicated that they worked for law firms. See Figure 4–13.

SALARIES BY SIZE OF LAW FIRM

Large law firms, which typically are located in the larger metropolitan areas, tend to offer the best paralegal salaries. The average salaries of paralegals in large law firms tend to be significantly higher than the salaries of paralegals in medium or small law firms. The lowest reported salaries are from paralegals who work for sole proprietors or very small law firms.

The NFPA Survey Results. The highest paid paralegals, according to the NFPA survey, were those who worked for law firms of over 200 attorneys. Respondents to the survey who were employed by law firms of over

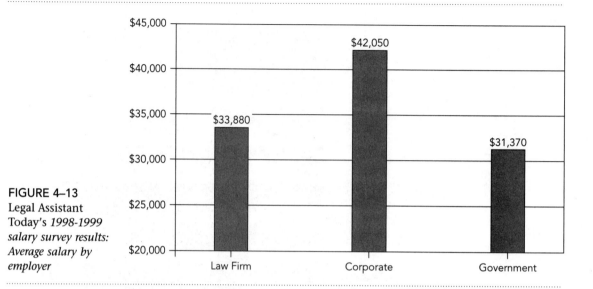

FIGURE 4–13
Legal Assistant
Today's *1998-1999
salary survey results:
Average salary by
employer*

200 attorneys reported an average salary of $38,974, compared with those who work for small law firms with no more than ten attorneys, who reported an average salary of $30,308. See Figure 4–14.

The NALA Survey Results. Again, the results of the NALA survey support the general trend that paralegals in larger law firms tend to earn significantly more than paralegals in small- to medium-sized law firms. See Figure 4–15.

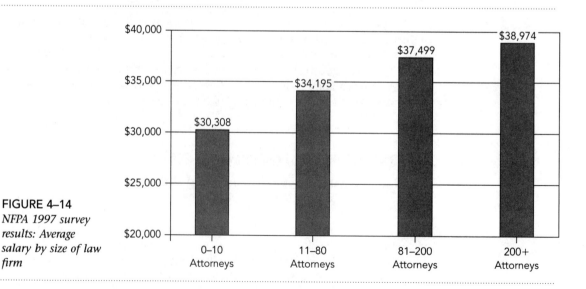

FIGURE 4–14
*NFPA 1997 survey
results: Average
salary by size of law
firm*

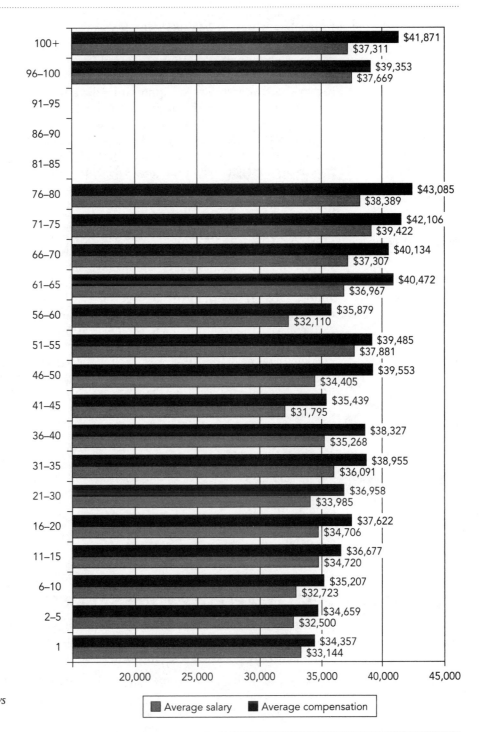

FIGURE 4–15
NALA 1997 survey results: Average salary and average compensation by number of attorneys in law firm

The highest reported average compensation by number of attorneys in the law firm was $43,085, which was reported by the paralegals who work for firms with between 76 and 80 attorneys. This figure is significantly higher than the figure reported by paralegals working for firms with more than 100 attorneys. However, only twelve paralegals responding to the NALA survey, or approximately 1 percent of the respondents, fall into the category of working for between seventy-six to eighty attorneys, so this figure may not be too accurate. More than 8 percent of the respondents to the NALA survey work for more than 100 attorneys, so the average salary of those individuals ($41,871) is probably relatively accurate. No paralegals responding to the NALA survey indicated that they worked for firms with between 80 and 96 attorneys. The lowest average reported compensation was $34,357, which is earned by paralegals who work for sole proprietors.

The *Legal Assistant Today* Survey Results. The results of the *Legal Assistant Today* 1998-99 salary survey support the findings of both the NFPA survey and the NALA survey. The average salary of the paralegal respondents to the magazine's survey who work for sole proprietors ($32,212) is almost $10,000 less than the average salary of paralegal respondents who work for law firms with fifty-one to 100 attorneys ($41,664). As with the NALA survey, the respondents to the *Legal Assistant Today* survey who work for large firms (fifty-one to 100 attorneys) earned somewhat more than paralegals who work for the very largest firms with more than 100 attorneys ($41,232).

Average Salary by Firm Size	
1 Attorney	$32,212
2 to 5 Attorneys	$33,800
6 to 10 Attorneys	$34,109
11 to 25 Attorneys	$37,227
26 to 50 Attorneys	$36,770
51 to 100 Attorneys	$41,664
101 or More Attorneys	$41,232

HOW YOUR SPECIALTY AFFECTS YOUR SALARY

Paralegals who specialize in certain areas of law tend to have higher salaries than paralegals who specialize in other areas of law. The specialties that pay better generally do so for the following reasons.

1. The practice of that area of law may be more profitable than other areas.
2. Demand may be high for paralegals who specialize in that area of law.

3. That area of law may require additional specialized training or experience.
4. The employers who specialize in that area of law may be in a category of employers that generally pay higher.
5. Paralegals who specialize in that area of law may be required to work a significant amount of overtime.

The specialties that tend to pay the best include the following.

- Corporate law
- Entertainment law
- Environmental law
- Insurance law
- Intellectual property
- Litigation
- Real Estate law
- Securities

Paralegals who specialize in the following areas of law generally report the lowest salaries.

- Bankruptcy
- Criminal law
- Family law
- Personal injury
- Probate
- Workers' compensation

THE NFPA SURVEY RESULTS

The 1997 NFPA survey compared the average salary among paralegals who specialize in the eight most common specialties. Of those, paralegals who specialize in the corporate area reported the highest average salary of $35,444. Paralegals who specialize in matrimonial law reported the lowest average salary of $25,622. See Figure 4–16.

THE *LEGAL ASSISTANT TODAY* SURVEY RESULTS

The *Legal Assistant Today* survey also measured the average paralegal salary by specialty. The results showed some similarity to the results of the NFPA survey. Both surveys counted the corporate specialty as among the highest paying, and both counted family law/matrimonial law and personal injury law as among the lowest paying specialties. Other correlations are not so clear. In general, it seems that a few of the specialties tend to pay on the higher end of the pay scale and a few tend to pay on the lower end of the pay scale, while the remaining specialties are not good indicators of the salary received. See Figure 4–17.

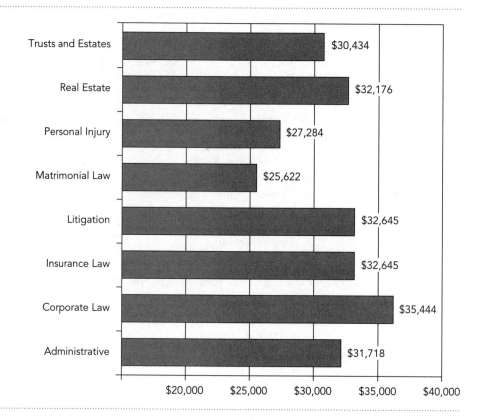

FIGURE 4–16
NFPA 1997 survey results: Average salary by specialty

THE NALA SURVEY RESULTS

The 1997 NALA survey compared the average total compensations of thirty different specialties. The NALA survey questionnaire requested respondents to indicate how much time they spent working in a particular area of law. Paralegals were asked to estimate their time spent on each of several different specialties and categorize it as:

Less than 20 percent of time
More than 20 percent of time; less than 40 percent
More than 40 percent of time; less than 60 percent
More than 60 percent of time; less than 80 percent
From 80 percent to 100 percent of time

Possibly because of the way the NALA survey collected paralegal specialty information, no significant correlation was found between salary and specialty. Taking into consideration the results of both its 1995 and 1997 surveys, the NALA survey analysts concluded that the data gathered in the survey "does not substantiate a notion that, generally, certain practice areas offer higher compensation levels."[8]

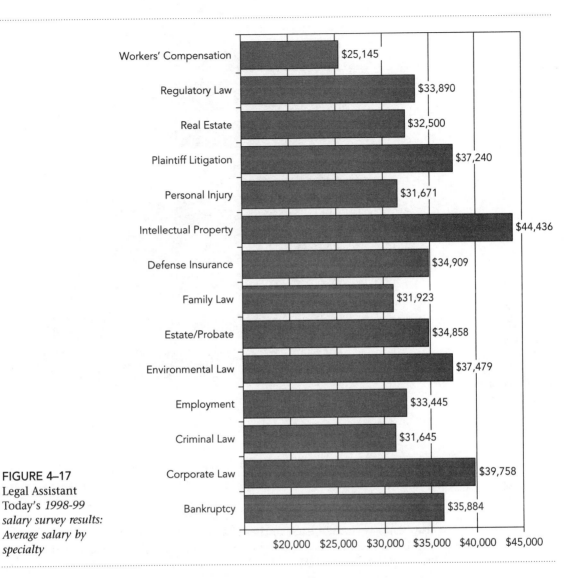

FIGURE 4–17
Legal Assistant Today's *1998-99 salary survey results: Average salary by specialty*

HOW YOUR BILLABLE HOURS AFFECT YOUR SALARY

The vast majority of paralegals who work for law firms bill time to clients. Generally, paralegals who bill the most hours have the highest average salary. The results of the 1997 NFPA survey indicated that paralegals who billed 2,001 or more hours per year had an average salary of $38,321, while paralegals who billed between 500 and 750 hours per year had an average salary of $27,352. Those paralegals who do not bill hours reported an average salary of $23,931. See Figure 4–18.

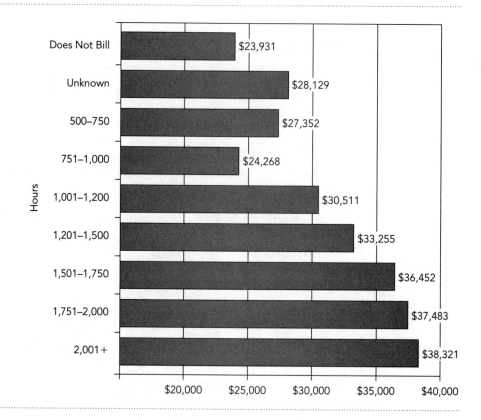

FIGURE 4–18
NFPA 1997 survey results: Average salary relative to billable hours

The only surprise in the data collected by the NFPA survey is that the paralegals who billed between 751 and 1,000 hours earned an average salary of $24,258, which is less than the average salary of the paralegals who billed between 500 and 750 hours. These numbers may be insignificant due to the low response rate in each of these categories. Only 2.7 percent of the paralegals who work in law firms reported that they billed between 500 and 750 hours per year, and only 3.9 percent reported that they billed between 751 and 1,000 hours per year.

The 1997 NALA survey did not measure average compensation by billable hours, and some studies have shown little or no correlation between billable hours and paralegal salaries.

BONUSES

If you accept a paralegal position with a law firm, you can probably expect an annual bonus in addition to your salary. Bonuses may be awarded to paralegals and other law firm or legal department personnel based on a number of different factors. Bonuses may be awarded at the end of each year or on an employee's anniversary. Your bonus may be calculated using a set formula based on years of service with an employer or it may be based on a variable, making bonuses somewhat unpredictable. Bonuses based on the firm's profitability each year or on your performance may be just as generous but less reliable.

THE NFPA SURVEY RESULTS

The 1997 NFPA survey measured the number of paralegals who work for specific types of employers and received bonuses. Over 80 percent of paralegals who work for law firms reported that they receive a holiday bonus or a bonus based on their years of service, billed hours, firm profits, or some other type of criteria.[9] Other types of employers are less likely to pay bonuses.

Type of Employer	Percent Paying Bonus	Average Bonus
City Government	17.6%	$ 201
Court	20%	$ 140
Federal Government	40.5%	$ 501
For-Profit Corporation	54.8%	$1,357
Freelance	36.2%	$1,266
Law Firm	82.3%	$1,532
Nonprofit Corporation	34.6%	$ 440
State Government	17.3%	$ 152

THE NALA SURVEY RESULTS

The NALA surveys do not measure separately the bonuses received by type of employer, but throughout the survey, salary and total compensation were measured. Total compensation includes salary and bonuses, so bonuses can be calculated from the compensation figures. According to the 1997 NALA survey, the average bonus awarded during 1997 was $2,062.

PARALEGAL BENEFITS

Paralegal respondents to the NFPA, NALA, and *Legal Assistant Today* surveys report a vast array of benefits. Your benefits will depend, in large part, on your employer. The federal government, for example, tends to offer a high level of benefits. Smaller law firms may offer fewer benefits. The following chart indicates the percentage of respondents to each survey who receive each particular benefit.

BENEFIT RECEIVED	1997 NFPA RESPONDENTS	1997 NALA RESPONDENTS	1997-98 LEGAL RESPONDENTS ASSISTANT TODAY
Cafeteria Plan (pre-tax premium or flexible benefit plans)	34.7%	N/A	N/A
Continuing Education Fees	49.9%	N/A	62.84%
Daycare Assistance	4.7%	2%	3.24%
Dental	48.6%	35%	
		15% (partial)	55.36%
Disability Insurance	47.5%	53%	51.12%
Employee Medical Insurance	51.8%	71%	90.02%
Entertainment Allowance	3.3%	N/A	N/A
Family Medical Insurance	10.6%	29%	N/A
Flex-Time	N/A	N/A	37.9%
Health Club	9.3%	N/A	N/A
Free Legal Representation	N/A	42%	28.43%
Leased Car	N/A	2%	N/A
Life Insurance	67.8%	67%	63.84%
Maternity Benefits	30.3%	51%	43.14%
Mileage Allowance	43.2%	N/A	N/A
Vision Insurance	22.2%	N/A	29.67%
Parking	31.2% (full)	65%	39.4%
	7.6% (partial)		
Pension or Retirement Plan	44.6%	73%	N/A
Professional Dues	65.9%	78%	60.09%
Profit Sharing Plan	28.2%	42%	N/A
Savings Plan/401(k)	64.5%	N/A	N/A
Seminars	61.2%	N/A	N/A
Paid Sick Leave	78.4%	N/A	N/A
Tuition Reimbursement	31.0%	N/A	N/A
Vacation	89.7%	N/A	N/A

Focus on Ethics: *Financial Matters*

As a paralegal, you may be in a position to see a lot of money change hands. You could be responsible for assisting at a corporate merger closing where several million dollars changes hands. You also could be assigned the bookkeeping of a trust account that holds thousands of dollars. You may see bills leave your office for tens of thousands of dollars in attorneys' fees—some of which are generated by you.

Any time both attorneys and clients are concerned with financial matters, attorneys must use the utmost care to follow the pertinent rules of ethics—many of which are designed to protect the client. With regard to safekeeping of a client's funds and trust accounting, the attorney has a fiduciary duty to the client. When it comes to assessing fees for legal services and billing clients, attorneys must deal fairly with the client and take into consideration their unequal positions.

The rules of ethics of each state include very specific rules for financial dealings between attorneys and their clients. The rules of ethics prescribe guidelines for safekeeping of a client's property, establishing reasonable fees for legal services, fee agreements, and fee splitting arrangements. Regardless of these safeguards, a high proportion of ethical complaints against attorneys concern financial matters, either mishandling of monies held by attorneys on behalf of clients or excessive or unfair billing.

Attorneys have the ultimate ethical responsibility for most financial matters, including billing and handling client funds. This does not mean, however, that the paralegal profession does not affect, or is unaffected by, the ethical rules concerning billing and other financial matters. Quite the opposite is true. Because clients generally are billed for the time paralegals spend working on their files, you must be familiar with the rules of ethics concerning billing and fee splitting. In addition, because paralegals often are assigned the bookkeeping and record keeping associated with accounting for client funds, it is imperative that you be familiar with the ethical rules applicable to attorneys concerning client funds and the rules for bookkeeping and record keeping of client funds.

EXCERPT FROM NFPA MODEL DISCIPLINARY RULES AND ETHICAL CONSIDERATIONS

. . . 1.2 A paralegal shall maintain a high level of personal and professional integrity.

. . . EC-1.2(c) A paralegal shall ensure that all timekeeping and billing records prepared by the paralegal are thorough, accurate, honest, and complete.

EC-1.2(d) A paralegal shall not knowingly engage in fraudulent billing practices. Such practices may include, but are not limited to, inflation of hours billed to a client or employer; misrepresentation of the nature of tasks performed; and/or submission of fraudulent expense and disbursement documentation.

SUMMARY

Most paralegals report being satisfied with their salaries and think they are paid fairly.[10] The overall national average salary for paralegals is somewhere between $34,000 and $34,500. This is up from the national average of $29,607 reported in 1991. Starting base salaries for beginning paralegals range between $20,000 and $30,000. The salary and benefits you can expect as you begin your paralegal career will depend on your employer, your education, and your location. Your specialty and billable hour requirements may also affect your salary. The average age and level of experience from the major surveys indicate that the respondents, on the whole, are a very experienced group of paralegals who have probably been in the work force for several years. This may suggest that older, more experienced paralegals value participation in these surveys more than their younger, less experienced counterparts. It may also be an indication of the maturing of a relatively young profession. With the average respondent to these surveys nearing retirement age within the next 25 years, it would seem that the demand for qualified, experienced paralegals will continue to increase at a faster rate than will the supply of experienced paralegals. Increasing demand over supply will put continual pressure on paralegal employers to offer increasingly attractive salary and benefits packages. All factors influencing the paralegal profession point to an increased demand and increasing responsibilities for paralegals, which will lead to increasing paralegal salaries in the future. According to a study performed by *Compensation & Benefits for Law Offices,* "Highly qualified paralegals who are able to bolster firms' plans for enhanced utilization are hard to come by. As a result, these staff can command top-dollar."[11]

CAREER TRACK

How does the information in this chapter measure up to your expectations and your need to earn a living? What is the average salary for paralegals in your area?

Now take a look at the factors that may determine your starting salary.

- For what type of employer would you prefer to work?
- Do you have related work experience?
- Do you possess any unique skills that potential employers will value?
- What specialty would you prefer?
- Do you have the requisite education and training?

All of these factors can influence your starting salary. For more information on salaries in your location, contact your state or local paralegal association. Appendix C is a directory of state and local paralegal associations.

The most current figures from all sources in this chapter can be accessed at **www.westlegalstudies.com**, the companion Website to this book.

ENDNOTES

[1] The NFPA 1997 Paralegal Compensation and Benefits Report is based on the 4,129 responses the NFPA received to its questionnaire.

[2] The data for this survey was collected during the latter part of 1997 from 2,607 participants.

[3] The 1998-99 *Legal Assistant Today* Survey measured responses from approximately 475 paralegals.

[4] National Federation of Paralegal Associations, Inc. Paralegal Compensation and Benefits Report (1997).

[5] *Money Magazine*, Best Cities 1996.

[6] *Ibid.*

[7] National Federation of Paralegal Associations, Inc. Paralegal Compensation and Benefits Report (1997).

[8] 1997 National Utilization and Compensation Survey Report. Copyright 1997. Published with permission of the National Association of Legal Assistants, 1516 S. Boston, #200, Tulsa, OK, 74119.

[9] National Federation of Paralegal Associations, Inc. Paralegal Compensation and Benefits Report (1997).

[10] Are They Paying You What You're Worth? *Legal Assistant Today's* 1997-98 Salary Survey Results, *Legal Assistant Today,* March/April 1998, p. 72.

[11] 97-12 *Compensation & Benefits for L. Off. 1, *11*

Feature   Pro Bono—Paralegals Who Work for Nothing

As a paralegal, you are in a unique position to make a difference—a difference in the life of a child, an elderly person, a homeless person, or someone else in need. Pro bono work may actually be the most rewarding work of your career.

The term *pro bono* means "for the good; used to describe work or services (e.g., legal services) done or performed free of charge."[1] Pro bono work is encouraged by the bar associations, by the paralegal associations, and by the management of most law firms and legal departments.

As a paralegal, you can volunteer your services independently for tasks that do not constitute the practice of law. You can also work with attorneys as part of a legal team to provide pro bono services. According to the ABA, more than 3 million hours of legal services are donated annually as pro bono work.[2] The ABA recommends a voluntary goal of 50 hours of pro bono work per lawyer per year.[3]

Many law firms and legal departments have pro bono committees that set the standards for pro bono participation by attorneys and paralegals of their firms, and they encourage a certain amount of pro bono work on firm time. They recognize that active pro bono programs in the law firm provide unique experience and training to attorneys and paralegals in the firm and that pro bono work can enhance the reputation of the firm in the community.

Although paralegals must not partake in activities that can be considered the practice of law, there are numerous ways in which paralegals are uniquely qualified to assist those in need. Some of the ways paralegals can offer their pro bono services include the following.

- Working as advocates for victims of abuse and domestic violence
- Acting as advocates for children within the court system or administrative agencies (for example, working with children who are limited by medically determined physical or mental conditions to see that the families of these children receive the SSI benefits they are due from the Social Security Administration)
- Assisting at legal aid clinics that strive to meet the legal needs of the poor, including assistance with divorces, bankruptcies, and landlord-tenant disputes.

---

[1] *Black's Law Dictionary, Abridged Sixth Edition,* (1991).
[2] Leader of the Pro Bono Pack, *ABA Journal,* October 1997.
[3] Court Weighs Required Pro Bono, *ABA Journal,* Februrary 1995.

- Working in homeless shelters and homeless legal clinics
- Assisting with the drafting of wills and other estate planning documents for indigent, sick, and elderly people
- Assisting with the legal work performed for nonprofit organizations
- Educating children regarding law-related careers
- Mentoring children and young adults in their communities

While you are helping others, you will also be helping yourself. Many pro bono programs offer free training to paralegals—training that may be valuable throughout your career.

There are also opportunities to gain recognition for your pro bono work. *The Affiliates* Pro Bono Award, granted by *The Affiliates* employment service and the NFPA, recognizes the pro bono efforts of paralegals by awarding an all-expense-paid trip to the NFPA fall convention, a plaque, and a $1,000 contribution to the pro bono project of the winner's choice.

If you want to volunteer your time for a good cause, there is no shortage of opportunities or resources. Most state and local paralegal associations have pro bono committees that work to match paralegal volunteers with pro bono opportunities. Your school, employer, and the state bar association may also assist in finding the right opportunity for you.

For more information, contact the following organizations.

The National Federation of Paralegal Associations Pro Bono Committee

www.paralegals.org/probono/home.html

American Bar Association Center for Pro Bono

(312) 988-5769

www.abanet.org/legalserv/probono.html

Paralegal Associations

"I can't imagine a person becoming a success who doesn't give this game of life everything he's got."

WALTER CRONKITE

INTRODUCTION

From your first consideration of the paralegal profession, and all through-out your paralegal career, you will find the information and support offered by various paralegal associations to be of tremendous value. Paralegal associations promote professionalism, offer continuing legal education to paralegals, set ethical guidelines for paralegals to follow, and offer assistance in many forms. There are two major national paralegal associations in the United States. In addition, most states have at least one state paralegal association and may have numerous local paralegal associations. Although membership in a paralegal association is not mandatory for paralegals, the associations have done much to assist paralegals and to shape the image of paralegals, both with attorneys and with the public in general.

Paralegal Profile

PROFILE ON SHARON K. ENGLE

Do not even think about this career if you are not detail-oriented.

Name and Location:	Sharon K. Engle, Wichita, Kansas
Title:	Legal Assistant
Specialty:	Litigation, Bankruptcy, and Copyright
Education:	Associate Degree in Paralegal Studies
Experience:	17 Years

Sharon Engle is the only paralegal at Raytheon Aircraft Company, an aircraft manufacturer, in Wichita, Kansas. Sharon received her legal assistant certification 13 years ago. As a director of the Kansas Association of Legal Assistants, she shares her experience with other paralegals.

Sharon has a tremendous degree of responsibility at Raytheon, where she reports to the general counsel, who is also a vice president and secretary of the corporation. Her work in litigation includes gathering documents, interviewing witnesses, and preparing responses to discovery requests. She also works in the bankruptcy area and prepares applications for copyright.

Sharon's work for the general counsel, who is also a corporate officer, means that she also has responsibility for several administrative tasks. These include reviewing all outside counsel legal statements for the corporation and its subsidiaries, tracking legal budgets, and updating the database of all litigation for Raytheon Aircraft Company and its subsidiaries.

The varied duties and degree of responsibility are Sharon's favorite part of her job. The administrative duties are her least favorite. Sharon's experience includes previous law office managing, litigation, and her current corporate experience. She has found all three areas interesting and, at times, exciting. Although she finds corporate work the most interesting, it is not necessarily the most exciting to her.

Sharon's advice to paralegal students?

Do not even think about this career if you are not detail-oriented. Obtain your degree and then your CLA (certified legal assistant) certification. After having accomplished all this, be prepared to work "long" hours and receive "short" payment until you've gained your experience.

P.S. I probably wouldn't change anything.

NATIONAL PARALEGAL ASSOCIATIONS

The two major national associations in the United States are the **National Association of Legal Assistants (NALA)** and the **National Federation of Paralegal Associations (NFPA)**. Although these two associations share many of the same concerns, they are separate organizations with separate and distinct philosophies. The main difference in the philosophies of the two paralegal associations is their positions on regulation. The NFPA supports a two-tiered licensing plan, which constitutes mandatory regulation, but recognizes that another form of regulation, such as certification or registration, may be appropriate in a given state. The NALA prefers self-regulation of paralegals through the adoption of standards for the profession and voluntary certification. The position of the paralegal associations with regard to regulation is discussed further in Chapter Six of this text.

THE NATIONAL ASSOCIATION OF LEGAL ASSISTANTS

The National Association of Legal Assistants (NALA) was formed in 1975 and has approximately 18,000 paralegal members through individual memberships and through its ninety state- and locally affiliated associations. Student membership is available to students who are pursuing a course of study to become legal assistants.

The NALA's efforts in the following areas are primary reasons for paralegals to join the organization.[1]

- Recognition of the legal assistant profession
- Identification of those within the profession
- Establishment of professional standards
- Research on the growth and development of the profession through biannual surveys
- Involvement in professional issues, including tracking state legislative activities and becoming involved in cases affecting the legal assistant career field

The NALA's Statement. According to the NALA, it is "the leading professional association for legal assistants, providing continuing education and professional certification programs for paralegals. Incorporated in 1975, NALA is an integral part of the legal community, working to improve the quality and effectiveness of the delivery of legal services."[2]

Advocate for the Legal Assistant Profession. The NALA monitors events affecting paralegals, and it represents paralegals on important national issues, including education standards and certification. An important part of the NALA's philosophy includes self-regulation through the issuance of the **Certified Legal Assistant (CLA)** credential to paralegals who meet certain education requirements and pass a comprehensive test. See Figure 5–1.

FIGURE 5–1

Benefits of becoming a certified legal assistant[3]

Over 25 percent of paralegals report that the CLA designation increased the following.

- Salaries
- Job responsibility
- Independence
- Credibility with clients
- Job satisfaction

Over 50 percent reported an increase in the following.

- Professional status
- Recognition from peers
- Respect from lawyers
- Respect from nonlawyers
- Awareness of professionalism and ethics
- Positive self-image

The NALA has served as an advocate for the legal assistant profession on numerous occasions by representing the philosophy of the association and the interests of its members. The NALA has filed **amicus curiae** briefs on issues concerning the awarding of legal assistant fees in certain court cases. In addition, it has filed opinions in several instances concerning matters of ethics, legal assistant utilization, and proposed regulation. The NALA was represented on the Commission on Nonlawyer Practice, a commission established in 1992 by the ABA to conduct research, hearings, and deliberations to determine the implications of nonlawyer practice for society, the client, and the legal profession. The Commission issued its report in 1995. More information on the Commission and its report can be found in Chapter Six of this text.

For further information on the NALA, contact the association at the following address.

National Association of Legal Assistants
1516 S. Boston, #200
Tulsa, OK 74119
Phone: 918-587-6828
Fax: 918-582-6772
E-Mail: **nalanet@nala.org**

You can also check out their Web site at **www.nala.org**. The NALA Web site includes information on memberships and other topics of interest to all paralegals. Available information includes the following items.

- Information concerning the paralegal profession and the NALA's philosophy
- News concerning current events affecting the NALA members and the paralegal profession in general
- Information concerning the Certified Legal Assistant Examination
- Information concerning ethics and the NALA's Code of Ethics and Professional Responsibility
- Links to affiliated associations and legal research sites
- Opportunities for continuing education

THE NATIONAL FEDERATION OF PARALEGAL ASSOCIATIONS

The National Federation of Paralegal Associations (NFPA) was formed in 1974, and its members consist primarily of state and local paralegal associations. The NFPA is a federation of sixty member associations representing over 17,000 individual members nationwide. Student memberships are available. Membership in some state associations automatically constitutes membership in the NFPA.

The NFPA has formally adopted the following purposes.[4]

- To constitute a unified national voice for the paralegal profession
- To advance, foster and promote the paralegal concept

- To monitor and participate in developments affecting the paralegal profession
- To maintain a nationwide communication network among paralegal associations and other members of the legal community

The NFPA Mission Statement. The NFPA Mission Statement, as adopted in March 1987, is as follows:

The National Federation of Paralegal Associations, Inc. (NFPA) is a nonprofit, professional organization comprising state and local paralegal associations throughout the United States and Canada. NFPA affirms the paralegal profession as an independent, self-directed profession, which supports increased quality, efficiency, and accessibility in the delivery of legal services. NFPA promotes the growth, development, and recognition of the profession as an integral partner in the delivery of legal services.

Advocate for the Paralegal Profession. Much like the NALA, the NFPA has acted as an advocate for the paralegal profession by promoting its philosophy and that of its members. The NFPA monitors legislation concerning regulation and other issues concerning paralegals and reports activity to its members. The NFPA has filed testimony with state and federal legislative bodies on issues that may have an impact on the paralegal profession. The NFPA also has filed amicus briefs with courts throughout the United States on issues that might affect the paralegal profession; and it has participated in judicial, legislative, and bar hearings concerning issues that affect the development and recognition of the paralegal profession. Since its inception, the NFPA has reviewed, been involved with, and/or commented upon proposed regulatory programs developed by at least fifteen different states.[5]

Recently, the NFPA has provided information to the Supreme Court of New Jersey's Standing Committee on Paralegal Education and Regulation and to the Utah State Bar Association when the issue of regulation arose in those states.

In addition to paralegal regulation, the NFPA has taken positions on issues involving paralegal ethics and fee recoverability. Many of the NFPA's positions on these issues can be found on their Web site at **www.paralegals.org.**

The NFPA offers the **Paralegal Advanced Competency Examination (PACE)** as a means for experienced paralegals to validate their knowledge to themselves and to their employers. The NFPA foresees that this test may someday be part of a mandatory regulation program. The NFPA began administering the PACE in 1997, and as of June 1999, 133 paralegals have passed the examination and become Registered Paralegals. See Figure 5–2.

For further information, contact the NFPA at the following address.

National Federation of Paralegal Associations
Post Office Box 33108
Kansas City, MO 54114
Phone: 816-941-4000; fax: 816-941-2725
E-Mail: **info@paralegals.org**

FIGURE 5–2
*The Paralegal
Advanced
Competency
Examination (PACE)*[6]

Offering experienced paralegals an option to
• validate your experience and job skills
• establish credentials
• increase your value to your organization and clients

The only examination of its kind, PACE
• was developed by a professional testing firm
• is administered by an independent test administration company
• provides results across practice areas, and when available, for state-specific laws
• offers the profession a national standard of evaluation
• is offered at multiple locations on numerous dates and at various times

PACE = Personal Advancement for the Experienced Paralegal

The NFPA also offers a wealth of information and services to its members and other interested paralegals at its Web site at **www.paralegals.org**. This information includes the following topics.

• Developments affecting NFPA members and all paralegals
• Survey results
• Legal ethics, including the NFPA's Model Code of Ethics and Professional Responsibility with Guidelines for Enforcement
• Publications and links to publications of interest to paralegals
• Job postings and networking opportunities
• NFPA's quarterly publication, *National Paralegal Reporter*
  Getting started with your education or your career
• Continuing education opportunities
• Pro bono opportunities
• Links to affiliated associations, legal research sites, and other sites of interest to paralegals

News concerning the latest developments at the NALA or the NFPA can also be found on the companion Web site to this text at **www.westlegalstudies.com**. See Figure 5–3.

STATE AND LOCAL PARALEGAL ASSOCIATIONS

Every state and several major cities have their own paralegal associations, which are invaluable resources to paralegals. Your most frequent personal involvement with paralegal associations will probably be with state and local paralegal associations, which may be affiliated with either of the national associations.

State and local paralegal associations typically hold monthly meetings that feature speakers on topics of special interest to paralegals. In addition, many periodically offer seminars and workshops. Membership in a state or

NATIONAL ASSOCIATION OF LEGAL ASSISTANTS	NATIONAL FEDERATION OF PARALEGAL ASSOCIATIONS
Prefers the title *legal assistant* to *paralegal*	Prefers the title *paralegal*
Defines *Legal Assistant* as follows: *Legal assistants, also known as paralegals, are a distinguishable group of persons who assist attorneys in the delivery of legal services. Through formal education, training, and experience, legal assistants have knowledge and expertise regarding the legal system and substantive and procedural law which qualify them to do work of a legal nature under the supervision of an attorney.*	Defines *paralegal* as follows: *A paralegal is a person qualified through education, training, or work experience to perform substantive legal work that requires knowledge of legal concepts and is customarily, but not exclusively, performed by a lawyer. This qualified person may be retained or employed in a traditional capacity by a lawyer, law office, governmental agency, or other entity or may be authorized by administrative, statutory, or court authority to perform this work. This qualified person also may be retained or employed in a non-traditional capacity, provided that such non-traditional capacity does not violate applicable unauthorized practice of law statutes, administrative laws, court rules, or case law.*
Has over 18,000 paralegal members through individual memberships and through its 90 state and local affiliated associations	Is a federation of 60 member associations representing over 17,000 individual members nationwide
Is headquartered at 1516 S. Boston, #200, Tulsa, OK 74119, phone 918-587-6828; fax 918-582-6772, e-mail nalnet@nala.org, Web site **www.nala.org**	Is headquartered in Kansas City, Missouri, mailing address: Post Office Box 33108, Kansas City, Missouri 54114, telephone 816-941-4000, fax 816-941-2725, e-mail info@paralegals.org., Web site **www. paralegals.org**
Prefers self-regulation of the paralegal profession through voluntary certification	Prefers a two-tiered licensing plan, which constitutes mandatory regulation, but recognizes that another form of regulation, such as certification or registration, may be appropriate in a given state
Offers the Certified Legal Assistant (CLA) credential to those who meet certain education requirements and pass a comprehensive test	Offers the Registered Paralegal (RP) credential to those who meet certain education requirements and pass the Paralegal Advanced Competency Examination (PACE).
Publishes *Facts & Findings*, a quarterly journal featuring how-to educational articles for legal assistants	Publishes *National Paralegal Reporter*, a quarterly journal for paralegals
	(Continued)

FIGURE 5–3
The national paralegal associations

NATIONAL ASSOCIATION OF LEGAL ASSISTANTS—cont'd	NATIONAL FEDERATION OF PARALEGAL ASSOCIATIONS—cont'd
Has adopted Model Standards and Guidelines for Utilization of Legal Assistants	Has adopted a Model Code of Ethics and Professional Responsibility and Guidelines for Enforcement
Has adopted a Code of Ethics and Professional Responsibility that is binding on its members	Has appointed The Ethics and Professional Responsibility Committee that responds to questions and renders opinions regarding ethical conduct, obligations, utilization, and/or discipline of paralegals

FIGURE 5–3
—continued

local association provides an excellent opportunity to network with other paralegals in the area. Most state and local paralegal associations publish newsletters on a monthly basis, and many run job banks for their members and potential employers.

Many of the state and local paralegal associations are divided into sections, to which you can choose to belong in addition to membership in the association itself. These sections represent paralegals with specific interests—some typical sections of paralegal associations include paralegals in litigation, corporate, entry-level, freelance, and probate. Appendix C is a directory of state and local paralegal associations.

Much like the national associations, the local and state paralegal associations often interact with the state bar associations and the state supreme courts to further the paralegal profession and help establish guidelines for utilization of paralegals.

PARALEGAL ASSOCIATIONS AND LEGAL ETHICS

Paralegals must be familiar with and abide by the code of ethics that is binding on the attorneys in the paralegal's state of employment. This code of ethics will be binding on the paralegal as an employee and agent of the attorney. In addition, the national, state, and local paralegal associations adopt codes of ethics specifically for their paralegal members.

THE NALA CODE OF ETHICS AND PROFESSIONAL RESPONSIBILITY

The NALA has established a Code of Ethics and Professional Responsibility as well as Standards and Guidelines for Utilization of Legal Assistants. The NALA members are bound by the Code of Ethics and Professional Responsibility and any violation of the Code is cause for removal of membership. The NALA-affiliated associations must adopt the NALA Code of Ethics and Professional Responsibility as their standard of conduct.

ETHICAL CONSIDERATION

Paralegals must abide by the rules of ethics that apply to the attorneys who supervise them. In addition, they must abide by the rules of ethics adopted by their paralegal association.

Code of Ethics and Professional Responsibility. The NALA's Code of Ethics and Professional Responsibility closely resembles the ABA's Code of Professional Responsibility. The NALA's code was initially adopted in 1975 and has been revised several times since. Canon 9 of the NALA's Code specifically states that legal assistants are governed by the bar association's codes of professional responsibility and rules of professional conduct.

Code of Ethics and Professional Responsibility of the National Association of Legal Assistants[7]

Canon 1

A legal assistant must not perform any of the duties that attorneys only may perform, nor take any actions that attorneys may not take.

Canon 2

A legal assistant may perform any task which is properly delegated and supervised by an attorney, as long as the attorney is ultimately responsible to the client, maintains a direct relationship with the client, and assumes professional responsibility for the work product.

Canon 3

A legal assistant must not (a) engage in, encourage, or contribute to any act which could constitute the unauthorized practice of law; and (b) establish attorney-client relationships, set fees, give legal opinions or advice, or represent a client before a court or agency unless so authorized by that court or agency; or (c) engage in, conduct, or take any action which would assist or involve the attorney in a violation of professional ethics or give the appearance of professional impropriety.

Canon 4

A legal assistant must use discretion and professional judgment commensurate with knowledge and experience but must not render independent legal judgment in place of an attorney. The services of an attorney are essential in the public interest whenever such legal judgment is required.

Canon 5

A legal assistant must disclose his or her status as a legal assistant at the outset of any professional relationship with a client, attorney, court, administrative agency or personnel thereof, or with a member of the general public. A legal assistant must act prudently in determining the extent to which a client may be assisted without the presence of an attorney.

Canon 6

A legal assistant must strive to maintain integrity and a high degree of competency through education and training with respect to professional responsibility, local rules and practice, and through continuing education in substantive areas of law to better assist the legal profession in fulfilling its duty to provide legal service.

Canon 7

A legal assistant must protect the confidences of a client and must not violate any rule or statute now in effect or hereafter to be enacted controlling privileged communications between a client and an attorney.

Canon 8

A legal assistant must do all other things incidental, necessary, or expedient for the attainment of the ethics and responsibilities as defined by statute or rule of court.

Canon 9

A legal assistant's conduct is guided by bar associations' codes of professional responsibility and rules of professional conduct.

THE NALA'S MODEL STANDARDS AND GUIDELINES FOR UTILIZATION OF LEGAL ASSISTANTS

In addition to the NALA's Code of Ethics and Professional Responsibility, the NALA has adopted Model Standards and Guidelines for Utilization of Legal Assistants. The NALA's ongoing study of professional responsibility and ethical considerations lead to the development of these standards and guidelines. The model "provides an outline of minimum qualifications and standards necessary for legal assistant professionals to assure the public and the legal profession that they are, indeed, qualified."[8] The full text of the Guidelines may be found in Appendix D at the end of this text.

THE NFPA'S MODEL CODE OF ETHICS AND PROFESSIONAL RESPONSIBILITY WITH GUIDELINES FOR ENFORCEMENT

The NFPA also has adopted a code of ethics for paralegals' guidance. The NFPA's Model Code of Ethics and Professional Responsibility was adopted in 1993 to "delineate the principles for ethics and conduct to which every paralegal should aspire."[9] In 1997, the NFPA supplemented its Model Code with Guidelines for the Enforcement of the Model Code of Ethics and Professional Responsibility.

As with other model codes, the NFPA's Model Code of Ethics and Professional Responsibility has no binding authority on paralegals. Many state paralegal associations have, however, adopted the NFPA's Model Code as their own code of ethics. The NFPA's Model Code follows the format of the ABA's Model Code and has eight canons. The canons are supplemented by Ethical Considerations. The full text of the NFPA Model Code of Ethics and Professional Responsibility with Ethical Considerations and Guidelines for the Enforcement may be found as Appendix E to this text. However, a list of the eight canons follows.

Model Code of Ethics and Professional Responsibility

1.1 A Paralegal Shall Achieve and Maintain a High Level of Competence.

1.2 A Paralegal Shall Maintain a High Level of Personal and Professional Integrity.

1.3 A Paralegal Shall Maintain a High Standard of Professional Conduct.

1.4 A Paralegal Shall Serve the Public Interest by Contributing to the Improvement of the Legal System and Delivery of Quality Legal Services.

1.5 A Paralegal Shall Preserve All Confidential Information Provided by the Client or Acquired From Other Sources Before, During, and After the Course of the Professional Relationship.

1.6 A Paralegal Shall Avoid Conflicts of Interest and Shall Disclose any Possible Conflict to the Employer or Client, as Well as to the Prospective Employers or Clients.

1.7 A Paralegal's Title Shall be Fully Disclosed.

1.8 A Paralegal Shall Not Engage in the Unauthorized Practice of Law.

THE NFPA'S ETHICS AND PROFESSIONAL RESPONSIBILITY COMMITTEE

The NFPA has appointed an Ethics and Professional Responsibility Committee for the purposes of accepting and responding to inquiries concerning ethical conduct, obligations, utilization, and/or discipline of paralegals.[10] This committee responds to inquiries from any paralegal, attorney, corporation, or government entity employing a paralegal, as well as from any court, legislature, or bar association. The committee issues opinions based, in large part, on the following factors.

- The NFPA Model Code of Ethics and Professional Responsibility
- Other policy statements and/or positions of the NFPA
- The ABA Model Guidelines for Utilization of Legal Assistant Services
- The ABA Model Rules of Professional Conduct
- The Code of Ethics adopted by the state from which the inquiry arose
- The ABA Model Code of Professional Responsibility
- Any published decision concerning paralegal and/or attorney ethics or discipline

The opinions issued by the NFPA Ethics and Professional Responsibility Committee are not binding. However, they may be used for guidance and as a persuasive argument in favor of the findings of NFPA. Opinions of this committee may be found on the NFPA's Web site at **www.paralegals.org** without the names of the concerned parties.

BENEFITS OF ASSOCIATION MEMBERSHIP

There are numerous benefits offered to members of national, state, and local paralegal associations. These benefits vary depending on your particular association. The importance of the various benefits to you will also vary depending on your position, your interests, and the current stage of your career.

ASSISTANCE IN CHOOSING A PARALEGAL SCHOOL

If you are just deciding on a career as a paralegal or choosing a paralegal school to further your education, the paralegal associations can help.

The NFPA offers a directory of paralegal schools by geographic location on its Web site, as well as information on how to choose a paralegal school. The NALA Web site also offers assistance on choosing a paralegal school.

Your state or local paralegal association may have a close relationship with the paralegal schools in your area. They may also be a good resource for information on choosing a paralegal school.

ASSISTANCE IN FINDING A PARALEGAL POSITION

Your state or local paralegal association may be the best resource you have for finding a paralegal position. Most paralegal associations operate job banks for member paralegals and employers in the community. In addition, job openings often are published in the newsletter of state and local paralegal associations.

The NFPA also has a national job bank. It lists paralegal positions by state and offers other advice and assistance for job seekers, including a directory of placement services.

ACCESS TO SALARY SURVEYS

As a member of a paralegal association, resources concerning paralegal salary and benefits surveys will become available to you. Both of the national paralegal associations conduct extensive salary and benefits surveys periodically, as do most of the state and local associations.

NETWORKING

Networking is an informal opportunity to learn about career opportunities and to get advice for problems you may encounter as a paralegal. It can be very important to your paralegal career. Other paralegals can be a great resource for advice on situations that you may face on your job. Paralegal associations offer numerous opportunities to network with other paralegals and with attorneys in your area. Networking opportunities are available through attending meetings and seminars and by serving on committees. The national organizations also provide networking opportunities via on-line chats and Internet list servs.

CONTINUING EDUCATION

One of the main functions of the national, state, and local paralegal associations is to offer continuing paralegal education. Continuing education can take on many forms, including luncheon seminars, two- to three-day seminars, evening classes, study classes for CLA or PACE, and even Internet courses and seminars. Most of these continuing education opportunities are courses taught by attorneys or by experienced paralegal specialists. They are designed specifically for paralegals. Paralegals who have passed the CLA or PACE are required to complete a minimum number of continuing education hours each year to retain their CLA or RP designations. Information on continuing education opportunities offered by paralegal associations is usually disseminated by the associations' newsletters or via their Web sites.

MENTORING PROGRAMS

Mentoring programs that give paralegal students the benefit of working with experienced paralegals are becoming increasingly popular. These programs are often coordinated through state and local paralegal association mentoring committees.

PRO BONO INVOLVEMENT

Pro bono work is a way for paralegals to give back to the community. It is also a great way for paralegals to expand their experience. Most paralegal associations take on the role of matching volunteer paralegals with those who need their services. Paralegal associations may act as coordinators and facilitators of volunteer programs.

At its fall convention each year, the NFPA Pro Bono Committee presents a pro bono workshop to offer information to paralegals interested in pro bono work. The NFPA also publishes a manual to assist paralegal associations in creating a pro bono program, as well as a directory of individuals and associations associated with pro bono work. If you are interested in volunteering your time as a paralegal, contact your local or state paralegal association or the NFPA.

KEEPING INFORMED ABOUT CURRENT EVENTS

The newsletters and other periodicals published by paralegal associations are one of the best ways to keep informed about current events that affect paralegals. The NALA publishes *Facts & Findings,* a quarterly journal featuring how-to educational articles for legal assistants. The NFPA publishes the *National Paralegal Reporter, a* quarterly journal for paralegals. State and local associations publish similar newsletters including items of local interest.

The Web sites of both the NFPA and the NALA, as well as Web sites of several state and local organizations, also publish news of interest to paralegals. Appendix C, a directory of paralegal associations, provides Web site addresses for the national associations, as well as for several state and local associations.

REPRESENTING YOUR INTERESTS WITH REGARD TO REGULATION

When state judiciary committees and legislatures are considering paralegal regulation, the rule makers and lawmakers often turn to the paralegal associations for information and advice. The NFPA and the NALA both present testimony, written and oral, at government hearings and meetings held by the bar associations to express the position of their members.

NATIONAL CONVENTIONS

Both the NALA and the NFPA hold national conventions for their members to give paralegals from across the nation an opportunity to network, share ideas, and discuss relevant issues. The national conventions usually are held at interesting locations and feature several speakers and events. The national conventions also offer unique continuing education opportunities.

OTHER BENEFITS

There are numerous other benefits available to members of paralegal associations, including eligibility for group health and life insurance and special discounts. The NFPA offers professional liability insurance to paralegal members who are not covered under the policy of an employer. The exact benefits you receive will depend on your particular association. It will also depend, in large part, on your involvement in the association. The more you put into your association, the more benefits you will receive. Your volunteer involvement with your state or national paralegal association can give you unique experiences in leadership, public speaking, and serving on a committee. It will also assure that you are up to date with the latest developments in the paralegal profession. See Figure 5–4.

OTHER ASSOCIATIONS OF INTEREST TO PARALEGALS

In addition to the paralegal associations, the undertakings of the bar associations and certain other associations are often of great interest to paralegals. The role of the ABA and the state bar associations in the practice of law in this country cannot be overlooked. Bar associations are responsible for regulating attorneys, proposing new legislation, and overseeing the continuing education of attorneys.

FIGURE 5–4

Benefits to belonging to a paralegal association

> **The associations offer the following benefits.**
>
> - Assistance in choosing a school
> - Mentoring programs
> - Job placement assistance
> - Salary surveys
> - Networking opportunities
> - Continuing education seminars and courses
> - Pro bono opportunities
> - Publications to keep you informed of current events
> - Ethical guidelines
> - Group insurance

THE AMERICAN BAR ASSOCIATION

A **bar association** is an organization of members of the bar of the United States or of a state or county. The primary function of bar associations is to promote professionalism and enhance the administration of justice. The American Bar Association (ABA) is the country's largest voluntary professional association of attorneys. More than half of the attorneys in this country are members of the ABA. Its influence in lawmaking and the practice of law, particularly through the development of model codes and guidelines, is substantial.

The ABA has had a significant effect on the paralegal profession. Its recognition of the field in 1968 with the creation of its Special Committee on Lay Assistants (later renamed the Special Committee on Legal Assistants) gave authenticity to the profession in the eyes of many attorneys and the public. The ABA now allows paralegals to become associate members. Although paralegal members do not have all the rights of attorney members, they are on the mailing list for publications that inform members about significant developments within the legal community, and they are invited to continuing legal education opportunities sponsored by the ABA.

Standing Committee on Legal Assistants. The Standing Committee on Legal Assistants (SCOLA) is a seven-member committee of the ABA created in 1968 to oversee all issues regarding education, training, and utilization of legal assistants. The SCOLA works to ensure the quality of paralegal education by developing standards for paralegal education programs and giving the approval of the ABA to those programs that meet their established criteria. The SCOLA also helps educate attorneys with regard to utilization of paralegals by offering the ABA Model Guidelines for Utilization to the states for adoption.

STATE BAR ASSOCIATIONS

Each state in the country has at least one bar association with the same general purpose as the national association. In many instances state bar associations are very prominent and influential within the legal community, and they are also influential with regard to state legislation. A state bar association plays a major role in the regulation of attorneys who are licensed to practice law within that state.

Many state bar associations have also taken an interest in the regulation of paralegals within their states, and the positions of the state bar associations with regard to the utilization of paralegals vary from state to state. Some states have invited paralegals to become associate members, as the ABA has done.[11]

LOCAL BAR ASSOCIATIONS

Larger communities also have local bar associations that can provide significant support to paralegals. Local bar associations may provide information, seminars, employment agencies, or job banks that may be of particular interest to paralegals.

AMERICAN ASSOCIATION FOR PARALEGAL EDUCATION

The American Association for Paralegal Education (AAfPE), formed in 1981, is an association for paralegal educators and institutions that educate paralegals. The AAfPE also concerns itself with matters of interest to paralegal students and paralegals. For example, the AAfPE offers assistance in choosing a paralegal education program, and it tracks legislation concerning the regulation of paralegals. More information concerning the AAfPE can be found on their Web site at **www.aafpe.org** or by calling 770-452-9877.

LEGAL ASSISTANT MANAGEMENT ASSOCIATION

The Legal Assistant Management Association (LAMA) is an international association formed specifically for managers of legal assistant programs in law firms, corporate legal departments, and government, judicial, and legal agencies. For further information on LAMA, call 770-457-7746, or visit their Web site at **www.lamanet.org**.

Focus on Ethics: Maintaining Integrity and Public Respect for the Legal Profession

Although attorneys are responsible, in many instances, for the ethical conduct of the paralegals they supervise, paralegals must follow their own set of ethical guidelines and rules and do their part to maintain the integrity of the legal profession in general and the paralegal profession in particular. As a paralegal, you must be certain your actions maintain and build on the integrity and public perception of the paralegal profession. You must avoid any form of criminal activity or misconduct, and you must report certain incidents of serious misconduct you witness, involving paralegals or attorneys, to the appropriate authorities.

Exactly what type of paralegal misconduct must be reported to authorities often remains a judgment call on behalf of the paralegal. It is clearly your ethical duty to report the misconduct of other paralegals when that misconduct may be harmful to clients, employers, or the paralegal profession as a whole, especially when that misconduct is continuing.

The NFPA Model Code of Ethics and Professional Responsibility requires reporting of the following types of paralegal misconduct.

(a) any action of another legal professional that clearly demonstrates fraud, deceit, dishonesty, or misrepresentation

(b) dishonest or fraudulent acts by any person pertaining to the handling of the funds, securities, or other assets of a client

The Model Code of Ethics and Professional Responsibility of the NFPA also states that "failure to report such knowledge is in itself misconduct and shall be treated as such under these rules."

If you have witnessed illegal or unethical behavior by a paralegal, and you have determined that you are required to report the behavior, you must next decide to whom that behavior should be reported. It may be most appropriate to report the behavior to your supervising attorney. If your supervising attorney is also responsible for supervising the paralegal you suspect of misconduct, you must remember that he or she could be held responsible for that paralegal's misconduct. The circumstances may also warrant reporting the misconduct to your paralegal manager or to an ethics committee within your law firm or corporate legal department. At other times, the behavior and circumstances may require you to go to the paralegal association, local or state bar association, or even to the prosecutor's office.

Who you report misconduct to will depend on the type of misconduct and the circumstances surrounding it. For example, if you witness a coworker paralegal stealing funds from a client trust account and falsifying documents to cover it up, you definitely must report this behavior. Your first step would probably be to report it to your supervising attorney or an ethics committee within your law firm or legal department, depending on your employer's policy.

One of the most difficult ethical dilemmas paralegals may encounter is discovering unethical behavior by the attorneys for whom they work. Suppose you witness one of the attorneys you work for shredding documents that have been requested by the opposing counsel in a civil lawsuit or you discover him or her borrowing money from a client trust account. Reporting unethical behavior could mean the loss of status or employment with the firm. Is it unethical to remain silent? Yes. Paralegals have an ethical duty to report misconduct of attorneys. The code of ethics for attorneys in nearly every jurisdiction requires attorneys to report misconduct by other attorneys. This duty then extends to paralegals.

There are measures short of reporting an attorney to the state's professional authority that you can take if you witness the unethical behavior by your attorney employer. You may feel it is more appropriate to bring the matter to the attention of the responsible individual or committee within the law firm. If this still does not produce positive results, the attorney should be reported to the ethics committee of the state bar association.

To date there have been no cases involving a paralegal's duty to report unethical or illegal behavior. However, it remains clear that if questioned by a court or an ethics committee of the state bar, you have a duty to report the full truth concerning any actions of which you have knowledge. Any time you are involved in testifying or reporting unethical attorney behavior, you must use extreme caution not to divulge confidential client information.

Every working paralegal has a responsibility to all members of the paralegal profession. You are responsible for conducting yourself in a professional and ethical manner. Especially because much of the public and a fair portion of the legal community does not know what to expect from paralegals, every paralegal represents the entire paralegal profession with his or her behavior.

CAREER TRACK

Your local and national paralegal associations can help you get your career off the ground. Are you familiar with the local paralegal association in your area? If not, see Appendix C to determine what paralegal associations operate in your area. Do you have a choice of more than one local association? With which of the national paralegal associations is your local association affiliated?

This is a good time to answer some of these questions and obtain information from your local paralegal association on paralegal careers in your area. Contact your local paralegal association to learn about the assistance they can offer to you.

GLOSSARY

Amicus Curiae A person who is not a party to a lawsuit but who petitions the court or is requested by the court to file a brief in the action because that person has a strong interest in the subject matter. Often shortened to *amicus*. Also termed *friend of the court*. (*Black's Law Dictionary, Seventh Edition*)

Bar Association An association of members of the legal profession. [Several state bar associations sponsor superb CLE programs.] (*Black's Law Dictionary, Seventh Edition*)

Certified Legal Assistant (CLA) Title granted by the National Association of Legal Assistants to paralegals who have passed the CLA examination and met other criteria of NALA.

National Association of Legal Assistants (NALA) National association of legal assistants (paralegals) formed in 1975, which currently represents over 18,000 members through individual memberships and ninety state- and locally affiliated associations.

National Federation of Paralegal Associations (NFPA) National association of paralegal associations formed in 1974; currently has more than fifty-five association members representing more than 17,000 individual members.

Paralegal Advanced Competency Examination (PACE) Test developed for the NFPA as a means of validating the knowledge and experience of paralegals who pass the test and meet with certain other criteria. Paralegals who pass the PACE are granted the title of Registered Paralegal (RP).

Pro Bono (Latin *pro bono publico* "for the public good") Being or involving uncompensated legal services performed especially for the public good [took the case pro bono] [50 hours of pro bono work each year]. (*Black's Law Dictionary, Seventh Edition*)

ENDNOTES

[1] Copyright 1999. Published with permission of the National Association of Legal Assistants, 1516 S. Boston, #200, Tulsa, OK 74119, **www.nala.org.**

[2] Ibid.

[3] Ibid.

[4] From the National Federation of Paralegal Associations Inc. Web site, Membership Information, at **www.paralegals.org** (July 14, 1998).

[5] NFPA, *Comments of the National Federation of Paralegal Associations, Inc., Regarding the Report of The Supreme Court of New Jersey Standing Committee on Paralegal Education and Regulation,* February 11, 1999.

[6] From the National Federation of Paralegal Associations Inc. **www. paralegals.org.**

[7] Reprinted with permission of the National Association of Legal Assistants, 1516 S. Boston, #200, Tulsa, OK 74119, **www.nala.org.** Copyright 1975, Revised 1979, 1988, and 1995.

[8] Copyright 1998. Published with permission of the National Association of Legal Assistants, 1516 S. Boston, #200, Tulsa, OK 74119, **www.nala.org.**

[9] National Federation of Paralegal Associations, Inc. Model Code of Ethics and Professional Responsibility Preamble (1993).

[10] National Federation of Paralegal Associations Inc. Guidelines for Rendering Ethics and Disciplinary Opinions (1995).

[11] The states of Alaska, California, Colorado, Connecticut, Florida, Illinois, Kansas, Michigan, Minnesota, Montana, Nevada, New Jersey, New Mexico, North Carolina, North Dakota, Ohio, Rhode Island, Texas, Utah, Virginia, and Wisconsin currently have parlegal members.

Guidelines for Utilizing Paralegals

One argument for the regulation of paralegals is that regulation will further define the role of the paralegal in providing legal assistance to the public and help paralegals avoid the unauthorized practice of law. Under some scenarios, regulating paralegals would expand their utilization while setting definite limits on what tasks they would be able to perform and what services they would be allowed to offer to attorneys and the public.

Short of regulating paralegals, many states have adopted guidelines for the utilization of paralegals. These guidelines are drafted for the benefit of attorneys and are meant to offer assistance in determining how best to utilize the services of paralegals without crossing the unauthorized practice of law line. The guidelines may be adopted as state statute or as part of the state's court rules. The state of New Hampshire has adopted such guidelines as Rule 35 of its Rules of the Supreme Court of New Hampshire, which follows.

New Hampshire Statutes Annotated Rules of Supreme Court of New Hampshire Administrative Rules 35 to 54

Guidelines for the Utilization by Lawyers of the Services of Legal Assistants Under the New Hampshire Rules of Professional Conduct

Rule 1.

It is the responsibility of the lawyer to take all steps reasonably necessary to ensure that a legal assistant for whose work the lawyer is responsible does not provide legal advice or otherwise engage in the unauthorized practice of law; provided, however, that with adequate lawyer supervision the legal assistant may provide information concerning legal matters and otherwise act as permitted under these rules.

Rule 2.

A lawyer may not permit a legal assistant to represent a client in judicial or administrative proceedings or to perform other functions ordinarily limited to lawyers, unless authorized by statute, court rule or decision, administrative rule or regulation or customary practice.

Rule 3.

Except as otherwise provided by statute, court rule or decision, administrative rule or regulation, or by the Rules of Professional Conduct, a lawyer may permit a legal assistant to perform services for the lawyer in the lawyer's representation of a client, provided:

  A. The services performed by the legal assistant do not require the exercise of professional legal judgment;

  B. The lawyer maintains a direct relationship with the client;

C. The lawyer supervises the legal assistant's performance of his or her duties; and

D. The lawyer remains fully responsible for such representation, including all actions taken or not taken by the legal assistant in connection therewith.

Rule 4.

A lawyer should exercise care that a legal assistant for whose work the lawyer is responsible does not:

A. Reveal information relating to representation of a client, unless the client expressly or implicitly consents, after consultation with the supervising lawyer and with knowledge of the consequences, or except as otherwise required or permitted, in the judgment of the supervising lawyer, by statute, court order or decision, or by the Rules of Professional Conduct; or

B. Use such information to the disadvantage of the client unless the client consents after consultation with the supervising lawyer and with knowledge of the consequences.

Rule 5.

A lawyer shall not form a partnership with a legal assistant if any of the activities of the partnership consist of the practice of law, nor practice with or in the form of a professional corporation or association authorized to practice law for a profit if a legal assistant owns an interest therein, is a corporate director or officer thereof or has the right to direct or control the professional judgment of a lawyer.

Rule 6.

A lawyer shall not share fees with a legal assistant in any manner, except that a lawyer or law firm may include the legal assistant in a retirement plan even if the plan is based in whole or in part on a profit-sharing arrangement.

Rule 7.

A legal assistant's name may not be included on the letterhead of a lawyer or law firm. A legal assistant's business card may indicate the name of the lawyer or law firm employing the assistant, provided that the assistant's capacity is clearly indicated and that the services of the assistant are not utilized by the lawyer or firm for the purpose of solicitation of professional employment for the lawyer or firm from a prospective client in violation of the relevant statutes or the Rules of Professional Conduct.

Rule 8.

A lawyer shall require that a legal assistant, when dealing with clients, attorneys or the public, disclose at the outset that he or she is not a lawyer.

Rule 9.

A lawyer should exercise care to prevent a legal assistant from engaging in conduct which would involve the assistant's employer in a violation of the Rules of Professional Conduct.

The American Bar Association has adopted Model Guidelines to assist the States in drafting their own guidelines. A copy of the Model Guidelines, with annotations and commentary, is available through the ABA Legal Assistants Department staff office. (Phone: 312/988-5616; Fax: 312/988-5677; e-mail: legalassts@abanet.org)

The Guidelines adopted in New Hampshire, as with most states that have adopted similar Guidelines, do not offer many specifics or much detail on the utilization of paralegals. However, until a consensus is reached on paralegal regulation, guidelines for utilizing paralegals may be the best guidance the attorneys you work for have to define the legal possibilities, and limits, of your position.

CHAPTER 6

Paralegal Regulation

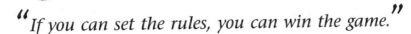

"If you can set the rules, you can win the game."

JOHN MCCORMACK

INTRODUCTION

Attorneys must be licensed and admitted to the bar in any state in which they practice—but who sets the national standards for and regulates paralegals? At this time, the answer is no one. There are currently no minimum education requirements for paralegals, nor are there mandatory rules for certification or licensing. In most jurisdictions, paralegals are subject to the same laws concerning the unauthorized practice of law as other nonattorneys. However, there is a movement underway in many states to change this. Regulation by means of registration, certification, or licensing is currently a hot topic. Possibly by the time you read this text, some of these issues will have been resolved. You must be aware of any licensing and certification requirements being considered and comply with any requirements in place in any jurisdiction in which you plan to work as a paralegal.

Paralegal Profile

PROFILE ON SHELBY SHRECK-BECK

I enjoy the fact that we are protecting the public by removing and sanctioning the dangerous and incompetent licensees from the profession.

Name and Location:	Shelby Shreck-Beck, Mt. Pleasant Mills, Pennsylvania
Title:	Legal Assistant II
Specialty:	Regulatory Law
Education:	Associate Degree in Paralegal Studies from Harrisburg Area Community College
Experience:	11 Years

Shelby Shreck-Beck is a busy and motivated paralegal who works for the Pennsylvania Department of State's Bureau of Professional and Occupational Affairs Prosecution Division. When she is not working to help regulate professionals in the state of Pennsylvania, Shelby enjoys the beach, reading, and spending time with her husband and 3-year-old daughter. Shelby is also a member of the Central Pennsylvania Paralegal Association.

The government agency that Shelby works for employs forty attorneys and eight paralegals. The Pennsylvania Department of State's Bureau of Professional and Occupational Affairs regulates twenty-seven licensing boards. Shelby manages nine boards, including those for real estate, real estate appraiser, medical veterinary, podiatry, physical therapy, optometry, landscape architect, and barber.

Shelby's work involves analyzing complaints against licensees and managing investigations. When the investigation of a licensee is complete, she prepares a written prosecution evaluation of the case. Her findings recommend a disposition of the case that may include a formal action, dismissal, issuance of a warning letter, psychiatric evaluation, participation in the Professional Health Monitoring Program, expert review, or emergency temporary suspension for the protection of the public.

Shelby also assists in preparing for any hearings that are held. She regularly participates in individual board or commission round table discussions with the attorneys, board counsel, and/or board representatives.

Shelby enjoys the diversity of her position. Her department receives different complaints against licensees every day. She also enjoys the fact that the department helps to protect the public by removing and sanctioning the dangerous and incompetent licensees from the profession. Her main frustration with her position is that politics sometime interfere with the process.

Shelby's advice to paralegal students?

I would advise paralegal students to stay focused. Never sell yourself short and keep the things you learn about clients confidential.

TYPES OF PARALEGAL REGULATION

There are several different means by which paralegals might be regulated. Paralegals may be required to be licensed, certified, or to register with certain state or local authorities. The exact definitions of *licensing, certification,* and *registration* vary among the proponents for each type of regulation. In the end, the definition may be prescribed by legislation.

DEFINING *PARALEGAL*

One frustration shared by the courts, members of the bar, and paralegals alike is the imprecise use of the terms *paralegal* and *legal assistant.* Although most state and local paralegal associations have adopted the definition supported by their affiliated national association, those associations are voluntary. In states where no formal definition of these terms has been adopted by law, anyone can call themselves paralegals or legal assistants. If no formal definitions of the terms exist, convicted felons, disbarred attorneys, individuals who have little or no education or formal training, and individuals who are otherwise unqualified can legally call themselves paralegals or legal assistants. Not only does this reflect poorly on the profession, but it can be confusing to potential paralegal employers and the unsuspecting public.

The exact definition of *paralegal* adopted by any state bar association, state court, or state legislature is important because the term is often defined by describing the qualifications for paralegals. Defining the term *paralegal* formalizes the profession and serves to educate the public with regard to paralegals and their role. It may also be a first step toward regulation in that state—defining the individuals who will be regulated. For example, the Supreme Court of South Dakota has adopted a definition that sets minimum qualifications and eligibility standards for paralegals assisting attorneys in South Dakota. SDCL, Section 16-18-34.1 establishes specific minimum education and training qualifications, and it provides that certain individuals, including those who have been convicted of a felony or disbarred from the practice of law, are ineligible to act as paralegals or legal assistants. The full definition of the term *paralegal* as adopted by the South Dakota Supreme Court can be found in Appendix A. Appendix A is a list of state-adopted definitions of the terms *paralegal* and *legal assistant.*

PARALEGAL LICENSING

A **license** is a privilege conferred on a person by the government to do something which he or she otherwise would not have the right to do. No form of licensing for paralegals is currently required in any state in this country. However, two types of licensing have been proposed and either one or both may be adopted in several states in the near future.

The first type of licensing requires that independent paralegals and legal technicians meet certain requirements and be licensed by the state. Independent paralegals and legal technicians offer their services directly to the public without the supervision of an attorney. Much of the regulation controversy involves legal technicians and independent paralegals.

The second type of proposed licensing covers a broader base of paralegals and requires all paralegals to meet certain requirements and be licensed in the state in which they work. If this type of licensing is adopted in any state in which you work, you must meet the licensing requirements of that state to work as a paralegal.

Limited licensure refers to a process currently utilized in a few jurisdictions that authorizes nonlawyers, who are often paralegals, the authority to perform certain, specific functions that are customarily performed by attorneys. One example of limited licensure is Rule 12 (Limited Practice Rule for Closing Officers) of the Washington Court Rules. This rule authorizes nonattorneys in the state of Washington who meet with certain conditions to perform specified functions incident to the closing of real estate and personal property transactions. The authorized functions, including preparation and completion of legal documents incident to the closing, are tasks traditionally considered to be the practice of law.[1]

PARALEGAL CERTIFICATION

Certain groups, including the NALA, endorse the voluntary **certification** of paralegals, as opposed to licensing. Contrary to licensing, which involves permission from a government to perform certain functions, certification is a means of self-regulation. Certification usually is considered a voluntary program, such as the CLA certification currently being granted by the NALA. Certification is granted to individuals who meet predetermined qualifications, usually in terms of education, experience, and passing a test established by the certifying group. Other groups have proposed voluntary certification by the state bar associations.

The Texas Board of Specialization, under authority of the Supreme Court of Texas, has been certifying experienced paralegals in six specific areas of law since 1994. The certification is strictly voluntary and granted only to paralegals who are qualified through education, experience, and by passing an examination. As of late 1999, 318 paralegals had been certified in civil trial law, criminal law, estate planning and probate law, family law, personal injury trial law, or real estate law.

PARALEGAL REGISTRATION

Some proposals for regulation provide for the **registration** of paralegals. If paralegal registration were required in a particular jurisdiction, paralegals who fall under certain categories (most likely those offering their services directly to the public) would be required to register with the county clerk, or some similar officer, in any county or state in which they work. In order to register properly, a paralegal would likely be required to meet certain education, bonding, and character requirements. Bonding requirements provide that paralegals must purchase a surety bond from an insurance or bonding agency in an amount prescribed by law. Bonding protects the public by providing coverage for damages to anyone who suffers financially due to the bonded individual's negligence or misconduct. It would not prevent the bonded paralegal from being personally liable for any damages he or she causes.

California recently has passed legislation requiring the registration of **legal document assistants,** paralegals who provide certain self-help services to individuals who represent themselves in a legal matter. The registration requirements do not apply to paralegals who work under the supervision of an attorney.

Although there are no licensing, certification, or registration requirements for traditional paralegals at this time, both the NALA and the NFPA support minimum education standards and voluntary testing for different types of **credentials.** The NALA and the NFPA do not share the same positions with regard to licensing and certification. Their positions are discussed later in this chapter.

Any legislation or rules proposed to regulate paralegals tend to spark controversy among groups with differing ideas and perceptions of the paralegal profession. Any proposed regulation must consider the benefits to paralegals and the public in the form of expanded services and protection, as well as the expense of regulation and the desires of some attorneys and paralegals who oppose regulation in any form.

ARGUMENTS FOR REGULATION

Proponents of paralegal regulation feel it will allow paralegals to expand their role without engaging in the unauthorized practice of law. They also believe regulation will promote the profession while protecting the public.

PROMOTING THE PARALEGAL PROFESSION

Many paralegals perceive a problem with the lack of established qualifications and standards for paralegals. They feel the profession as a whole suffers when there are no minimum requirements for paralegals. Many paralegals welcome the possibility of regulation to establish qualifications and standards for all paralegals and to increase the role of paralegals in providing legal services. They feel regulation will benefit the paralegal profession by increasing its credibility with the public, attorneys, and the courts.

Some proponents of regulation also point out that attorneys themselves would benefit from a regulatory scheme that would expand and clarify the role of the paralegal. When hiring paralegals, attorneys could be certain that licensed or certified paralegals had met certain established criteria. In addition, expanding and codifying the role of the paralegal would assist attorneys in fully utilizing paralegals—without fear of assigning them the unauthorized practice of law.

It is not uncommon in matters that are litigated for attorneys' fees to be awarded to the prevailing party. Fees for time spent on the file by paralegals are usually recoverable, so long as the paralegal's work is legal in nature, supervised by an attorney, and clearly documented. In addition, the paralegal must be an individual *qualified* by education and experience.

The problem, at times, is in determining who is qualified as a paralegal. With no established qualifications and standards, attorneys must prove the qualifications of their paralegals for their fees to be recoverable. Regulation of paralegals would establish the qualifications individuals must have to be paralegals and to have their time billed. In Hawaii, one federal court judge has proposed a local rule adopting a certification policy for paralegals who work on federal court cases. The certification rule would provide that court approval for fees generated by paralegal time would only be granted for those paralegals who are certified.[2]

AVOIDING THE UNAUTHORIZED PRACTICE OF LAW

The codes of ethics and state statutes prohibit paralegals from engaging in the unauthorized practice of law, but they often fail to define that term with any detail. Some activities routinely performed by traditional paralegals may be considered the unauthorized practice of law if their attorney supervision is insufficient. Independent paralegals constantly run the risk of engaging in the unauthorized practice of law. To compound the problem, unauthorized practice of law statutes and rules are often not enforced consistently.

Many who favor regulation feel that it would define the role of the paralegal and give paralegals adequate guidance to expand their role, without fear of engaging in the unauthorized practice of law. Under some proposals, regulation would mean that independent paralegals would be required to quit offering some of the services they currently provide, while traditional paralegals would be allowed to expand their list of permissible activities.

ETHICAL CONSIDERATION

Paralegals must be careful to avoid activities that are considered the *practice of law*, including giving legal advice, representing clients in court (under most circumstances), and preparing and signing legal documents (without attorney supervision).

EXPANDING AFFORDABLE LEGAL SERVICES AND PROTECTING THE PUBLIC

Some who argue for regulation feel that the expansion of the role of traditional paralegals will allow attorneys to delegate more of their work and keep their fees down. Others point out that there are numerous routine legal services that can be rendered by independent paralegals and legal technicians at fees much lower than those traditionally charged by attorneys. They feel that regulation would expand the role of independent paralegals, making needed legal services more affordable and more available to the public and thus providing a valuable service to society.

Many supporters of regulation feel strongly that paralegals, especially independent paralegals and legal technicians, provide a valuable service by allowing greater access to the law by lower- and middle-income individuals who may not be able to afford or otherwise seek out legal services. These proponents cite studies indicating that about three-quarters of the legal needs of low-income Americans remain unmet. According to Patricia Seitz, a past president of the Florida Bar Association, "Constitutionally, we cannot close off someone who is filling such a need, unless we are able to provide an alternative at an equally affordable price."[3]

Many members of the bar agree with Deborah Rhode, professor of law and director of the Keck Center on Legal Ethics and the Legal Profession at New York University School of Law. Rhode feels that regulating paralegals and allowing paralegals more freedom to offer services to the public is an important and necessary step toward meeting the needs of lower- and middle-income clients. According to Rhode, "Change is inevitable, and the bar's long-term interest lies in constructively assisting the reform process, not trying to prevent it."[4]

Some proponents of regulation feel that the only reason the paralegal profession has not yet been regulated is that state and local bar associations have fought against a perceived threat to their monopoly. Independent paralegals argue, and some members of the bar admit, that much of the concern coming from attorneys is based on self-interest. When legal technicians or independent paralegals are allowed to perform many of the tasks traditionally reserved for attorneys, they pose an economic threat to attorneys. It has been estimated that as much as $2 billion is spent annually in the United States on routine legal problems that nonlawyer specialists and self-help technology can often resolve.[5]

Proponents for regulation acknowledge that there is a potential for problems when paralegals offer even limited services directly to the public—problems with unethical behavior, incompetent advice and service, and lack of malpractice insurance. However, they feel the best way to combat these problems is to impose regulation that will mandate ethical behavior and a certain level of competency. Regulation can also be imposed to require all independent paralegals to be bonded and carry a certain level of malpractice insurance. Finally, regulation may grant authority to state or local officials to oversee regulatory compliance of paralegals and issue sanctions for failure to meet with regulations. See Figure 6–1.

FIGURE 6–1

Arguments in favor of paralegal regulation

> • The role of the paralegal will be expanded—keeping legal services more affordable.
> • Licensing paralegals will give the profession credibility in the eyes of the public and the legal community.
> • Regulation will provide much needed standards and qualifications for paralegals.
> • Regulation will further define permissible paralegal activities and help paralegals and their supervising attorneys to avoid the unauthorized practice of law.
> • Regulation will help attorneys to prove the qualification of their paralegals when seeking court approval for legal fees.
> • Regulated paralegals will be able to offer routine legal services to the poor whose needs may otherwise go unmet.
> • Paralegal regulation will help to prevent unethical and unqualified paralegals from offering their services to the public.

ARGUMENTS AGAINST REGULATION

Opposition to regulation comes from a diverse group of members of the legal community. Those who oppose paralegal regulation include attorneys, judges, and some paralegals themselves. Opponents to paralegal regulation argue that it is unnecessary and would increase legal fees and negatively impact the paralegal profession.

REGULATION IS UNNECESSARY

Many of those opposed to regulation hold the opinion that regulation of paralegals is an unnecessary expense and burden. They feel paralegals should work under the supervision of an attorney, who is ultimately responsible for their work, and that much of the current work of independent paralegals and legal technicians constitutes the unauthorized practice of law. Some opponents to regulation argue that only attorneys who are duly admitted to the bar are qualified to offer services of a legal nature to the public and that the public should be protected from these individuals who are *practicing law* without a license. They feel the need to protect the public outweighs the good done by legal technicians who provide low-cost services. Therese A. Cannon, education consultant for the ABA Standing Committee on Legal Assistants has pointed out that "issues do arise even in the simplest of transactions that a nonlawyer cannot handle or does not recognize."[6]

REGULATION WOULD INCREASE LEGAL FEES AND HAVE A NEGATIVE IMPACT ON THE PROFESSION

One common argument against regulation of paralegals is that the costs associated with regulation, including the creation of regulatory agencies, would be burdensome and would eventually be passed on to the client—effectively increasing legal fees. They fear that the costs also would be a hardship for paralegals and that regulations imposing strict qualifications may discourage potential paralegals from entering the profession.

Under certain regulatory schemes, attorneys would be allowed only to hire paralegals who have been licensed, registered, or certified. Many attorneys want the freedom to hire any individuals they choose as paralegals, especially if their firm offers extensive training.

Much of the proposed legislation to license paralegals and allow them to offer limited legal services directly to the public is dying in committee, often due to strong lobbying efforts of the state and local bar associations.[7] Detractors from the proposed regulation include both paralegals who prefer no regulation or voluntary regulation and members of the bar who feel that the licensure or regulation of the legal profession should be reserved for attorneys.

- Services performed by regulated paralegals may constitute the unauthorized practice of law.
- Paralegals should be working only under the direction of attorneys who are responsible for their work and hold the only license necessary.
- If paralegals are regulated, they will assume too much responsibility.
- If paralegals offer legal services to the public at a cost much less than attorneys, the income of attorneys will be jeopardized.
- Regulation of paralegals that will allow them to provide limited legal services directly to the public will not adequately protect the public from unethical and unqualified paralegals.
- The qualifications imposed by regulation will discourage potential paralegals from entering into the profession.
- The cost of regulation may be burdensome to paralegals and their employers and eventually may be passed on to the client.

FIGURE 6–2
*Arguments against
paralegal regulation*

William F. Hoffmeyer of the Pennsylvania Bar Association's Unauthorized Practice of Law Committee seems to be one of the attorneys who feels that too many paralegals are treading in the territory of licensed attorneys. Hoffmeyer's position is that "a paralegal by definition assists an attorney,"[8] and therefore no licensure is required. Hoffmeyer does not agree that independent paralegals are filling a need in the market. According to him, "there are a large number of young lawyers who couldn't get a job [with a firm] who have their own office. These young attorneys may charge $50 or $75 an hour, which is less than the paralegals are charging. The bar hasn't done enough to advertise to the public affordable legal services."[9] See Figure 6–2.

THE ABA'S POSITION

In 1992, the ABA established the Commission on Nonlawyer Practice, which consists of sixteen lawyers and nonlawyers having diverse geographic and professional backgrounds, to conduct research, hearings, and deliberations to determine the implications of nonlawyer practice for society, the client, and the legal profession. A part of the Commission's task was to consider the advisability and necessity of some type of regulation for paralegals. The Commission heard testimony in Washington, D.C., New York, Minneapolis, and seven other cities and collected extensive data from the testimony of witnesses, written submissions, and independent documents to form the basis for its findings and recommendations.

The Commission examined the nonlawyer activity in law-related situations by self-represented persons, **document prepares**, paralegals, and legal technicians.

The report issued by the Commission recognized two urgent goals: increasing access to affordable assistance in law-related situations and protecting the public from harm from persons providing assistance in law-related situations.

The Commission further concluded that when adequate protections are in place, nonlawyers, including paralegals, have important roles to perform in providing affordable access to justice.

The Committee recommended:[10]

1. That the bar associations, courts, law schools, and governments should continue to find new and improved ways to provide access to justice and help the public meet its legal needs.
2. That the range of activities of traditional paralegals should be expanded, with lawyers remaining accountable for their activities.
3. That the individual states should consider allowing nonlawyer representation of individuals in state administrative agency proceedings, and that nonlawyer representers should be subject to the agencies' standards of practice and discipline.
4. That the ABA should review its ethical rules, policies, and standards to ensure that they promote the delivery of affordable competent services and access to justice.
5. That the activities of nonlawyers, including independent paralegals, who provide assistance as authorized by statute, court rule, or agency regulation should be continued, subject to review by the regulating entity.
6. That states should adopt an analytical approach in assessing possible regulation for nonlawyers and activities performed by those nonlawyers. The criteria for the analysis should include the risk of harm presented by the nonlawyers, whether consumers can evaluate the qualifications of the nonlawyers, and whether the net effect of the proposed regulation will be a benefit to the public.
7. That State Supreme Courts should take the lead in examining specific nonlawyer activities within their jurisdictions with the active support and participation of the bar and the public.

In summary, the Bar Association supports a position that includes the expansion of the paralegal's role under the supervision of attorneys and leaves the issues of regulation and licensing to the individual states.

THE NFPA'S POSITION

In 1992, the NFPA passed a resolution that endorses a two-tiered regulatory scheme consisting of licensing and specialty licensing at the state level as the preferred form of regulation. The NFPA resolution outlines standards for the profession, including a minimum level of education, continuing legal education courses, requirements for experience, and standards of ethics and character. The NFPA concurs with the position of the ABA Commission on Nonlawyer Practice by supporting regulation so long as the role of paralegals is expanded through regulation. The following is a portion of the NFPA position on regulation of the paralegal profession. [11]

> The NFPA has adopted a position to endorse regulation of paralegals as long as paralegals would be able to do more under the regulatory plan than they were previously doing. Included within NFPA's position on regulation for paralegals working in an expanded role are provisions for

> - A preference for a two-tiered licensing plan, which constitutes mandatory regulation
> - Standards for ethics
> - Standards for education
> - A method to assess advanced competency of paralegals
> - Establishing a disciplinary process
> - Defining those tasks that paralegals may perform in numerous specialty areas of law

THE PACE

The Paralegal Advanced Competency Examination (PACE) was developed for the NFPA as a means for paralegals to validate their knowledge to themselves and their employers. Also, the members of the NFPA feel that with the increasing numbers of states considering regulation of paralegals, the PACE may be one means for establishing competency for future regulation and licensing requirements. Unlike the NALA, which promotes the voluntary certification through its CLA exam, the PACE is not intended to be used in place of regulation but as a part of a regulation scheme. According to the NFPA, "it is not the intention of NFPA members to use PACE as a voluntary certification process. PACE is to be used in conjunction with a regulatory plan that will permit experienced paralegals to perform at higher levels of responsibility than now permitted."[12]

PACE is not required by the NFPA or any state-regulating agency at this time. PACE is a two-tiered test that may be taken by experienced paralegals who meet certain education requirements to "validate experience and job skills, establish credentials, and confirm their value to the legal industry."[13] Tier One of the examination tests critical thinking skills and problem solving abilities, including general legal and ethical questions. Tier Two tests knowledge in specific legal practice areas. The NFPA's stated purposes of PACE are as follows.

- To provide the groundwork for expanding paralegal roles and responsibilities
- To provide the public and legal community with a mechanism to gauge the competency of the experienced paralegal
- To be used in states considering regulation of experienced paralegals

The PACE may be taken only by paralegals who have two years of work experience. Education requirements for taking the PACE are as follows.

Tier I Requirements
- A minimum of four (4) years' work experience as a paralegal if application is made within the global grandparenting period (through December 31, 2000) **OR**
- A bachelors degree and completion of a paralegal program within an institutionally accredited school (which may be embodied in the bachelors degree), and a minimum of two (2) years' work experience as a paralegal

Tier Two Requirements
- Successful completion of the first tier, **AND** one of the following:
- A minimum of six (6) years' work experience as a paralegal, if application is made within the global grandparenting period (through December 31, 2000)
- A bachelors degree and completion of a paralegal program within an institutionally accredited school (which may be embodied in the bachelors degree) and a minimum of four (4) years' experience as a paralegal.

Qualified paralegals who pass the PACE are referred to as Registered Paralegals (RP). Registered paralegals must complete twelve hours of continuing education every two years to maintain their status. At this time, no jurisdiction requires paralegals to pass the PACE.

THE NALA'S POSITION

A top priority of the NALA since its formation has been the establishment of certain standards for the profession. The NALA developed a voluntary certification program with a designation of Certified Legal Assistant (CLA) for those who meet certain education requirements and pass the CLA examination. As of January 1998, there were over 9,000 Certified Legal Assistants in the United States and over 700 Certified Legal Assistant Specialists. Over 19,000 legal assistants had participated in the CLA program.[14]

THE CLA EXAMINATION

Requirements for CLA designation include successful completion of a two-day comprehensive examination based on federal law and procedure covering communications, ethics, human relations and interviewing techniques, judgment and analytical ability, legal research, and legal terminology. In addition, the test covers substantive areas of law, including the American legal system, administrative law, bankruptcy law, business organizations/

corporate law, contracts, family law, criminal law and procedure, litigation, probate and estate planning, and real estate law. Paralegals are tested on the American legal system and four of the aforementioned areas of substantive law. The NALA offers certification to qualified paralegals who pass the examinations. In addition, specialty certification is available in the areas of bankruptcy, civil litigation, corporations/business law, criminal law and procedure, intellectual property, estate planning and probate, and real estate law for students who pass additional testing requirements in those areas. Specialty certification specific to the states of California, Florida, and Louisiana is also available.

According to the NALA, the CLA program establishes and serves as a:

- National professional standard for legal assistants
- Means of identifying those who have reached this standard
- Credentialing program responsive to the needs of legal assistants and responsive to the fact that this form of self-regulation is necessary to strengthen and expand development of this career field
- Positive, ongoing, voluntary program to encourage the growth of the legal assistant profession, attesting to and encouraging high level of achievement

To be eligible to take the CLA examination, paralegals must meet one of the following three education requirements.

1. Graduation from a legal assistant program that is:
   - Approved by the American Bar Association; or
   - An associate degree program; or
   - A post-baccalaureate certificate program in legal assistant studies; or
   - A bachelors degree program in legal assistant studies; or
   - A legal assistant program that consists of a minimum of sixty semester hours (900 clock hours or 225 quarter hours) of which at least fifteen semester hours (90 clock hours or 22.5 quarter hours) are substantive legal courses

2. A bachelors degree in any field plus one year's experience as a legal assistant. Successful completion of at least fifteen semester hours (or 22.5 quarter hours or 225 clock hours) of substantive legal courses will be considered equivalent to one year's experience as a legal assistant

3. A high school diploma or equivalent plus seven (7) year's experience as a legal assistant under the supervision of a member of the bar, plus evidence of a minimum of twenty (20) hours of continuing legal education credit to have been completed within a two (2) year period prior to the examination date

The CLA credential is awarded for five years, provided the Certified Legal Assistant submits proof of participation in the required fifty hours of continuing legal education. Becoming a Certified Legal Assistant is not a re-

FIGURE 6–3
Summary of positions on the regulation of paralegals

THE AMERICAN BAR ASSOCIATION COMMISSION ON NONLAWYER PRACTICE	THE NATIONAL ASSOCIATION OF LEGAL ASSISTANTS	THE NATIONAL FEDERATION OF PARALEGAL ASSOCIATIONS
Supports a position that includes expansion of the paralegal's role under the supervision of attorneys and leaves the issues of regulation and licensing to the individual states. Encourages authorizing nonlawyer representation of individuals in state administrative agency proceedings.	Supports minimum education and competency standards for paralegals and voluntary certification of paralegals (as opposed to mandatory regulation). Offers the Certified Legal Assistant examination and the CLA designation as a means of voluntary certification.	Supports a two-tiered regulatory scheme at the state level that includes mandatory licensing and specialty licensing. Offers the PACE as one means to establish competency as part of future regulation of paralegals.

quirement in any jurisdiction in the United States. However, according to the NALA, surveys of legal assistants consistently show that paralegals with the CLA designation are better paid and better utilized in a field where attorneys are looking for a credible, dependable way to measure ability. The CLA credential is recognized by the ABA and by more than forty-seven legal assistant organizations. Over 1,000 applicants per year take the NALA's CLA examination.

The NALA offers this voluntary test and voluntary certification as an alternative to mandatory licensing or regulation. The NALA's position is that all legal assistants should work under the supervision of a licensed attorney who is responsible for their work and that voluntary certification is the best means of giving credibility to paralegals. See Figure 6–3.

DEVELOPMENTS ACROSS THE NATION

Across the country, more and more responsibilities are being taken on by paralegals, both within law firms and legal departments and independently. The acceptance of paralegals is growing rapidly. Already several administrative agencies allow paralegals to represent clients before their governing boards under certain circumstances. As the profession continues to expand, some type of regulation probably will be inevitable. Many states are attempting to tighten control of paralegals through new or existing unauthorized practice of law statutes. Others are studying the feasibility of outright licensing or certification of paralegals. Following is a review of some of the more recent developments in legislation and regulation regarding paralegals and the unauthorized practice of law as of the end of 1999. Be aware that new legislation is being introduced continually. For the latest developments in paralegal regulation across the country and in your state, check out the companion Web site to this text at **www.westlegalstudies.com**.

CALIFORNIA

In California, a new law was adopted in 1998 to regulate legal document assistants.[15] Legal document assistants provide or assist in providing, for compensation, self-help services to the public. The self-help services that may be provided by legal document assistants include the following.

(1) Completing legal documents in a ministerial manner, after being selected by a person who is representing himself or herself in a legal matter, by typing or otherwise completing the documents at the person's specific direction

(2) Providing general published factual information that has been written or approved by an attorney pertaining to legal procedures, rights, or obligations to a person who is representing himself or herself in a legal matter, to assist the person in representing himself or herself

(3) Making published legal documents available to a person who is representing himself or herself in a legal matter

(4) Filing and serving legal forms and documents at the specific direction of a person who is representing himself or herself in a legal matter

Legal document assistants may not provide any kind of advice, explanation, opinion, or recommendation to a consumer about possible legal rights, remedies, defenses, options, selection of forms, or strategies. A legal document assistant shall complete documents only in the manner prescribed by statute.

Effective January 1, 2000, legal document assistants must meet with certain education and experience requirements and they must register with the county clerk of the county in which they work each year. If the legal document assistant meets all requirements, the clerk issues an identification card, which includes an identification number that the legal document assistant must include on all documents he or she prepares. Legal document assistants or any other type of paralegal working under the direction of members of the California State Bar need not register or otherwise be concerned with the requirements of this statute.

FLORIDA

In Florida, the bar association's Board of Governors has approved a change to the Supreme Court Rules to prohibit individuals not supervised by attorneys from using the titles *paralegal, legal technician,* or a similar name. The rule amendment also provides that paralegals and legal assistants working for attorneys may perform some tasks outside the direct presence of the attorney.

HAWAII

A proposal has been made in Hawaii for the regulation of paralegals by local court rule requiring certification for all qualified paralegals who work on federal court cases. No formal action has been taken at this time.

MAINE

In the spring of 1999, the Maine statutes were amended to include a definition of the terms *paralegal* and *legal assistant.* These amendments provide that individuals using these titles must perform specifically delegated substantive legal work for which an attorney is responsible.

MONTANA

In Montana, the state bar association recently has organized a new paralegal section and is inviting paralegals to apply for membership. Section membership is available to paralegals who meet specified education requirements and who affirm that they do not provide legal services directly to the public. As members of the Paralegal Section of the State Bar of Montana, paralegals will be eligible for most of the bar association benefits available to attorney members, and they will be recognized by the bar as being qualified paralegals. All paralegal members must abide by the Rules of Professional Conduct adopted by the bar, and they must complete ten hours of continuing legal education each year.

NEW JERSEY

In 1998, the Standing Committee on Paralegal Education, a committee appointed to make recommendations on paralegal regulation to the New Jersey Supreme Court, released its report based on a five-year study. The Committee recommended, among other things, that paralegals within the state of New Jersey be brought under the jurisdiction of the New Jersey Supreme Court and be licensed. The committee recommended that paralegals meet established education requirements and pass an ethics examination as a prerequisite to licensure.

In 1999, the Court declined to follow the recommendations of its Committee and concluded that "direct oversight of paralegals is best accomplished through attorney supervision rather than through a court-directed licensing system." The Court further determined that the Rules of Professional Conduct applicable to attorneys in that state "should be modified to describe more comprehensively the obligations imposed on attorneys by their use of paralegals."[16]

OREGON

In 1997, a house bill was introduced in Oregon that would allow independent paralegals to provide legal assistance or advice so long as they are registered with the Department of Consumer and Business Services. The bill also created the Independent Paralegal Advisory Board to assist the Department of Consumer and Business Services in establishing the requirements for certification as an Independent Paralegal. Although this bill died in committee, it may be a look at things to come.

UTAH

The Utah State Bar Legal Assistant Division has made a recommendation to the bar for mandatory licensing of legal assistants. The Utah Board of Bar Commissioners is considering this report.

WISCONSIN

A Paralegal Practice Task Force has been formed in Wisconsin for the purpose of exploring the role of paralegals in the state. The task force will be considering a proposal by the Paralegal Association of Wisconsin for licensure of paralegals.

Focus on Ethics: Paralegals and the Unauthorized Practice of Law

All paralegals, whether regulated or not, must avoid the unauthorized practice of law. As the level of paralegal responsibility increases, so does the paralegal's risk of being found guilty of the unauthorized practice of law (UPL). This has always been of special concern to independent paralegals, who do not always work under the direct supervision of attorneys.

The authority to practice law is granted to attorneys through the issuance of a license by each state or territory in the United States and by each federal court. Licensing qualifications vary among jurisdictions but usually include meeting minimum education, citizenship, residence, age and character requirements, as well as passing a bar examination. Anyone who practices law without the proper license is considered to be guilty of the unauthorized practice of law.

Unauthorized individuals are prohibited from practicing law because it is assumed that they do not have the necessary knowledge and skill to represent others adequately in matters of a legal nature. Unauthorized practice of law rules are designed to protect the public from "rendition of legal services by unqualified persons."[17] Courts have enforced unauthorized practice of law statutes by stating that it is clear that their purpose is to ensure that "laymen would not serve others in a representative capacity in areas requiring the skill and judgment of a licensed attorney."[18]

WHAT CONSTITUTES THE UNAUTHORIZED PRACTICE OF LAW?

Rules prohibiting the unauthorized practice of law can be found in the codes of ethics of each state. Although they vary, in general these rules prohibit attorneys from practicing law in any jurisdiction where they are unauthorized, and they prohibit attorneys from assisting lay persons in the unauthorized practice of law.

The practice of law generally includes giving legal advice, preparing or signing legal documents (without attorney supervision), setting fees for legal services, and representing another before a court or other tribunal (unless authorized by statute or administrative rule to do so).

All states have statutes providing that only duly licensed attorneys may practice law in that state. Most of these statutes do not define the practice of law but leave that up to the state's courts. If you are concerned with the unauthorized practice of law in your state, you may need to research both the state statutes and the case law interpreting those statutes.

In many states, the bar association appoints a committee to oversee the enforcement of unauthorized practice of law rules. The bar association and committee both derive their power from the state's highest court. Most actions against individuals are brought by committees of the state's bar association.

TRADITIONAL PARALEGALS

As a traditional paralegal, you can use your knowledge of the law and legal procedure to assist attorneys in various ways. Drafting legal documents and performing other law-related services may at first glance appear to be practicing law. However, if you work under the supervision of an attorney who is ultimately responsible for your actions, you are merely assisting attorneys with their practice of law. Rarely does the question of unauthorized practice of law arise in these circumstances.

According to the ABA's Special Committee on Legal Assistants, a lawyer may permit a legal assistant to assist in all aspects of the lawyer's representation of a client, provided that the following procedures are followed.

- The status of the legal assistant is disclosed
- The lawyer establishes the attorney-client relationship
- The lawyer reviews and supervises the legal assistant's work
- The lawyer remains responsible
- The services performed become part of the attorney's work product
- The services performed by the legal assistant do not require the exercise of unsupervised legal judgment
- The lawyer instructs the legal assistant concerning standards of client confidentiality[19]

INDEPENDENT PARALEGALS

Most of the real controversy surrounding paralegals and the unauthorized practice of law concerns independent paralegals—paralegals who offer their services directly to the public without attorney supervision. Many of the services offered by independent paralegals are self-help services. These services include furnishing and completing forms and offering self-help information written by attorneys to members of the general public. The independent paralegals do not represent individuals in legal matters; instead they assist their customers with self-representation. Whereas it is clear that, in most instances, individuals have the right of self-representation, the role of a lay person in assisting them is less clear.

Independent paralegals are in constant danger of crossing the unauthorized practice of law line. For example, in most jurisdictions it is legal for independent paralegals to sell legal forms, sample legal forms, and printed material drafted by attorneys that explain legal practice and procedure to the public in general. However, if the independent paralegal dispenses legal advice, in addition to the legal forms, he or she probably will be committing the unauthorized practice of law. In Michigan, the Court has ruled that "the advertisement and distribution to the general public of forms and documents utilized to obtain a divorce together with any related textual instructions does not constitute the unauthorized practice of law."[20] However, offering counsel and advice in addition to the forms and documents *is* considered the unauthorized practice of law in that state.

If you are considering employment as an independent paralegal, you must be very sure of the precedence for independent paralegals in your state. You must know how the unauthorized practice of law has been defined in your state and be exceedingly careful that your services never meet that definition. In addition, you must be aware of any registration requirements in your state. For the latest developments in your state, keep current with your local paralegal association.

AVOIDING THE UNAUTHORIZED PRACTICE OF LAW

There are certain activities that all paralegals must be cautious to avoid and some general rules to follow so as not to engage in the unauthorized practice of law.

- Always disclose your status as a paralegal, including on letterhead and business cards.
- Make sure that legal documents and any correspondence that may express a legal opinion that you prepare are reviewed, approved, and signed by your supervising attorney.
- Communicate important issues concerning each case or legal matter on which you are working with your supervising attorney, and be sure that your work is reviewed and approved by an attorney.

- Never give legal advice.
- Never discuss the merits of a case with opposing counsel.
- Never enter into fee agreements for legal services or agree to represent a client (on behalf of your supervising attorney or law firm).
- Never represent a client at a deposition, in a court of law, or before an administrative board or tribunal (unless paralegals or other lay persons are specifically authorized to appear by the court's rules).

SUMMARY

With all the interest in paralegal regulation, some type of regulation appears inevitable. It also appears likely that regulation will take place at the state level. Questions remaining to be answered include the following.

1. Who (within each state) should regulate paralegals? The state bar associations? The Judiciary? The Legislature?
2. Exactly who should be regulated—all paralegals or just those offering their services directly to the public?
3. What qualifications should be imposed on licensed or certified paralegals?
4. Should licensing or certification be mandatory or voluntary?
5. What type of services should regulated paralegals be allowed to offer?
6. How far toward the practice of law should regulated paralegals be allowed to go?

It is quite likely that individual states will continue to struggle with these questions—and that many answers will become law in the near future.

CAREER TRACK

As you begin your paralegal career, it will be important to follow developments in the state in which you work regarding the regulation of paralegals. Chances are that during your paralegal career, regulation will affect you directly. You can follow the developments in your state by keeping current with information published by your local and national paralegal associations. New developments in paralegal regulation will also be reported at the companion Web site to this text at **www.westlegalstudies.com**.

Does your state or local paralegal association have an official opinion regarding regulation? Paralegal associations often are asked to submit their position when legislation is being considered. To make your opinion on the matter count, become active in your local and national paralegal association and help to represent the interests of all paralegals in your state.

GLOSSARY

Certification Form of self-regulation whereby an organization grants recognition to an individual who has met qualifications specified by that organization.

Credentials Documentary evidence of a person's qualifications; commonly in the form of letters, licenses, or certificates.

Document Preparer An individual who prepares or assists in the preparation of legal documents at the direction of an individual who is representing himself or herself in a legal matter.

Legal Document Assistant Individuals recognized in California who are authorized to provide or assist in providing, for compensation, self-help legal services to the public.

License Permission by competent authority, usually the government, to do an act which, without such permission would be illegal or otherwise not allowable. Permission to exercise a certain privilege, to carry on a particular business, or to pursue a certain occupation.

Registration The process by which individuals or institutions meeting with certain requirements list their names on a roster kept by an agency of government or by a nongovernmental organization. Registration provides the public with a list of individuals or institutions who have met with certain requirements.

Self-Represented Person A person who represents himself or herself for the purpose of resolving or completing a process in which the law is involved.

ENDNOTES

[1] Washington Local Rules of Court and West's Washington Court Rules, Part I, rule 12. (1997).

[2] Nakaahiki, Victorialei (Nohea, "Hawaii Paralegals Head Toward Certificate Through Federal Court," *Hawaii Bar Journal,* August 1998.

[3] Garcia, Mike Jay, "Key Trends in the Legal Profession," *Florida Bar Journal,* May 1997.

[4] Rhode, Deborah L., "Professionalism in Perspective: Alternative Approaches to Nonlawyer Practice," *New York University Review of Law and Social Change,* 1996.

[5] Ibid.

[6] "Shades of Regulation," *ABA Journal,* June 1997.

[7] "State Bills Apply Sundry Standards to Independent Paralegals," *ABA Journal,* June 1997.

[8] Kimmel, Sherri, "Stemming the Tide of Unauthorized Practice", *Pennsylvania Lawyer,* May/June 1998.

[9] Ibid.

[10] ABA Commission on Nonlawyer Practice, Nonlawyer Activity in Law-Related Situations, a Report with Recommendations (1995).

[11] From the Statement of the National Federation of Paralegal Associations, Inc. for the new *Roles in the Law II: Improving Citizen Access to Justice,* from the NFPA Web site, **www.paralegals.org** (1996).

[12] *NFPA Response to the ABA Commission on Nonlawyer Practice,* from the NFPA Web site, **www.paralegals.org** (November 1997).

[13] *The Paralegal's Partner in Progress,* from the NFPA Web site, **www.paralegals.org** (March 1998).

[14] NALA Web site, **www.nala.org/cert.htm** (March 1998).

[15] West's Annual California Business and Professional Code §6400 (1999).

[16] Supreme Court of New Jersey Administrative Determinations, Report of the Committee on Paralegal Education and Regulation, May 18, 1999.

[17] *Annotated Model Rules of Professional Conduct,* American Bar Association Comment to Rule 5.5 (1996).

[18] *State, ex. Rel. Porter v Alabama Funeral Services, Inc.,* 338 So.2d 812 (Alabama, 1976).

[19] A.B.A. Special Committee on legal Assitants "Proposed Curriculum for Training Law Office Personnel." (preliminary draft 1971).

[20] *State Bar of Michigan v. Cramer,* 249 NW2d 1 (Mich. 1976)

Feature   **Stress Management**

Nothing gives one person so much advantage over another as to remain cool and unruffled under all circumstances.

Thomas Jefferson

One skill that will almost certainly be required of you as a paralegal is the ability to handle stress. Every job involves some level of stress. If the paralegal profession involved no stress whatsoever, it would not be very interesting or challenging. The goal of stress management is not to eliminate stress but rather to deal with it effectively. Everyone has personal methods of dealing with stress. Some, such as substance abuse and excessive absence from work, are destructive. Here, however, are suggestions of several constructive ways to deal with the stress you will encounter on your job.

1. If your workload looks overwhelming and is causing you stress, make a list of the things you need to do and prioritize them. It may not be as bad as you think.
2. Tackle the problem. Stress can sometimes give you excess nervous energy. Use it to your advantage by working late to get caught up if you are stressed about getting behind with your workload.
3. If you are stressed about a particular assignment, talk it over with the responsible attorney, the paralegal manager, or someone else who might be able to help you with the problem.
4. Take a break. Leave the situation for a quick change of scenery and to regain control. Things should look better when you return.
5. Take a walk on your lunch break. Exercise and fresh air can do wonders to alleviate stress.
6. Make time for exercising and taking care of yourself. Forty-five minutes of vigorous exercise every day will not only improve your outlook, but you will sleep better at night.
7. Talk the stress-causing problem over with someone. A friend or relative who will lend a sympathetic ear is usually preferable to a co-worker. Keep in mind the rules of confidentiality, though; never identify clients or specific legal problems outside the law office.

Above all, take care of yourself and get help if you need it to control your stress, before it controls you. For more information on stress management, check with your local bookstore or library. There are also Web sites dedicated to stress management. Following is a list of some of the more popular books concerning stress management in the workplace (and elsewhere).

- *Don't Sweat the Small Stuff...And It's All Small Stuff*, Richard Carlson, Thorndyke Press (1997)
- *How to Stay Cool, Calm & Collected When the Pressure's On: A Stress-Control Plan for Businesspeople*, John E. Newman, AMACOM (1992)
- *Relax—You May Only Have a Few Minutes Left*, Loretta LaRoche, Villard (1998)
- *Stress for Success: The Proven Program for Transforming Stress into Positive Energy*, James E. Loehr, Random House (1997)
- *The Working Women's Guide to Managing Stress*, J. Robin Powell and Holly George-Warren (Editors), Prentice Hall (1994)

You may also want to try these Web sites for information on stress management and links to other stress management sites.

- The Web's Stress Management and Emotional Wellness Page
  imt.net/~randolfi/StressPage.html
- Job Stress Help
  jobstresshelp.com/links.htm
- 4Stress—a guide to stress relief from 4anything.com
  www.4stress.com/main/shtml

CHAPTER 7

Skills and Personal Traits of Succesful Paralegals

"Few things are impossible to diligence and skill. Great works are performed not by strength, but perseverance."

SAMUEL JOHNSON

INTRODUCTION

To be a successful paralegal, you must have both knowledge and skill. A *skill* is defined as "ability to use one's knowledge effectively in doing something; developed or acquired ability."[1] Despite the extreme diversity of the paralegal profession, there are some skills that are expected of all paralegals. The paralegal's title is, in some respects, defined by the possession of these skills. Educating you with regard to all the required skills is beyond the scope of this chapter and this text. Instead, this chapter will introduce and define the skills you will need and suggest resources for learning any of these skills you feel you have not yet mastered. This chapter then concludes with a look at the character and personality traits commonly possessed by successful paralegals.

Paralegal Profile

PROFILE ON KELLY WALTER McKEE

I enjoy working for a firm that utilizes technology such as the Internet, document scanning, Westlaw, and various databases to perform factual and legal research.

Name and Location:	Kelly Walter McKee, Denver, Colorado
Title:	Legal Assistant
Specialty:	Litigation
Education:	Bachelor of Arts in Political Science from the University of Colorado–Boulder; Paralegal Certificate from the Denver Paralegal Institute
Experience:	3 Years

Kelly McKee is a litigation paralegal for the Denver office of Hogan & Hartson, L.L.P. Hogan & Hartson employs thirty-six attorneys in Denver, approximately 500 attorneys in Washington, D.C., and 650 in all their offices worldwide. Although Kelly is supervised by eight litigation attorneys in the Denver office, he reports to a paralegal manager in the firm's Washington, D.C. office via a weekly workload report.

Kelly specializes in litigation, and his work includes organizing and managing large quantities of documents for discovery, pre-trial and trial; docketing and calendaring deadline dates and filings; research on Westlaw and the Internet; and drafting various types of legal documents, including memoranda, motions, pleadings, discovery responses, orders, and agreements.

Kelly enjoys the variety in the types of cases he has the opportunity to work on, including appeals, complex commercial, education, healthcare fraud, white collar crime, trademark, and employment law. However, he indicates that working with document management and production tasks can be somewhat mundane.

Kelly also enjoys working for a firm that utilizes the latest technology. Currently he is working on a project to establish a link between his law firm's Colorado Springs and Denver offices via a custom case management database, case and budget planning templates, and potential use of their intranet site for document viewing and searching.

Kelly's advice to paralegal students?

Imagine the possibilities. Every area of our lives involves legal implications. Use your previous experiences as a stepping stone into an area of law, or move in an entirely new direction.

SKILLS IMPORTANT TO ALL PARALEGALS

If you are planning a career as a paralegal, it is very important to acquire the skills that potential employers will be looking for—and the skills that will contribute to your continued success. The skills you must acquire will depend, in part, on the specialty you choose. For example, a litigation specialist may rely heavily on interviewing and investigating skills, while a securities law specialist may rely more heavily on research and writing skills. Employers will often hire entry-level paralegals who have mastered the general paralegal skills and offer them the opportunity to learn new skills specific to the practice on the job.

> Because the law is complex and often ambiguous, paralegals must be intelligent with an analytical and logical mind. They must be able to recognize and evaluate relevant facts and legal concepts. Paralegals have the ability to organize, analyze, communicate, and administer. Other interpersonal skills that serve paralegals are resolving conflicts, negotiating, and relating well with various types of persons, often when those persons are in distress.[2]

Whereas there may be some disagreement as to exactly what skills paralegals must possess, most employers, educators, and working paralegals would agree that competent paralegals possess the following types of skills.

- Organizational skills
- Communication skills
- Analytical skills
- Computer skills
- Legal research skills
- Interpersonal skills
- Interviewing and investigation skills

You will want to be sure that you possess all of these skills as you begin your search for your first paralegal position (Figure 7–1).

ETHICAL CONSIDERATION

Paralegals have an ethical responsibility to perform their work competently and diligently.

ORGANIZATIONAL SKILLS

As a paralegal, you must possess excellent organizational skills. Paralegals must have the ability to organize their work assignments, as well as important court dates and other deadlines. In addition, you must have the skill required to organize files and numerous documents for which you may be given responsibility. In a recent survey of more than 200 attorneys conducted by The Affiliates, a staffing service that specializes in project attorneys and legal support personnel, organizational ability was the number one quality preferred by attorneys in the paralegals they hire.[3]

Organizing Your Work and Assignments. Paralegals often are assigned numerous tasks with various priorities and due dates that must be worked on each day. Time management is one skill you cannot do without. You must have an organized calendar and scheduling system for recording, prioritizing, and tracking your assignments to see that all deadlines are met.

You will want to organize your tasks throughout the day for maximum efficiency. For example, if you will need several files throughout the day, you will make the most of your time by planning ahead and making one trip to the file room first thing in the morning for all files or by making one request to the file clerk.

You may be assigned the responsibility of tracking deadlines for the files assigned to you or for the entire firm. According to a recent survey, placing deadlines on the calendar was the third most common responsibility assigned to the paralegals who responded. Case management was the sixth most

---

Most Important Skills

- Organization
- Communication
- Interpersonal
- Computer Literacy

FIGURE 7–1

Most important skills desired in paralegals (From The 1998 ABA Utilization of Legal Assistants Among Private Practitioners Survey)

commonly assigned task. Do not underestimate the importance of these tasks.[4] Failure to properly note a matter or event on the appropriate calendar is the single most frequent reason for malpractice claims against attorneys.[5]

Consistently checking and updating your own system, be it manual or electronic, is the only way to be sure you are managing your time, your work, and your assignments effectively.

Organizing Your Files. Most legal work in the form of documents and letters will be organized in file folders. Several individuals may be assigned to the same case or legal matter and may need to access the file folder. Paralegals must keep their work organized within each file in compliance with the standard procedure of the law firm or legal department. For example, it is standard procedure in some firms to bind legal documents on the left-hand side of the file folder and bind correspondence on the right. All documents are kept in chronological order so you can start in the back and read the history and progress of the case or glance at the top of the file for the latest developments. Documents that are not filed or are misfiled within a client's file may be overlooked. Missing documents can have serious consequences and will cause problems if the attorneys and other individuals working on a file are unaware of their presence and content. At a minimum, it will be a source of irritation for everyone involved. Paralegals must learn the system for organizing client files and must organize any file they are working on consistently.

Organizing Documents. The work of many paralegals requires the preparation and maintenance of numerous documents, including exhibits, corporate documents, and closing documents. Paralegals responsible for numerous documents and other items are often required to produce them within seconds. An attorney in the courtroom does not want to wait ten minutes for a disorganized paralegal to search through files for the required exhibit. When a client is waiting to turn over a $2 million check at a closing, she does not want to wait for the paralegal to dig through stacks of closing documents to find the correct one. Many law firms and legal departments use computer software designed for document tracking and organization, while others rely strictly on manual systems. In some instances, it may be up to you to create your own system for organizing documents for closings or large litigation files. In any event, you must draw on your organizational skills to organize, track, and retrieve important legal documents (Figure 7–2).

Paralegal educators recognize the importance of organizational skills. Although courses are not offered in organizational skills, many paralegal courses require you to develop and practice such skills. According to the AAfPE, paralegal education programs should develop the student's ability to do the following.

1. Categorize information
2. Prioritize information
3. Organize information
4. Use time efficiently

Publications

Complete Idiot's Guide to Organizing Your Life, Georgene Muller Lockwood, Macmillan Publishing Company (1996)

First Things First: To Live, to Love, to Learn, to Leave a Legacy, Stephen Covey, A. Roger Merrill, and Rebecca R. Merrill, Simon & Schuster Trade (1995)

How to Be Organized in Spite of Yourself, Sunny Schlenger and Roberta Roesch, Signet (1990)

How to Get Organized When You Don't Have the Time, Stephanie Culp, F & W Pub. (1986)

How to Make the Most of your Workday, Jonathan and Susan Clark, Career Press (1994)

The Organized Executive, Stephanie Winston, Warner Books (1994)

The Overwhelmed Person's Guide to Time Management, Ronni Eisenberg and Kate Kelly, Plume/Penguin (1997)

The Personal Efficiency Program: How to Get Organized to Do More Work in Less Time, Kerry Gleeson, John Wiley & Sons, Inc. (1994)

Time Management for Dummies, Jeffrey J Mayer, IDG Books Worldwide (1995)

Web Sites

Mind Tools Time Management Skills
www.mindtools.com/page5.html

FIGURE 7–2
Resources to help you get organized

COMMUNICATION SKILLS

The smartest paralegal in the world will be inadequate if he or she is unable to communicate effectively. As a paralegal, you must have excellent communication skills for communicating with attorneys, clients, and other individuals. You must have basic communication skills, including good grammar and a good vocabulary, and you must be able to communicate effectively in writing, on the telephone, and in person.

The basic communication skills you must possess to be a successful paralegal include the ability to do the following.

1. Speak in clear, concise, and grammatically correct English—one to one, in a group, and sometimes in front of an audience
2. Use appropriate language to persuade others
3. Use appropriate legal terminology to communicate complex legal issues
4. Demonstrate excellent active listening skills and accurately interpret nonverbal communication
5. Use appropriate nonverbal communication
6. Read quickly with comprehension
7. Write in clear, concise, and grammatically correct English
8. Adapt the nature and level of your communication to maximize understanding in the intended audience, including those with different levels of education and different cultural backgrounds

FIGURE 7–3
Tips for demonstrating effective communication skills when meeting with clients

- Be prepared for your meeting; bring notes to assist you.
- Be sure to smile at the client and offer a warm greeting, including a handshake.
- Use active listening skills—nod and offer verbal agreement when appropriate.
- Make frequent eye contact (without staring).
- If you do not know the answer to a client's question—say so and offer to find the answer.
- Note your client's level of understanding when you are describing legal issues; use an appropriate level of vocabulary and description.
- Do your best to project a professional, confident, and approachable manner.
- Speak clearly and use appropriate vocabulary.
- Do not yawn, scratch, or fidget.

ETHICAL CONSIDERATION

In all communication with clients, paralegals must be sure to identify themselves as *paralegals,* so it is not assumed that the paralegal is an attorney.

Effective In-Person Communication. Your in-person communication will include meeting with and speaking to attorneys, your co-workers, and possibly clients. According to a recent survey, 80 percent of paralegals participate in attorney/client meetings at least occasionally[6]. For that reason, it is imperative that you have effective personal communication skills. You must have the ability to communicate clearly, concisely, and politely. Your nonverbal communication must match your spoken words (Figure 7–3).

Your first true test of effective personal communication skills will be during your job interviews. You will want to be sure you have the necessary skills mastered prior to that time. You may find it helpful to capitalize on any opportunities you have at school to speak and practice effective communication either in small groups or in front of an audience—such as a speech course. Following are some references you may find useful to assist you in gaining effective communication skills.

- *Communicate with Confidence: How to say it Right the First Time and Every Time,* Dianna Daniels Booher, McGraw-Hill (1994).
- *How to Get Your Message Across: A Practical Guide to Power Communication,* Dr. David Lewis, Souvenir Pr Ltd. (1997).
- *How to Say It: Choice Words, Phrases, Sentences, and Paragraphs for Every Situation,* Rosalie Maggio, Prentice Hall Trade (1990).
- *How to Say it at Work,* Jack Griffin, Prentice Hall Press (1998).
- *How to Talk So People Listen,* Sonya Hamlin, Harper & Row, Publishers (1988).

- *I'd Rather Die Than Give a Speech,* Michael M. Klepper, Irwin Professional Pub (1993).
- *Lifescripts: What to Say to Get What You Want in 101 of Life's Toughest Situations,* Stephen M. Pollan and Mark Levine, Macmillan Publishing Company, Inc (1996).
- *Say What You Mean/Get What You Want: A Businessperson's Guide to Direct Communication,* Judith C. Tingley, AMACOM (1996).
- *Straight Talk: Turning Communication Upside Down for Strategic Results at Work,* Eric E. Douglas, Consulting (1998).
- *Thinking on Your Feet: How to Communicate Under Pressure,* Professional Business (1996).

Effective Written Communication. As a paralegal, writing will be a significant part of your work every day. Paralegals responding to a recent survey indicated that drafting correspondence and pleadings were among their most commonly assigned tasks. Paralegals spend more of their time drafting correspondence than any other single task.[6]

In addition to basic communication skills, your paralegal career will require that you are proficient with legal terminology and the basics of legal writing. Your skill as a writer can have a significant impact on the outcome of a legal matter, even a court case. Paralegals are often given writing assignments that busy attorneys only briefly review. Many individuals, attorneys included, are not comfortable with the written word and struggle with writing through their entire careers. Your superior writing skills can be an important asset to any legal team of which you are a member (Figure 7–4).

Legal writing varies from general business writing in that legal writing often requires that specific formats be followed, especially for documents that will be filed with the court. In addition, effective legal writing necessitates a thorough knowledge of legal terminology. While it is important to use proper legal terminology to express yourself, it is just as important to avoid **legalese.**

Some of the specific writing skills you will need as a paralegal include the ability to do the following.

1. Use the appropriate format and content in drafting client correspondence and legal documents
2. Write clear and concise interoffice memoranda to report legal research findings in an appropriate format
3. Adapt standardized forms found in form books, form files, or a computer data bank
4. Use appropriate citations for sources

Quality paralegal education programs offer courses in legal writing and communications. In addition, legal writing and communication is often the topic of continuing education for paralegals. Written resources to assist you with your legal writing and communication include tips and advice found in periodicals such as *Legal Assistant Today* magazine, as well as the following books.

General Writing Assistance

1. *The Chicago Manual of Style: The Essential Guide for Writers, Editors, and Publishers, 14th Edition* (1993).
2. *Elements of Style,* William Strunk, E.B. White (1995).
3. *Elements of Grammar,* Margaret D. Shertzer (1996).
4. *Elements of Correspondence,* Mary Ann DeVries (1996).
5. *Prentice Hall Style Manual: A Complete Guide with Model Formats for Every Business Writing,* Mary Ann DeVries (1992).
6. *Style: Ten Lessons in Clarity & Grace,* Joseph Williams, (1996).
7. *The Merriam-Webster Dictionary: New Edition* (1994).
8. *The New American Roget's Thesaurus in Dictionary Form,* Albert H. Morehead, Philip Morehead (1974).

Legal Writing Assistance

1. *Black's Law Dictionary, 7th Edition,* West Publishing (1999).
2. *Clear and Effective Legal Writing,* Veda R. Charrow, Myra K. Erhardt, Robert Charrow (1995).
3. *A Dictionary of Modern Legal Usage,* Bryan A. Garner (1994).
4. *The Elements of Legal Style,* Bryan Garner (1991).
5. *The Elements of Legal Writing,* Martha Faulk (1997).
6. *Expert Legal Writing,* Terri Leclercq, Thomas R. Phillips (1995).
7. *The Lawyer's Guide to Writing Well,* Goldstein and Lieberman (1991).
8. *Legal Research and Writing,* Statsky (1998).
9. *Legal Thesaurus/Dictionary,* William P. Statsky, J.D. (1998).
10. *Legal Writing,* Steve Barber, Delmar Publishers (1998).
11. *Practical Legal Writing for Legal Assistants,* Celia Elwell and Robert Smith (1998).

You may also want to try out these Web sites for useful information to help improve your writing and communication skills.

1. An Elementary Grammar Guide **www.robinsnest.com/grammar.html**
2. Elements of Style by William Strunk – On-Line Version **www.bartleby.com/141/index.html**
3. Guide to Grammar and Writing **webster.commnet.edu/HP/pages/darling/original.htm**
4. K-State College of Arts and Sciences On-Line Resources about Writing **www.k-state.edu/artsci/write.html**
5. The Writing Center—Basic Prose Style and Mechanics **www.rpi.edu/dept/llc/writecenter/ web/text/proseman.html**

- Use outlines to organize your thoughts.
- Follow your office format for memoranda and other legal documents.
- Be concise.
- Use the active voice (instead of the passive) whenever possible.
- Consider your audience.
- Keep sentences short.
- Use a new paragraph for each separate idea.
- Avoid legalese.
- Proofread.
- Use proper footnotes.

FIGURE 7–4
Tips for effective legal writing

ANALYTICAL SKILLS

The ability to read and understand legal documents and legal research materials is only the beginning. The ability to analyze and summarize those documents probably will be equally important to you. As a paralegal, you often will be responsible for analyzing a given set of facts and summarizing them for the attorneys for whom you work or for clients. Documents surrounding a case can take up thousands of pages. Paralegals are often responsible for reading and analyzing documents and summarizing them for the attorneys for whom they work. The ability to analyze legal documents and put their content into a format that clients can understand is also a valuable skill to have.

As a paralegal, you may be required to use your analytical skill for **legal analysis**—applying the law to a given set of facts. Most of legal analysis concerns the analysis of **case law** or **statutory law**. A process commonly used for legal analysis is the **IRAC Analysis**. The steps used in the IRAC Analysis are as follows.

1. **Issue:** Identify the issue and define the precise legal question at hand.
2. **Rule:** Research the law and identify the rule (or law) that governs the issue.
3. **Analysis/Application:** Determine how the law applies to the issue.
4. **Conclusion:** Summarize your findings in a conclusion.

In addition to your analytical skills, legal analysis also will require excellent legal research and writing skills, as well as a comprehensive understanding of the law.

Paralegal education programs generally do not offer courses in analytical thinking or legal analysis. However, legal analysis may be taught as a subject of a legal research or legal writing course. In addition, a quality paralegal education should teach students to apply analytical thinking throughout their education.

According to the AAfPE, paralegal education programs should be able to demonstrate that their courses incorporate learning strategies, which develop their students' abilities to complete the following tasks.

1. Analyze a problem by identifying and evaluating alternative solutions
2. Logically formulate and evaluate solutions to problems and arguments in support of specific positions
3. Identify interrelationships among cases, statutes, regulations, and other legal authorities
4. Apply recognized legal authority to a specific factual situation
5. Recognize when and why varied fact situations make it appropriate to apply exceptions to general legal rules
6. Determine which areas of law are relevant to a particular situation
7. Apply principles of professional ethics to specific fact situations
8. Distinguish evidentiary facts from other material and/or controlling facts
9. Identify factual omissions and inconsistencies

COMPUTER SKILLS

Computer skills are an absolute necessity in the modern law firm or legal department. According to a 1999 survey, almost 99 percent of responding paralegals are using computers on a daily basis.[7] Most employers will consider for hire only paralegals who are computer literate and have experience with at least a few basic computer software programs, including word processing programs. The number of different functions performed by computers is also on the rise. Whereas just a few years ago computer use in law firms was limited to word processing, now, at many law firms, all attorneys and paralegals have personal computers at their desks that serve a wide variety of purposes. As a paralegal, you may need to use at least some of the following computer applications on the job.

1. Word processing
2. Billing and timekeeping
3. Westlaw or Lexis legal research
4. Internet legal and factual research
5. Spreadsheet applications
6. E-mail communication
7. Database creation and processing

Most software applications used by law firms are relatively easy to learn. Training is often provided online or by the vendor. Even though that is the case, it is still a plus if you are familiar with software applications that are popular in law firms. According to 1998 surveys conducted by the ABA

Technology Resource Center,[8] the most popular software applications for law firms are as follows.

	Large Firms	Small Firms
Suite	Microsoft Office	Corel WordPerfect Suite
Practice Management	Elite	
Docketing	CompuLaw	
Document Assembly	Hot Docs	Hot Docs
Document Management	Docs Open	Worldox
Litigation Support	Summation Blaze	Folio Views
Time and Billing	Distributed Time Entry (DTE)	Timeslips
Online Research	Lexis	Westlaw
Case Management		Amicus Attorney

Almost without exception, paralegal education programs include training on various types of computer software that are found commonly in law firms and legal departments. The AAfPE recommends that paralegal education programs include courses in law-related computer skills and that students be taught the following skills.

1. Use of the basic features of at least one commonly used word processing program, database program, and spreadsheet program
2. Use of the basic features of a computer-assisted legal research program and other electronic resources

If you find you are ready to begin your job search but lack the necessary computer skills, there are numerous resources available. Many computer hardware and software vendors offer training on their products. Several types of computer programs can be self-taught (if you have a computer at your disposal).

LEGAL RESEARCH SKILLS

Although it is important to have a knowledge of the basic concepts of law; it is just as important to know where to find the law. Legal research is a skill used by nearly every paralegal. That does not mean that paralegals spend all their time with dusty, old law books in law libraries writing legal briefs and memoranda. Legal research also encompasses research done by computer and by telephone. It includes checking a simple procedure in a handbook or manual. Understanding the basics of what is required to perform adequate legal research is of the utmost importance to every paralegal.

Regardless of whether you are researching with the aid of books, periodicals, computers, or the telephone, all your resources will be either primary sources of law, secondary sources of law, or finding tools. Primary and secondary law and finding tools can all be found in bound volumes in law libraries, on computer disk, through computer services such as Westlaw and Lexis and, increasingly, on the Internet (Figure 7–5).

Primary sources of law are the **binding authority.** The most common categories of primary sources of law include judicial decisions (cases), statutes, and administrative rules and regulations.

Secondary sources of law are sources that discuss and analyze the law; they are not actual law themselves. Legal encyclopedias, legal practice manuals, **treatises,** and law review articles are all secondary sources of law. Although secondary sources of law are not binding, for three reasons they can be as important as primary law to a paralegal who is performing legal research.

First, secondary sources have educational value. When asked to research an area of law with which you are unfamiliar, often the best way to begin is to learn the basics of that areas of law. A secondary source such as a legal encyclopedia is a logical place to start in that instance.

Second, secondary sources are often valuable finding tools. The same sources that seek to educate the reader on a specific topic can lead to other sources, including primary sources, on that topic.

Third, secondary law can be persuasive. When the primary sources of law fail to provide a definitive answer to a question of law, prestigious and well-respected secondary sources of law can be used to support your case.

Finding tools are not really sources of law, but they are a means to find pertinent law. Because case law is constantly changing, with new court decisions being published all the time, case law is organized chronologically. When you consider the problem of finding a case that relates to the topic you are researching, keeping in mind that all cases for the last hundred years or so have been recorded in chronological order with no regard to subject, it is easy to understand the importance of finding tools. Finding tools for case law include digests, indexes, and computerized research tools.

PRIMARY SOURCES OF LAW	**SECONDARY SOURCES OF LAW**	**FINDING TOOLS**
Case Law	Law Review Articles	Digests
Statutory Law	Legal Encyclopedias	Indexes
Administrative Rules and Regulations	Treatises	Annotations
Constitutions	Legal Practice Manuals	Citators
Administrative Agency Decisions		Computerized Legal Research Systems
Rules of Court		
Executive Orders		
Treaties		
Attorney General Opinions		
Ordinances		

FIGURE 7–5
Sources of law

Statutory finding tools include citators, indexes, and computerized systems. Finding tools for secondary sources of law include law library cataloging systems, indexes, and computerized research tools.

Cite checking is a research-related task with which paralegals must be familiar. This task involves reviewing cites within legal documents to verify case citations, check the history of the cases, and conform the cites to the proper form. This is an important process, especially when the document being cite checked is to be submitted to a court. Paralegals often use specialized computer software to aid them in this task.

Without exception, quality paralegal training programs will offer at least one course in legal research. Continuing education courses and in-house training can help you keep your legal research skills current. The AAfPE recommends that paralegal programs include courses on legal research and that the following skills be taught.

1. Use of the resources available in a standard law library to locate applicable statutes, administrative regulations, constitutional provisions, court cases, and other primary source materials.
2. Use of LEXIS, WESTLAW, and/or other computer-assisted legal research programs to locate applicable statutes, administrative regulations, constitutional provisions, court cases, and other primary source materials.
3. Use of the resources of a standard law library to locate treatises, law review articles, legal encyclopedia, and other secondary source materials that help to explain the law.
4. The ability to "cite check" legal resources. Your paralegal training must include legal research training, particularly computerized legal research. Your legal research skills should include a familiarity with the Internet and some of the vast legal research resources it offers. Increasingly, the Internet is becoming one of the preferred methods of conducting both factual and legal research. Some paralegals even specialize in Internet research (Figure 7–6).

INTERPERSONAL SKILLS

Having good interpersonal skills is crucial to a successful career as a paralegal. You must be able to communicate, empathize, and interact with individuals with diverse backgrounds and education. Employers value an employee's attitude and ability to get along with others almost more than any other skill.

As a paralegal, you will probably have supervisory authority over one or more individuals. Experienced paralegals working on large cases or projects often are responsible for supervising several people at once. You must have excellent interpersonal and managerial skills. In addition, you must have the skill to be an effective team member. Teamwork is strongly emphasized in most workplaces today.

CITY AND COUNTY LAW

Municipal Code Corporation
www.municode.com/database.html

EXPERTS
ExpertPages
www.expertpages.com/about.htm

FEDERAL LAW

Code of Federal Regulations
www.access.gpo.gov/nara/cfr/cfr-table-search.html

Federal Court Locator
vls.law.vill.edu/compass

Federal Register
www.access.gpo.gov/su_docs

Securities Exchange Commission EDGAR Database
www.sec.gov

Supreme Court Decisions, United States
supct.law.cornell.edu/supct/

Thomas
Legislative Information on the Internet
thomas.loc.gov

United States House of Representatives Law Library
law.house.gov

United States Code
www4.law.cornell.edu/uscode

United States Department of Justice
www.usdoj.gov

Oyez Oyez Oyez
United States Supreme Court Multimedia Database
oyez.nwu.edu

FORMS

Forms, Business and Legal
www.geocities.com/CapitolHill/1802/buslegal.html

GENERAL REFERENCE AND LEGAL RESEARCH LINKS

Arizona Lawyer's Guide to the Internet
www.azstarnet.com/~frey

Attorney's Toolbox
www.mother.com/~randy/tools.html

Introduction to Basic Legal Citation
www.law.cornell.edu/citation/citation.table.html

Cornell University's Legal Information Institute
www.law.cornell.edu

FindLaw
www.findlaw.com

FIGURE 7–6
Top Web sites for legal research

CITY AND COUNTY LAW—cont'd

Hieros Gamos
www.hg.org.

Law Encyclopedia
www.lectlaw.com/ref.html

Law Journals, Articles and Abstracts
www.findlaw.com/03journals/index.html

LawsOnline
www.lawsonline.com

Legal Dictionary
www.lectlaw.com/ref.html
www.islandnet.com/%7Ewwlia/diction.htm

Legal Online
www.legalonline.com

Online Legal Periodicals—Free
www.usc.edu/dept/law-lib/legal/journals.html

Virtual Chase
www.virtualchase.com

WWW Virtual Law Library
www.law.indiana.edu/law/v-lib/lawindex.html

Yahoo
www.yahoo.com/Government/Law

LEGAL ETHICS

Practicing Attorney's Home Page
www.legalethics.com

MAPS

Mapquest
mapquest.com

PARALEGAL ASSOCIATIONS

National Association of Legal Assistants
www.nala.org

National Federation of Paralegal Associations
www.paralegals.org

STATE LAW

State Statutes and Legis. Info
www.prairienet.org/%7Escruffy/f.htm

UNIFORM LAWS

Uniform Laws/Codes Official
www.law.upenn.edu/bll/ulc/ulc.htm

Uniform Acts Adopted by States
www.lawresearch.com/CFCODE2.htm

FIGURE 7–6
—Continued

The AAfPE recognizes the following interpersonal skills as being important to the paralegal.

1. Establishing rapport and interacting with lawyers, clients, witnesses, court personnel, co-workers, and other business professionals
2. Being diplomatic and tactful
3. Being flexible and adaptable
4. Being assertive without being aggressive
5. Working effectively as part of a team when appropriate
6. Working independently and with a minimal amount of supervision when appropriate

While you do not always need to be wearing a happy face at work, you will need to have strategies for dealing with difficult individuals and situations, and you must have the ability to handle your stress without taking it out on your employer, co-workers, or clients.

Everyone at some point in his or her career must work with a difficult person. The problem may be a personality conflict or just a bad attitude on the part of one or more individuals. If you are involved in a conflict that causes you stress or impedes your progress on the job, it is best to deal with the problem quickly and directly. In most instances, it is preferable to address the person face-to-face and politely ask to talk it out. Often, simply communicating with the other individual can resolve misunderstandings.

INTERVIEWING AND INVESTIGATING SKILLS

Although interviewing and investigating are two skills often associated only with litigation, they are in fact used in all areas of law by paralegals. Interviewing and investigating are two distinct skills that often go hand in hand. Excellent interviewing skills are needed to conduct a thorough investigation in litigation matters. Both interviewing and investigating skills involve gathering facts for a lawsuit or for other legal services that will be performed for a client.

Most paralegals, from time to time, will have the opportunity to interview clients for any one of numerous reasons. Often paralegals will attend the initial client interview to take notes, or a paralegal will meet with the client before or after the attorney does to collect and record details such as names and addresses. The main goal of most paralegal/client interviews is to obtain the necessary facts and information to allow the attorney to analyze the situation and serve the client's legal needs properly. In addition, paralegals may be asked to interview witnesses and others to obtain pertinent facts and testimony regarding a client's case.

Your personal communication skills will be of the utmost importance during the interviewing process. When you are meeting with a client for the purpose of an interview, do not forget that your active listening skills will be just as important as your speaking skills (Figure 7–7).

1. Do not interrupt the client when he or she is speaking but show that you are listening by maintaining eye contact and nodding when appropriate.
2. Restate the facts and feelings the client is trying to express to you in short and simple terms and by making summary responses.
3. Avoid obviously correcting the client when he or she has misstated a fact or belief.
4. When you would like the client to expand on a statement, encourage the client by repeating the statement. For example, suppose that an estate-planning client is telling you about a family situation and says, "My daughter has four children." If you repeat the client's statement as a question, "Your daughter has four children?," chances are the client will continue by telling you the names and ages of the grandchildren.
5. When you have information as to the procedures that will be followed on the client's file, wait until the client is done relating all facts to you, then relate the procedures directly to the information given to you by the client.
6. Observe the client's body language to understand what the client is feeling, not just what the client is saying.
7. Keep an open mind. Do not presume that you know what the client is feeling or what he or she will say next. Ask questions.
8. Be sympathetic and sensitive without expressing an opinion or being patronizing.
9. Do not be judgmental.
10. Immediately following interviews, while it is still fresh in your mind, prepare a written summary, including any details not on your client interview form.

FIGURE 7–7

Tips for demonstrating active listening when interviewing a client

The law firm or legal department you work for may have several standard client interview forms that vary depending on the purpose of the interview. If not, you may want to create your own so you do not overlook any necessary client information. The questions on standard forms often lead to answers that, in turn, lead to further pertinent questions concerning each client's particular circumstances. Do not be afraid to go out of the box and ask additional questions. The form is just a tool to begin the interviewing process. The client interview form (Figure 7–8) may be used as an intake form for a new litigation client.

The term *investigating* may conjure up mental visions of trench coats and black fedoras. In fact, the term **investigate** means to inquire; to look into; to make an investigation. When the term is taken literally, much of any paralegal's work involves investigating. Whether you are searching for witnesses and evidence for a trial or trying to locate the registered office of a corporation, you must have excellent investigative skills.

Much of a litigation investigation involves collecting the pertinent **evidence** to prove a client's case. In litigation, a fact is not a fact until it has been proven. The litigation investigation is really a two-fold project: first to find the facts, then to find the evidence to prove the facts. Evidence is the means by which any matter of fact may be established or disproved, including testimony, documents, or physical objects. The law and rules of evidence determine what evidence is to be admitted or rejected in the trial of

---

PERSONAL DATA

Name:
Home Address:
Address for Billing:
Home Telephone:
Work Telephone:
Fax Number:
Date of Birth:
Social Security No.:
Driver's License No.:
Spouse's Name:
Spouse's Work Phone:
Employer:
Address:

INFORMATION RELATING TO CLAIM

Type of claim (EEOC, med. malpractice, etc.):
Date of incident leading to claim:
Brief statement of incident (or attach statement):
Itemize damages incurred to date:
Do you anticipate additional damages? If so, describe:
Name and address of any doctors you have seen:
Identity, address, and phone of any potential witnesses:
Description and location of any documents or correspondence pertinent to litigation:
Have you made any statements to anyone (orally or in writing) regarding this case? If so, describe.
Do you have any insurance that covers this claim? If so, please describe.
Have you been served with any papers relating to this case?
Have you heard from any lawyers concerning this case?

PRIOR LITIGATION

Type of litigation:
Date and place of litigation:
Outcome of litigation:
Attorney representing you:

FIGURE 7–8
Client interview form

---

a civil action or a criminal prosecution and what weight is to be given to evidence which is admitted.

There are several forms of evidence, including **testimonial evidence**, **documentary evidence**, **real evidence**, and **demonstrative evidence**. A thorough litigation investigation seeks to uncover all forms of evidence that exist to support the facts concerning a matter. (See Figure 7–9.)

The AAfPE recommends that paralegal students be taught to do the following.

1. Identify witnesses or potential parties to a suit
2. Conduct an effective interview and record appropriate accurate statements

- Client statements
- Witness statements
- Photographs
- Police reports
- Documents obtained from the client
- All types of discovery
- Newspaper articles and notices
- Business records
- Government records
- Employment records
- Hospital records
- Court records
- Automobile registrations (Department of Motor Vehicles)
- Property tax records (County Assessor's Office)
- Public library resources
- Internet

FIGURE 7–9
Sources of evidence

3. Gain access to information that is commonly kept by government agencies
4. Prepare releases and requests to gain access to medical and corporate records

Most paralegal programs offer courses in interviewing and investigation, as is recommended by the AAfPE. If one is not offered in the program you have chosen, you will have to rely on your communication skills, the advice of experienced paralegals or others in your office, and other resources provided by experts.

CHARACTER AND PERSONALITY TRAITS OF EFFECTIVE PARALEGALS

The paralegal profession includes a fairly diverse group of individuals. However, there are a set of character and personality traits that most successful paralegals possess. This section discusses the personality traits commonly found among the most successful paralegals.

It is important to examine your own character and personality traits from time to time to see how they match with your chosen profession and the lifestyle that accompanies it. For example, perhaps you feel that you do not always act with tact and diplomacy. Your personality is such that you always speak your mind with little regard for the feelings of the person you are addressing. This aspect of your personality may have served you well to this point, but you will need to learn to control it on the job to be a successful paralegal. A paralegal without diplomacy runs the constant risk of insulting someone. Insulting the wrong person could cause your law firm to lose a client, or it could cause you to lose your job. Diplomacy is a trait you will have to work to acquire to keep your job and to be successful.

The following character and personality traits are traits you will want to work on and strive for to achieve your optimal success.

- Common sense and good judgment
- Assertiveness
- Diplomacy
- Patience
- Perseverance
- Self-motivation
- Confidence

Whereas it is important for paralegals to have specific knowledge and skills, to be successful, you must have good common sense and judgment as well. You cannot be trained or educated for every possible situation that you will encounter as a paralegal; you will need your common sense and good judgment to get you through situations for which you cannot possibly prepare. For example, as a corporate paralegal you may be asked to incorporate a subsidiary for one of your corporate clients. The responsible attorney has asked you to incorporate the business as soon as possible under the name Kay Enterprises. Your common sense tells you that you should check to make sure the name is available for use in the state in which you will be incorporating. Your good judgment will tell you whether or not a similar alternative name will be acceptable if Kay Enterprises is not.

To be successful in the legal field, you must be assertive (without being overly aggressive). You must have the ability to present your opinion and to ask questions when necessary. In addition, you must be assertive enough to say "no" to an assignment when prior commitments make it impossible for you to get the assignment done on time. At times, some attorneys may appear to be imposing and unapproachable; you must have the assertiveness to speak up when necessary.

Diplomacy is a requirement for success in any work environment, but especially for paralegals. Tact and diplomacy are needed when dealing with attorneys and clients who often are under a great deal of stress.

Patience is a virtue, and it is very important to paralegals. The job of paralegals often requires that work be completed quickly, even when answers and information come slowly. At times, the completion of your work will be dependent on information for which you will be forced to wait—information from attorneys, clients, public officials, and others who may disregard the fact that you are waiting. You must use patience and perseverance when dealing with such situations.

As a paralegal, you will not have constant supervision. Most paralegals strive to be competent and trusted by their employers to the extent where very little supervision is required. This being the case, you will be more valuable to your employers if you are self-motivated and able to take responsibility for your work without requiring direction at every step.

Confidence is a requirement for success as a paralegal, especially as your experience and client contact increase. Clients and attorneys will not feel comfortable dealing with a paralegal who shows no confidence in his or her work. You must have the confidence to trust your work and to ask questions when necessary.

Focus on Ethics: *Competence and Diligence*

ATTORNEY COMPETENCE AND DILIGENCE

Attorneys have an ethical duty to represent their clients with competence and diligence. Competent representation requires attorneys to have the legal knowledge, skill, thoroughness, and preparation reasonably necessary to represent their clients.

Diligent representation requires attorneys to pursue matters on behalf of their clients with commitment and dedication. Attorneys must pursue each client's matter, despite any obstruction or personal inconvenience to the attorney, with zeal through whatever legal and ethical means appropriate, without procrastination.

Attorneys who do not provide competent and diligent representation of their clients are violating the codes of ethics that apply to them, and they may be subject to disciplinary action. In addition, they may be liable for legal malpractice if a disgruntled client brings a civil lawsuit against the attorney.

Most paralegals assist attorneys who represent clients. As part of the legal representation team, paralegals must be aware of the standards for competence and diligence applied to attorneys. All paralegals have an ethical duty to perform their work competently and to assist attorneys in providing competent and diligent representation to their clients.

PARALEGAL COMPETENCE AND DILIGENCE

As a paralegal, you must be certain you have the requisite knowledge and skill to perform the tasks that have been assigned to you. If you do not possess such skill, you must work to educate yourself, ask for help, or both. It is important that you do not misrepresent the level of your knowledge and skill. To do so can have serious consequences to you, the attorneys for whom you work, and the clients they represent. You must be diligent in the completion of your assignments. Attorneys will rely on your ability, skills, and diligence to get work done thoroughly and on time. A lack of competence and diligence on your part can lead to serious consequences, such as missed court dates or deadlines. You, your supervising attorneys, and their clients could all suffer.

STANDARDS FOR PARALEGAL COMPETENCE

Paralegal competence is a sensitive issue with many paralegals because there are no nationally recognized standards. With virtually no education requirements for the profession, paralegals are leery of those unqualified individuals who misrepresent themselves as paralegals and work against the professional image of the entire profession. Most agree that a competent paralegal has a basic knowledge of the American legal system and possesses the skills discussed in the preceding chapter

Both the national paralegal associations have been working to combat this problem by requiring a certain level of competence in their codes of ethics and by providing tests to identify competent paralegals and give them credibility. The NALA recommends that legal assistants establish their competence by obtaining a Certified Legal Assistance (CLA) designation, and the NFPA recommends that paralegals prove their competence by passing their Paralegal Advanced Competency Examination (PACE), thereby obtaining the Registered Paralegal designation (RP).

MAINTAINING COMPETENCE

It has never been easier for paralegals to maintain competence in their profession. Although new laws are being adopted at a rapid rate and the legal environment is constantly changing, there are numerous continuing education options available—even to busy paralegals. Continuing education courses are offered by national, state, and local paralegal associations, as well as by private organizations. Paralegals are also often invited to attend many continuing legal education opportunities that are designed for attorneys. Courses can be taken by attending seminars, by watching seminars on video, by listening to audio tapes, and increasingly, over the Internet.

CAREER TRACK

This chapter identified the skills that will be important to you as a paralegal. Do you possess these skills? You will want to do everything in your power to add as many of these skills to your resume as possible—if not literally, then by demonstrating the use of these skills through actions and experiences. For example, it is one thing to say that you have excellent writing skills and quite another to say that you were editor of your college's school newspaper, that you have had articles published in a trade journal, or that you have received a writing award.

You must plan your education to acquire as many desired skills as possible. If, for example, you find that Microsoft Word is the legal industry standard for word processing software in the area in which you will be working, you will want to have the ability to operate that software. If you cannot pick up training on that specific software through your current paralegal educa-

SKILLS	GOALS	STRENGTHS	WEAKNESSES	PLAN FOR ACHIEVING
Organizational				
Communication				
Analytical				
Computer				
Legal Reasearch				
Interpersonal				
Interviewing and Investigating				

EXAMPLE

SKILLS	GOALS	STRENGTHS	WEAKNESSES	PLAN FOR ACHIEVING
Organizational	Attain excellent organizational skills	Good at working with paper and organizing files	Need to work on time management skills	Read one book on time management before the end of school. Follow plan.
Computer	Become proficient in computerized legal research and litigation support software.	Class on computerized research. Experience on Internet and Lexis.	Never worked on Westlaw. No training on litigation support software.	Complete Westlaw Training. Contact Summation Blaze and Folio Views distributors for information on training.

FIGURE 7–10
Skills chart

tion program, perhaps you will want to register for a short course on this software at another facility.

The chart in Figure 7-10 may help you assess your current skills to make sure you have a plan for acquiring any skills you currently lack.

GLOSSARY

Binding (Mandatory) Authority Previous decisions of a higher court in the same jurisdiction or statutes that a judge must follow in reaching a decision or a case.

Case Law The collection of reported cases that form the body of law within a given jurisdiction. Also written case law; case-law. Also termed *decisional law; adjudicative law; jurisprudence; organic law. (Black's Law Dictionary, Seventh Edition)*

Demonstrative Evidence Physical evidence offered for viewing by the judge or jury.

Documentary Evidence A document or other writing that tends to establish the truth or falsity of a matter at issue. When oral evidence is given, it is the person (usually the witness) who speaks; when documentary evidence is involved, it is the document that "speaks."

Evidence The means by which any matter of fact may be established or disproved. Such means include testimony, documents, and physical objects. The law of evidence is made up of rules that determine what evidence is to be admitted or rejected in the trial of a civil action or a criminal prosecution and what weight is to be given to admitted evidence.

Investigate To inquire; to look into; to make an investigation.

IRAC An acronym used to refer to a common legal analysis process. It is composed of the first letter of the descriptive term for each step of the process—*Issue, Rule, Analysis/ Application, Conclusion.* This process is the identification of the issue, followed by the presentation of the governing rule of law, the analysis/application of the rule of law, and the conclusion.

Legal Analysis The process of applying the law to a given set of facts.

Legalese Legal jargon, including specialized words or phrases, used by lawyers instead of plain talk, when it serves no purpose.

Real Evidence Physical evidence, as opposed to testimony; demonstrative evidence.

Skill Ability to use one's knowledge effectively in doing something; developed or acquired ability.

Statutory Law That body of law created by acts of the legislature in contrast to constitutional law and law generated by decisions of courts and administrative bodies.

Testimonial Evidence Oral evidence elicited from a witness.

Treatise A book or set of books that provide an overview, analysis, or summary of a particular type of law.

ENDNOTES

[1] *Merriam Webster Dictionary* (1995).

[2] National Federation of Paralegal Associations, *NFPA Roles and Responsibilities,* **www.paralegals.org** (July 17, 1997).

[3] Savidge, Traci, Nit-Picks Wanted, *Legal Assistant Today,* March/April 1999, p. 22.

[4] National Association of Legal Assistants, *1997 National Utilization and Compensation Survey Report* (1997).

[5] Hunt, Stacy, *Legal Assistant Today,* Oops! Everything You Wanted to Know About Legal Malpractice, But Were Afraid to Ask, September/October 1998, p. 72.

[6] National Association of Legal Assistants, *1997 National Utilization and Compensation Survey Report* (1997).

[7] *Legal Assistant Today* Technology Survey 1999, *Legal Assistant Today,* March/April 1999, p. 55.

[8] American Bar Association Legal Technology Resource Center, *1998 Small Law Firm Technology Survey* (1998), and *1998 Large Law Firm Technology Survey (1998).*

Feature Need A Job . . . Get An Attitude!

When employers are hiring paralegals, what do they look for? We know they look for the required education, experience, and skills. We have already identified and discussed these requirements. But employers also look for less tangible attributes when hiring paralegals.

Although your potential employer may not even be conscious of doing so, he or she will be judging you on your professional image and your personality. But most of all, your potential employer will be looking to hire someone with the right attitude. Employers agree almost unanimously that the right attitude is essential for a successful employee. According to Richard Nelson Bolles, author of *What Color Is Your Parachute?* "Employers will hire someone with lesser skills, who has the right attitude, rather than a more-skilled person with a bad attitude."[1]

Exactly what is meant by attitude? Attitude is the mental state that you bring to your work and to the people with whom you work. It is your enthusiasm for your work and your willingness to help others on the job. Employers and human resource professionals agree that an employee with a great attitude will be, in the long run, much more valuable than an employee with superior skills and experience and a poor attitude.

Employers have learned that hiring employees with the right attitude increases morale among the entire office and cuts down on employee turnover. For this reason, many employers are requiring applicants to take personality tests to eliminate candidates whose personalities may be problematic or incompatible with the firm culture. Other firms and corporations assess an applicant's attitude based on the opinion of the interviewer and others who have the opportunity to meet with the paralegal during interviews. So not only do you need a good attitude, you need to be able to demonstrate that attitude to those you meet during your interviews. To demonstrate your good attitude, you will want to do the following.

- Express a positive outlook. Do not be negative about past experiences or expected future experiences. Instead of "I need a new job, because my current job is really boring," try "I have really enjoyed my current position and the people I work with, but I feel it is time for a new challenge."

---

[1] Richard Nelson Bolles, *The 1998 What Color is Your Parachute?,* Ten Speed Press (1997).

- **Show that you are willing to help others.** Mention, if appropriate, that you would be willing to stay late to help others on your team, or in the office, if necessary. Discuss other experiences you have had with teamwork—and how you have enjoyed them.
- **Let the interviewer know that you have a "Can Do" attitude.** If the interviewer is explaining an extremely difficult project that must be completed by the new paralegal they hire, let the interviewer know that you feel that the project would be a challenge—and that you are up to the challenge.
- **Show your openness to change.** When discussing your past experience, be sure to express that you are willing to take on new challenges and look at doing things in a different way.
- **Show enthusiasm.** You can show your enthusiasm with your speech and body language. Look alert and interested at all times during the interview. Also, you can demonstrate your enthusiasm for the position by following up on your interview promptly with a thank-you note and with a phone call about a week later.
- **Smile!** You can be both friendly and professional.

CHAPTER 8

Your Job Search

"*The average person puts only 25% of his energy into his work. The world takes off its hat to those who put in more than 50% of their capacity and stands on its head for those few and far between souls who devote 100%.*"

ANDREW CARNEGIE

BEGINNING YOUR SEARCH

The task of finding a paralegal position may seem a bit confusing and overwhelming at first. As is demonstrated by the number of books in the "Career" section of any bookstore, there are a variety of methods of finding employment and numerous places to begin your search. It is important for you to choose a realistic plan for finding the right position. You may want to use the "shotgun" approach and try every possible avenue available to you or you may decide on a more conservative approach, using one source at a time. Whatever your style, it is important to tackle your job search methodically. Keep track of the positions for which you apply, and follow up until you receive a final response or accept a position. A spreadsheet such as the one in Figure 8-1 may be useful for keeping track of your progress. In

Name of Firm or Company	Name of Contact at Firm or Company	Source of Info.	Resume Sent	Follow Up	Interview Date	Thank you Letter Sent	Second Interview Date	Follow Up Letter Sent	Result
ABC Electric	Samantha Lee, Personnel Administrator	Classified Ad Mainstreet Times, 11/5	11/8	11/20— Position Filled					
Tilton & Jablonski	Pamela Pearson, Paralegal Manager	NFPA Posting on Internet	11/8	11/20— Position not filled 12/10— Position not filled— Letter on the way	1:30 12/29 with Pamela Pearson, at 1210 Main Street, Suite 110	12/30	9:00, 1/3, with Tim Lewis and Karen Stillwater, attorneys	1/5 letter to Tim Lewis and Karen Stillwater	Job offer rec'd. 1/10!
Blithe and Bellson, Ltd.	Kathleen Jargins, Director of Personnel	"Hiring Paralegals" per: Linda at Association Meeting	12/5	12/15 Rec'd. Letter. Not currently hiring. Will keep resume. Follow up 1/5 if necessary					
Brown & Jacobson	Mr. Ira Keningston, Office Administrator	12/13 Posting at School Placement Office	12/15	10:30 A.M. Tuesday, 12/23, with Mr. Kenington	10/24	None. Rejection letter rec'd. 12/28			

FIGURE 8–1   *Job search spreadsheet*

addition, you will want to keep a file with copies of all your job search correspondence and any related items.

Your job search process will include the following activities.

- Identifying and using your resources for information about positions
- Researching potential employers
- Preparing your resume and cover letter
- Interviewing for positions
- Evaluating and accepting an offer

Some of the resources that will help you find a position include your school placement office, classified ads in newspapers and other periodicals, and the Internet. A large percentage of positions are never advertised and will only be found by effective **networking** or by targeting potential employers. You may also decide that the services of an employment agency or legal placement service will aid your job search. See Figure 8–2.

SCHOOL PLACEMENT OFFICES

School placement offices are a great place to begin your job search. Some schools boast of the percentage of paralegal graduates they place in jobs after

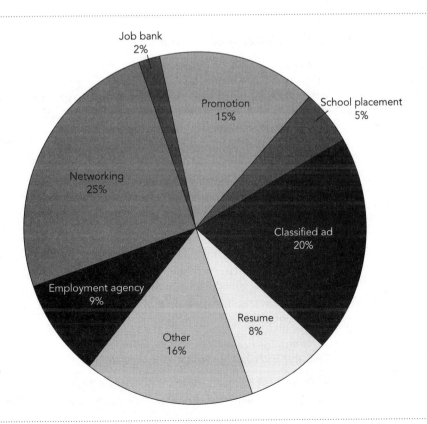

FIGURE 8–2
Method of attaining current paralegal position[1]

graduation, and they are eager to keep that percentage high. The personnel within school placement offices often have an ongoing relationship with recruiters from corporations and law firms who appreciate their free service. They are in a good position to match individuals with particular jobs.

In addition to matching students with prospective employers, the career services and placement offices of many colleges offer the following services.

- Assisting students with resume and cover letter preparation
- Placing students in internships
- Distributing student resumes to potential employers
- Assisting potential employers in finding qualified candidates within the school
- Weekly job postings
- Career counseling
- Providing resources on the job market and locating a position
- Offering seminars on career-related topics

School placement offices also can be a valuable resource for experienced paralegals looking for a more advanced position. Experienced paralegals often can use the placement services of their alma maters when seeking employment.

NEWSPAPERS AND OTHER PERIODICALS

The classified ads of your local newspaper and periodicals published by local bar associations and paralegal associations are usually a good resource when seeking paralegal employment. According to a recent survey of legal administrators, 53 percent of the administrators indicated that they usually use advertisements to locate paralegal candidates for job openings.[2] Listings of available paralegal positions may be under "paralegal" or "legal assistant" headings. Positions requiring paralegal skills also may be listed under various other titles. "Legal technician," "child support specialist," or "trademark specialist" are examples of some possibilities. See Figure 8–3.

When answering a newspaper or periodical ad, be sure to follow the instructions. For example, when the ad requests resumes, send a resume—do not call or appear in person.

Before responding to an ad, be sure to do some preliminary research on the hiring law firm or company. This could prevent you from wasting time applying to an employer for whom you do not really want to work. In addition, such research may help you to customize your resume and cover letter to the position. See Figure 8–4.

THE INTERNET

Job searching on the Internet is becoming an increasingly viable option. As of 1998, an estimated 100,000 Web sites included some job listings or in-

Paralegal – Government	Corporate/Securities	TRADEMARK PARALEGAL
Office	Paralegal	International electronics company seeks paralegal to assist in clearing, acquiring, maintaining, and protecting trademark rights of the corporation.

Paralegal – Government

Office

Attorney General's office is seeking a paralegal to work on large, complex, interrelated constitutional cases. Experience with computerized litigation support, while not required, would be helpful. If interested call 555-9325.

Corporate/Securities Paralegal

Busy law office with focus on serving corporate clients, as well as employment, contract, and securities law seeks an experienced paralegal to handle broad range of responsibilities.

Applicants must be computer-literate and proficient with online services such as the Internet, Westlaw and Microsoft Office (Word and Excel). Please send your resume, via fax, to 555-4938.

TRADEMARK PARALEGAL International electronics company seeks paralegal to assist in clearing, acquiring, maintaining, and protecting trademark rights of the corporation.

Responsibilities include database research, preparation of trademark applications and registrations; reviewing packaging, and advertising materials for trademark infringement.

Qualifications include: ability to use a variety of computer databases; attention to detail and organization; strong written and oral communication skills; work effectively with people and under pressure and time costraints with ability to prioritize; bachelors degree and/or paralegal certificate from ABA-approved program.

We offer a competitive salary and comprehensive benefits. For consideration, forward your resume and salary history to Brighton Electronics, P.O. Box 4837, Brighton, OH 98374.

FIGURE 8–3
Sample classified ads

- Do not overlook newspapers and periodicals directed toward paralegals and other legal professionals as a source of classified ads.
- Remember to look under all possible categories in the ads, including Paralegal, Legal Assistant, Corporate Legal Assistant, and others listed under specialty titles.
- Read the ad carefully and follow the directions.
- Be sure to respond to the individual indicated in the ad.
- Be sure to mention the ad you are responding to in your resume cover letter.
- If the ad you are responding to requests your salary requirements, give an approximately $5,000 salary range of what is acceptable to you. Ignore this request if you feel it will be to your detriment.
- Be sure to save a copy of any ad to which you respond.

FIGURE 8–4

Tips for finding a job through the classified ads

formation.[3] More and more positions are being listed over the Internet where they can be accessed freely. Not only are there several Web sites that list job openings, there are also several sites on the Internet that offer career advice, assist with your resume preparation, and allow you to post your resume for potential employers. Using the Internet can be an especially effective manner for finding a position if you are looking to make a move out of town. See Figure 8–5.

Considering that there are thousands of Web sites advertising positions and the fact that a disproportionately high number of the listed positions are in the computer and high-tech fields, searching the Internet for a job can be overwhelming. You may do well to start with a gateway site—one that contains links to numerous other Web sites—or to limit your search to a Web site that specializes in positions for the legal profession. Following is a sample of some of the Web sites you may find helpful. These are some of the larger sites and sites that specialize in positions in the legal field. Each of these sites lists positions for paralegals, at least from time to time.

America's Employers
www.americasemployers.com
This comprehensive site offers advice on launching your career and preparing your resume. In addition, this site includes links to several sources listing over 50,000 positions, including a link to the Classified section of *Law Journal Extra,* which typically advertises several paralegal positions.

- Search job banks for postings of available positions 24 hours a day
- Post your resume for prospective employers
- Network with other paralegals and potential employers
- Research a potential employer
- Advice on career planning from career counselors
- Advice on interviewing
- Advice on preparing a resume and cover letter

FIGURE 8–5

Tips for finding a job through the classified ads

Best Jobs U.S.A.

www.bestjobsusa.com

This Web site, established by the publishers of *Employment Review* magazine, has an extensive job databank with over 11,000 job listings. In addition, it includes information on career fairs, company profiles, and resume posting.

Career Magazine

www.careermag.com

Career Magazine is a comprehensive site offering links to several different categories of resources for the job seeker, including a job opening database, a resume bank, employer profiles, products and services for career management, articles and news for the job seeker, The Career Forum (a moderated discussion area), Career Links, and *Career Magazine* demographics.

Career Mosaic

www.careermosaic.com

This gateway career site boasts more than 3.9 million visitors per month, up to 418 database queries, and over 70,000 current job openings.[4] It includes searches by industry and by employer. In addition, this site leads to information on online job fairs and career advice sites.

Career Path

www.careerpath.com

The Career Path Web site features job postings from employment ads of the nation's leading newspapers, as well as from the Web sites of leading employers. Career Path gives you the option of posting a confidential resume for the perusal of potential employers. This site is particularly useful if you are considering relocating. You can view jobs listed in want ads of nearly sixty newspapers throughout the United States.

The Federal Jobs Digest

www.jobsfed.com

This Web site lists all currently available positions with the federal government, and it gives you the opportunity to post your resume for prospective federal employers.

Headhunters

www.headhunter.net

This mega site lists over 150,000 jobs (including numerous jobs for paralegals) nationwide.

JobBank USA MetaSEARCH

www.jobbankusa.com/search.html

JobBank USA offers a Job MetaSEARCH page that accesses the Internet's largest job databases, as well as a page for job seekers to post their resumes.

Job Hunters Bible

www.jobhuntersbible.com/

This is an extensive gateway Web site offering advice and links to sites under the following categories: Job Listings, Resume Posting, Career Counseling, Contacts, and Research.

LawInfo.Com Career Center
jobs.lawinfo.com
This Web site is designed specifically for attorneys, law students, and paralegals. It offers assistance with preparing an electronic resume and posting it for potential employers. This site also provides a job directory that includes paralegal positions.

NFPA Career Center
www.paralegals.org
The online Career Center of the National Federation of Paralegal Associations offers nationwide paralegal job listings for paralegals, as well as additional career resources.

National Law Journal's Employment Site
www.lawjobs.com
This site is the Law Employment Center of the *Law Journal Extra* periodical. It includes legal job listings, a listing of law firms, and several links to legal job-related articles, legal directories, surveys, and cites.

The Riley Guide
www.dbm.com/jobguide/
This Web site offers links to several employment opportunity and job resource sites compiled by Margaret F. Dikel, author of *The Guide to Internet Job Searching.*

In addition to the larger sites on the Internet that post listings for numerous law firms and corporations, several law firms and corporations have their own sites where they post their current openings. Do not forget to search the Internet for specific law firms and corporations in your area that are potential employers.

If you find a job you are truly interested in over the Internet, the next step you must take is to determine how to respond to the posting. Read the job posting carefully to see if the employer is requesting a response by e-mail, by telephone, or by U.S. Mail. For more information on sending your resume via e-mail, see the Electronic Resume section later in this chapter.

Although job searching on the Internet may be convenient for you, limiting your job search to the Internet may mean missing several promising opportunities that are not advertised via that medium. According to a recent survey of law office administrators, only 2 percent indicated that they used the Internet to identify paralegal candidates. While this number may have grown since the survey, you will probably not want to use the Internet as the exclusive means for your job search. You may want to combine your Internet search with other job seeking methods, such as networking.

NETWORKING

Networking is an excellent way to get started in your paralegal career, as well as advance after you have some experience. According to a recent survey of working paralegals, nearly 25 percent of the respondents indicated that they obtained their current positions through networking.[5] *Networking* means getting out into the community and meeting people who share your background and interests. If you have the opportunity to get to know several paralegals and attorneys, you will have several contacts when you look for a position or need a personal reference.

To illustrate the importance of effective networking, imagine a staff meeting of the litigation department at one of the leading firms in your hometown. The paralegals, attorneys, and the office administrator have been discussing the increase in workload and the need for additional help. The most likely reaction of the office administrator, who will probably have the task of initiating the search for a new paralegal, is to turn to the paralegals in the room and say, "Does anyone know a qualified paralegal who is looking for a litigation position?" If you have been networking, your name could be the next topic of discussion.

Paralegal associations are a great place for networking, and most associations accept student members. Joining a paralegal association allows you to meet and share concerns with other paralegals in your area. It can also lead to information about job opportunities that are never advertised. Paralegal and bar association continuing education seminars are also good places to meet individuals who share your interests. By attending seminars on topics that interest you, you can increase your knowledge in the field while forming future contacts.

Performing voluntary work for legal clinics and other nonprofit organizations is another great way to network. In addition, it can be rewarding and a great way to gain experience.

Electronic networking is a relatively new phenomenon that is gaining popularity as more and more people gain access to the Internet. Approximately 20 percent of the population currently has access to the Internet, and that number is growing exponentially. There are a variety of networking opportunities available on the Internet—probably the most fruitful are the career-specific chat rooms and list servs that focus on topics of interest to those in the legal profession. It may take some exploring to find the right online networking opportunities for you. You may want to start at the NFPA Web site, **www.paralegals.org**. This site hosts online chats, provides access to listservs, and offers a directory for paralegals. See Figure 8–6.

TARGETING POTENTIAL EMPLOYERS

Another approach to seeking paralegal employment is to target a specific employer or group of employers and aggressively seek a position with those firms, corporations, or government agencies. For example, if you have a specific law firm in mind that you would like to work for, you can call to find out the appropriate individual to send your resume and cover letter to. Your resume can be followed up by a telephone call a few days later. If you are willing to wait for an opening, let them know.

You may target specific employers by word of mouth—by talking with other paralegals who recommend the firms or legal departments in which they are employed. Another approach is to target firms that specialize in a

---

Possible Networking Contacts:
- Co-workers
- Fellow students
- Fellow members of paralegal associations
- Teachers
- Friends
- Family
- Social acquaintances

Possible Networking Opportunities:
- Paralegal association meetings
- Social gatherings with others in your field
- Seminars and continuing education
- Paralegal student organization meetings
- Internet chat groups and list servs for paralegals and others interested in the field

FIGURE 8–6
*Networking
opportunities*

---

specific area of law. Many law firm directories have listings of attorneys by state and city, including their names, addresses, and areas of specialty. Another source is the local news and newspapers. Law firms that are in the news because they are involved in big projects and big cases may well be in need of additional paralegal help. If you are interested in corporate law and mergers and acquisitions, you may want to target the legal departments of corporations that are in the news because of an upcoming merger or acquisition. If you are interested in criminal law, you may want to target attorneys who are in the news because they are involved in highly visible criminal representations.

Informational Interviews. After you have a list of potential employers to target, you may want to take your targeting strategy one step further by conducting **informational interviews** with the appropriate personnel managers from the law firms or corporations you have selected. An *informational interview* (in contrast to an employment interview) is an interview with the person responsible for hiring for an organization with the aim of obtaining general information about careers with the organization, even if no positions are currently available. Because of the time involved, this is an extraordinary measure that is not possible in every instance. Large law firms that have personnel departments and corporate personnel departments may be the most likely to grant informational interviews.

An informational interview can benefit the paralegal in at least three ways. First, the paralegal conducting the interview can gain valuable insight as to exactly what types of positions are, or may become, available within the firm or corporation, as well as what qualifications the potential employer is looking for. Second, the informational interview is good practice for actual employment interviews, as positions may become available. Third, and probably most important, an informational interview could be a foot in the door when a position becomes available within the firm or corporation. An impressed personnel manager may remember an interested candidate with whom he or she has had an informational interview and contact that individual for an employment interview when a position becomes available.

The interviewer at an informational interview is the paralegal; the interviewee is the personnel manager or the individual in charge of hiring for the organization. The questions put to the interviewee should include general questions about the organization, its practice, the number of paralegals it employs, the work it performs, its common practice for hiring paralegals, and the qualifications the organization looks for in potential paralegal employees. This is an opportunity to do a self-check to determine whether you have the skills employers are looking for, or if you need to acquire additional skills.

EMPLOYMENT AGENCIES AND SERVICES

Employment agencies are also a valuable resource for those seeking employment as paralegals. Bar associations and paralegal associations often have their own employment agencies or placement services. In addition, private employment agencies that specialize in the placement of law office personnel operate in most cities.

Bar Associations and Paralegal Associations. Many state and local bar associations have their own employment services that specialize in the placement of law office personnel, including paralegals. These services may be free or charge a minimal fee. In addition, paralegal associations often offer their own job banks as a benefit to their members. Attorneys who are hiring paralegals often contact the local paralegal association to get the word out that they will be accepting resumes for a particular position.

Private Employment Agencies. There are a variety of private employment agencies in every major city in this country. These agencies may charge a fee to the individuals they place, or they may charge a fee to the employer who hires their candidates. Still other employment agencies are willing to negotiate the terms of payment as a condition of employment. A growing number of employment agencies specialize in the placement of law firm personnel, including paralegals. For a legal employment service agency near you, see your local telephone directory.

If you set up an appointment with an employment agency, think of it as a preliminary interview. Dress as you would for an employment interview, and bring extra copies of your resume, writing samples, and references to the interview. The better you sell yourself to the employment agency, the better they can sell you to prospective employers.

RESEARCHING POTENTIAL EMPLOYERS

When you apply for a position, you should be familiar with the firm or the corporation to which you are applying. If you get called for an interview, you must find out what you can about the law firm or corporation to prepare yourself. If you are interviewing with a law firm, you may want to begin with *Martindale-Hubbell, West's Legal Directory,* or another legal directory to find out how many attorneys work for the firm, who the attorneys are, and what their specialties are. Your local library can be of assistance when you are looking for information on corporations or law firms. If you have computer access, do not forget to check the firm's or company's Web site and to use the other online resources available. If you know anyone within the firm or corporation, ask him or her about the organization and the position. You are not expected to know everything there is to know about a firm before attending an interview, but being somewhat familiar with the firm will help you to ask intelligent questions.

Following is a list of some of the resources you may want to use to research your potential employers.

Researching Law Firms and Attorneys (Including Legal Departments)

Martindale Hubbell
Information on law firms and all lawyers admitted to state bars in the United States

West's Legal Directory

The American Law Guide
Information on the top 200 law firms and major legal centers in the United States

Lawyers Register by Specialties and Field of Law
Listing of U.S. attorneys by specialty
State bar association directories
Many state bar associations publish directories of all admitted attorneys

Who's Who in American Law

Directory of Corporate Counsel

Dun's Marketing Service Books

Law Office.Com from West Legal Directory
www.lawoffice.com

Attorney Finder
www.attorneyfinder.com

Lawyers.com from Martindale-Hubbell
www.lawyers.com

Researching Corporations

Hoover's Online
www.hoovers.com

ComFind
www.comfind.com

Business Researcher's Interests
www.brint.com
CompanyLink
www.companylink.com

Standard and Poor's
Description of publicly held corporations and their records

Researching Nonprofit Corporations

Internet Nonprofit Center
www.nonprofits.org

YOUR RESUME

How important is your resume? Consider this: In a one- or two-page document, you have the opportunity to "sell" yourself to a potential employer. It may be the first step in a new career that could change your life. On the other hand, with a poorly written or constructed resume, you will never get your foot in the door.

Some of the important factors that must be considered when preparing a resume include its appearance, its content and style, and the items that often accompany a resume—the cover letter, writing samples, and personal references.

Your resume is the showcase for your skills. The layout and appearance of your resume itself can demonstrate your organizational, analytical, and communication skills. You will want to find ways to demonstrate the other skills you possess within the text of your resume.

APPEARANCES

When you apply for a paralegal position, your resume usually will be your first impression on a potential employer. First impressions are important. When a resume lands on the desk of a busy attorney or law office administrator, who may have hundreds of resumes to review, your resume must have a neat, professional appearance just to get read.

Resumes should be no longer than one or two pages. They should be neatly typed or reproduced on high-quality bond paper—either white or another light color, not a bold or bright color. You may want to have your resume professionally printed. If you have a computer with word processing capabilities and a quality printer at your disposal, you may choose to print your own. If you do, be sure to choose fonts and type size that will give your resume an interesting, but professional, look.

Your resume should be proofread carefully several times. Try reading it aloud to yourself, or enlist the help of a colleague or friend for this task. Many law firms have a collection of poorly written resumes containing typographical or grammatical errors that are maintained as a joke. Do not let your resume become a joke.

Be sure to deliver your resume in the appropriate manner with a cover letter. If you are responding to an ad, follow the directions. If the ad requests applicants to fax a copy of their resume—fax a copy of your resume (and cover letter). If you do not have a fax machine at your personal disposal, there are several businesses that will fax documents for you. If you are mailing your resume, be sure to mail it (unfolded) in a properly addressed, quality 9" by 12" envelope.

YOUR RESUME CONTENTS

Your resume is your opportunity to promote yourself, but you have only a maximum of two pages to do it in. Resumes must be concise, accurate, and to the point. The format you use will be a unique version of one of several standard formats, including the chronological, functional, blended, or electronic format.

Regardless of the format you choose for your resume, it will probably contain a combination of at least some of the following information.

- Personal information
- Career objectives
- Summary of qualifications
- Work experience
- Educational experience
- Special skills
- Memberships and affiliations

Personal Information. This section should include your name, address, and telephone number or numbers. It is not necessary to include personal information such as your height, weight, age, or marital status. Be sure to include all information a prospective employer will need to reach you to schedule an interview. Photographs are not recommended.

ALEXANDER MICHAELS
CERTIFIED LEGAL ASSISTANT
1238 Elm Street, Burlington VT 02314
Phone: (201) 873-4732
E-mail: amichaels@hotmail.com

Career Objective. If you choose to include an objective in your resume, it should be a specific statement to let your potential employer know that your objectives match the position being offered. Your objective usually will include the type of position you desire, the type of employer, and the geographical location in which you want to work.

Paralegal position in the corporate legal department of a large corporation in Toledo, Ohio.

Do not indicate that you are looking for an entry-level position as a paralegal. Many resumes are automatically screened out if they contain the words *entry level.* If you are actively seeking two or more different types of positions, you may want to have more than one version of your resume prepared, with appropriate career objectives for specific potential employers and positions.

If your main objective is simply to get a foot in the door of a particular firm or company and you are willing to consider more than one type of position, you may want to leave this optional objective statement off of your resume.

Summary of Qualifications. When you submit your resume to a potential employer, the first individual reviewing your resume may be someone assigned the task of reviewing hundreds of resumes to select a few candidates who possess the minimum requirements for a position. You want to be sure to highlight your specific qualifications for the position you are seeking in a leading section of your resume. This paragraph is often titled *Summary of Qualifications* or *Highlights.* You will make it easy for your potential employer to spot your best skills and qualifications if you list them as bullet points at the beginning of your resume. If possible, you may want to tailor this section on your resume to highlight the qualifications you possess that most closely match those sought for each position. Consider the following as items of information you may want to include in this section.

- Your relevant education
- Number of years experience in the field
- Specific relevant achievements
- Special skills and knowledge
- Certifications

Summary of Qualifications

- Certified Legal Assistant
- Graduate of Texas University Paralegal Program (an ABA-approved Paralegal Education Program)
- Two Years Varied Experience in the Legal Field
- Fluent in Spanish
- Proficient with both Westlaw and Lexis

Work Experience. This section is a description of your work experience, usually beginning with the most recent and working back in time. You need go back only two or three positions, unless you have earlier work experience that you would like to emphasize. If you are preparing a chronological resume, each entry in this section should include the dates that you were employed in that position, the title of your position, the name and address of your employer, and a brief description of your work with that employer. The description of your work should not merely be a routine job description. Rather, it should list your duties and highlight your accomplishments on the job. Use action words, such as established, communicated, initiated, and organized, to show what you have accomplished. Be specific and include figures and appropriate buzzwords where applicable. For example, compare the following paragraphs describing the same work.

Indexed documents for large litigation project.

---

or

Designed and maintained indexing system of nearly 1,200 discovery documents for multimillion-dollar product liability suit.

In addition, it is appropriate at times to give a brief description of the company you worked for if the company would not be known by your potential employer. Usually just one sentence will suffice. For example: "Investment Opportunities Incorporated is a multimillion-dollar real estate investment corporation." If your work experience is unrelated to the paralegal position you are applying for, stress any skills you have learned from those positions that could be helpful in a paralegal position. For example, if you have experience as an assistant manager in a restaurant, you might want to emphasize your organizational skills, your leadership skills, and your ability to manage others.

Educational Experience. If you do not have impressive, pertinent work experience, but you do have a paralegal degree or certificate, your educational experience should be listed before your work experience. This education section may include each degree you have earned, the name and address of each school you have attended since high school, the dates you attended that school, your graduation date or expected graduation date, and your major areas of study. You may also include a short list of legal specialty classes you would like to emphasize. You may report your grade point average if you feel it will work to your advantage (usually if 3.0 or above), as well as any honors and distinctions you have been awarded.

EDUCATION

Bachelor of Science – Paralegal Studies   California State University
Awarded May 1999 (GPA 3.8)   Hayward, CA 94542
Legal Specialty Courses Completed: Basic law, legal research and writing, business law, litigation and civil procedure, advanced litigation, business organizations, computers for paralegals, and legal ethics.

Special Skills and Qualities. In this section you should list any special skills that may be pertinent to the position for which you are applying. Some of these skills may include the following.

1. Specific computer proficiencies
2. Foreign language fluency
3. Sign language capability
4. Leadership and management qualities

SPECIAL SKILLS

- Fluent in German
- Proficient with both Macintosh and IBM personal computers

Memberships and Affiliations. If you are a member of pertinent organizations, such as your state paralegal associations, you may want to include that information as well.

AFFILIATIONS

Voting member of the Alabama Association of Legal Assistants and the National Association of Legal Assistants

Personal References and Transcripts. Personal references and school transcripts should not be included in a resume. However, if space permits, you may want to note at the end of your resume that such information is available upon request.

YOUR RESUME STYLE

Again, this is *your* resume. Your qualifications, experience, and skills may not fit neatly into a pre-formatted sample. However, a look at some samples can be helpful in getting you started. Most resumes are prepared in one of four basic formats.

Chronological. Traditionally, most resumes have been prepared in chronological format. **Chronological resumes** focus on a chronological description of work experience and education experience, in reverse chronological order. The headings of a typical chronological resume may include the following.

- Personal Information
- Objective or Summary of Qualifications
- Education
- Work Experience
- Special Skills and Qualities
- Memberships and Affiliations

Depending on how much room you have left at the end of your Work Experience section, you may decide to leave out any of the last two sections. If you do, be sure that skills you want to draw attention to are mentioned in a previous part of your resume. If you feel your work experience is more valuable than your education, feel free to include that first in your resume.

A resume in the chronological format may be right for you if you have a continuous stream of work experience and education experience that ties closely to the position you are currently searching for. See Appendix F-1 for sample chronological resumes.

Functional. The **functional resume** format focuses on your skills and achievements. The chronological listing of your previous employers and education is de-emphasized, and your skills and achievements from your work experience and education are highlighted. This type of resume often is used by individuals who have specific skills and achievements they want to emphasize, as well as by individuals who have gaps in their work experience and education to which they do not necessarily want to draw attention.

The headings of a functional format may include the following.

- Personal Information
- Objective
- Skills
- Achievements
- Past Employers
- Credentials

If you are returning to the work force after a long absence or if your past work experience is irrelevant or unfavorable, you may want to use the functional formal. However, many experts caution that some personnel managers and hiring attorneys do not like this format in a resume and feel that it is hard to read or may indicate possible problems with past employment—such as job hopping or being fired from one or more positions. See Appendix F-2 for a sample functional resume.

Blended Format. The **blended resume** uses a combination of the chronological and functional formats, emphasizing achievements and skills in the beginning and then providing a chronological listing of your work experience and education. The headings of a blended format resume may look like this.

- Personal Information
- Summary of Qualifications
- Relevant Experience
- Work History
- Education
- Memberships and Affiliations

You may prefer the blended resume format if you have relevant skills and achievements you want to emphasize and a steady stream of relevant work and education experience. The blended resume format is the style currently preferred by many career advice experts. For samples of resumes prepared in the blended format, see Appendix F-3.

ELECTRONIC RESUMES

Your experience and circumstances probably will determine if you choose to follow the chronological, functional, or blended format for your resume. Whatever style you choose, you may also need an **electronic format** for special submissions. If you are submitting a resume over the Internet, via e-mail, or submitting a resume that will be scanned, there are special formatting rules you must follow to make sure that your resume is read and that it has the best possible appearance.

E-mailing Your Resume. If you submit your resume by e-mail, you will need a plain text resume prepared specifically for e-mailing. The following are some steps to take to send your resume by e-mail. They will work with most word processing software applications.

1. Prepare a version of your resume saved in *plain text.*
2. Proof the plain text version of your resume and correct formatting as necessary.
3. Copy the plain text version of your resume.
4. Prepare your e-mail cover letter using the normal format.
5. Use the job title (as advertised) as the subject line of your e-mail message.
6. Paste the plain text version of your resume into the body of your cover letter e-mail message.
7. Proof your letter and resume, and make any necessary changes before you send.
8. Print or save a copy of your e-mail message and plain text resume for your files.

Do not send your resume as an attachment, as the chances of it getting lost or never opened are too great. After you have pasted the plain text version of your resume in your e-mail, you will want to proof it again and work on the format. Make sure that the spacing and line breaks are correct. Your resume should be accompanied by a properly formatted cover letter that includes any information requested in the job posting.

Posting Your Resume on the Internet. If you are posting your resume on the Internet, you must submit it in the format prescribed by the Web site you are posting to. Most Web sites that post resumes request either that you e-mail a plain text resume following the same steps listed above or that you complete an e-form (a fill-in-the-blanks form posted on their Web site) and click on a button to submit the information.

While the content of your resume need not be significantly different for posting on the Internet, you may need to make a few changes. Think about how your potential employer will be searching for the resumes of qualified candidates. The potential employer will probably be searching by key word for a few significant skills and qualifications that are required for the position they are trying to fill. You must make sure you use key words, either in the body of your resume, in a separate section at the beginning or end of your resume called Key words, or in the specified blank to be filled in on an e-form resume.

Key words: paralegal, Certified Legal Assistant, Westlaw, bachelors degree, legal research, litigation, database, deposition digesting, interviewing, investigating, legal writing

Once you post your resume on the Internet, it becomes a public document. If you are concerned about your current employer learning that you are searching for a new position, you definitely will want to check on who has access to the posted resumes. Resumes posted on some Web sites may only be accessed by registered employers. Other Web sites may offer more accessibility. If you are trying to keep your search a secret, you may decide that posting on the Internet does not offer the confidentiality you need.

The Scanned Resume. More and more of the largest law firms and corporations are using electronic scanners to screen the resumes they receive. These scanners read the resumes that large human resources departments receive and choose those resumes from individuals who have the key education, skills, and experiences for which the firm or corporation is currently looking.

If you are submitting a resume that you know will be scanned, you will want to format it to make it as easy as possible for the scanner to read it. Fancy formatting and type styles are not read well by scanners. In addition, you will want to be sure to include the key words in your resume that the scanner will pick up to indicate that you are qualified for the position for which you are applying.

Here are some specific tips to follow if you know your resume will be scanned.

- Use appropriate key words throughout your resume or, at least, in a *summary of qualifications* paragraph. Consider any information you have about the position (such as from an ad for the position) when choosing your key words.
- Use white 8½″ by 11″ paper—no more than two pages.
- Do not use italics or fancy typefaces.
- Use standard typefaces such as Times, Courier, and Helvetica.
- Use a font size of 10 or 12 (12 is preferred) for the body of your resume, and 14 or 16 for the headings.
- Use boldface or all capital letters to set headings apart.
- Do not use fancy graphics, such as double columns and underscores.
- Be sure to include all the pertinent information you typically would include in your resume.
- Remember, if your resume makes it past the scanner, it eventually will be seen by human eyes.

Most small- to medium-size law firms and legal departments do not use electronic scanners. If you are unsure about whether you should be preparing your resume for an electronic scanner, it is OK to call the human resource department, or other appropriate individual, to find out.

Appendix F-4 is a sample resume prepared in an electronic format. Further advice on preparing resumes for sending by e-mail, posting on the Internet, or being read by a scanner can be found in several of the Web sites previously listed in this chapter.

> - Your resume should be no longer than two pages.
> - Choose the correct resume format to fit your experiences, skills, and the position for which you are applying.
> - Focus the reader's attention by using an *Objective* or *Summary of Qualifications* section.
> - Use bullet-points to clarify lengthy paragraphs.
> - Use 12-point type if possible, 10 point if necessary.
> - Use high-quality white or light-colored bond paper.
> - Customize your resume for different types of positions you apply for.
> - Use bold and italic type appropriately—do not over-use them.
> - Proofread carefully several times.

FIGURE 8–7
Tips for preparing your resume

CUSTOMIZING YOUR RESUME

You must consider your resume a fluid document—ever changing as you acquire new skills and experiences. If you do not have your own personal computer, you will want to store a copy of your resume on disk so that it can be readily updated as necessary. Also, do not forget that subtle customizations to your resume for each position you apply for can make a big difference. Resumes that contain the specific skills an employer is looking for will receive special attention. If you have a good idea what the employer is looking for before you send in your resume, you will want to customize your resume to put an emphasis on those particular skills.

The importance of a good resume cannot be overstated. If you are in doubt, seek help with your resume. Numerous reference books on how to prepare resumes can be found in any bookstore or library. In addition, your school, your advisor, or a professional service can be of great help when assembling a resume. See Figure 8–7.

THE COVER LETTER

Your cover letter is yet another opportunity to sell yourself to a potential employer. Your challenge is to keep your letter short and to the point, and yet personalize it to fit the position and the potential employer. You will want to be sure to mention any connection you have with the firm—such as "I followed the Smith v. White case closely, and I was very impressed with the work done by your firm." You also will want to be sure to mention any specific skills you have that apply to the position. "I think my legal research skills and extensive experience on Westlaw will allow me to make an immediate contribution to your litigation department." Although you may want to refer to certain highlights of your resume in your cover letter, do not make your cover letter too lengthy by repeating information already in your resume.

> • Keep your letter short—no more than one page.
> • Use quality stationery that matches your resume.
> • Prepare on a word processor with a quality printer.
> • Close your letter with "Sincerely,"
> • Do not forget to sign your letter.
> • Make sure your letter is addressed to the correct individual.
> • Your cover letter should include an introduction—why you are sending the letter.
> • Your cover letter should include a paragraph indicating why you are qualified for the position.
> • Your cover letter should include a paragraph requesting specific action—"Please call me at your convenience for an interview."
> • If you have some unique qualification you want to emphasize, include it in a P.S.

FIGURE 8–8

Tips for preparing an effective cover letter

Resumes should always be accompanied by cover letters that include the following information.

1. The name of the position for which you are applying
2. How you learned of the position
3. A brief summary of your qualifications for the position
4. Why you would like the position
5. A request for an interview

Your cover letter is also the first writing sample you are providing to a potential employer. Your writing should be concise and to the point. Do not forget to double check your spelling and grammar. Always be sure to obtain the correct name, title, and address of the individual to whom you are sending the letter. Your cover letter should be prepared on quality bond paper that matches your resume. It should be signed, placed on top of your resume, and mailed in a 9" by 12" envelope or delivered by another specified means. See Figure 8–8; also, see Appendix G to this text for sample cover letters.

WRITING SAMPLES

Writing samples should not be included with your resume and cover letter. However, if you get called for an interview, be sure to bring writing samples with you. Your writing samples should demonstrate your ability to draft accurate and concise legal documents, as well as your ability to communicate well with others. Therefore, include several different types of legal documents and pieces of correspondence or general writing. You may use samples that were school assignments, and you may use samples gleaned from previous work experience.

ETHICAL CONSIDERATION

Be sure to protect the confidentiality of any former client or employer by rewriting samples without actual names or personal information.

PROFESSIONAL REFERENCES

You also should be prepared for interviews by having a list of professional references ready. Professional references should include the individual's name, address, and telephone number. Professional references should be people with whom you have worked or possibly school instructors. Those acting as references for you should always be consulted before their names are given out. In addition to being polite, this will give your references some time to think about what they would like to say to your prospective employer instead of sounding surprised when they get the call.

THE INTERVIEW

The whole purpose of your resume is not to get you a job; it is to get you an interview. A successful interview will get you the position you want. Do not be intimidated by the interviewing process. Interviewing is a skill that you can master. You can be prepared by doing your research, knowing what you want to say and how you want to say it, and dressing for the part. In addition, you must know what to expect from the initial interview, the second interview, and how to follow up after an interview.

KNOW WHAT YOU WANT TO SAY

Before you ever attend an interview, be aware of your strengths and weaknesses. Rehearse ways to demonstrate or describe your strengths during the interview. For example, if you feel that you are particularly helpful and easy to work with, you may want to mention that at your previous employment you worked with a great group of people and you really enjoyed the team atmosphere. Practice ways to overcome any possible objections to your skills or qualifications. For example, if the interviewer points out that their firm uses Lexis for their legal research and you have no experience or training, point out that you learned Westlaw quite quickly and feel you could pick up Lexis quickly as well.

Rehearse the interview in your mind. Think about the questions typically asked during interviews and how you want to answer those questions. One commonly asked question that interviewees often have trouble answering is "Where do you want to be five years from now?" Even if you are unsure, it is better to have a tentative answer than none at all. Remember, no one is going to hold you to your answer five years from now.

It is important to keep in mind the important things about yourself that you would like to convey during the interview. Do not get sidetracked and start rambling. The interview is a two-way street, let the interviewer speak when appropriate (usually about half the time). Also, it is a good idea to bring a list of questions for the interviewer with you so that you can ask everything you want to know before the interview is over.

Do not be afraid to sell yourself. Without being too overbearing, the interview is the time for you to point out ways your particular skills can benefit the potential employer.

KNOW HOW YOU WANT TO SAY IT

Almost as important as what you say in an interview is the manner in which you say it. Interviewers try to spot certain traits during interviews—many times subconsciously. If you are well-prepared with what you want to say about yourself and what you want to find out about the firm, you can focus on your manner during the interview. Some traits that you should try to display include the following.

- Professionalism
- A positive attitude
- Friendliness
- Honesty
- Poise
- Enthusiasm
- Excellent communication skills
- Initiative
- Intelligence
- Resourcefulness
- Assertiveness
- Excellent listening skills

DRESS THE PART

When applying for a paralegal position, dress like a paralegal. Dress like a paralegal who is going to the most important business meeting of his or her career. Although the general trend in the work place is toward a more casual and relaxed dress code, most law firms and legal departments have not been quick to follow suit. The dress code for most attorneys and paralegals is still a suit for women and a suit and tie for men. Even if this is not the case every day of the week in a firm you will be interviewing with, this is how you will want to dress for the interview. One or two quality suits will be an excellent investment as you begin your career as a paralegal. In addition, do not forget details such as a professional-looking briefcase or portfolio to carry your documents and well-polished or well-maintained shoes.

DRESSING FOR A SUCCESSFUL INTERVIEW

WOMEN
- Conservative dark-colored suit with white or pastel blouse
- Clean, well-kept medium-heeled or flat pumps
- Clean, well-groomed hair
- No more than one set of earrings and one ring on each hand
- Keep fragrance to a minimum
- Clean, trimmed fingernails, clear or light-colored polish

MEN
- Conservative dark blue or gray suit with white shirt and conservative silk tie
- Clean, polished, dark shoes
- Clean, well-groomed hair
- No earrings or other visible body piercing
- Keep fragrance to a minimum
- Clean, trimmed fingernails

Be sure to allow extra time to get to the interview, especially if you do not know exactly where the firm or corporation is located or where to park. You may also want to stop in the rest room for one last mirror check before entering the office right on time (not too early). Before you leave for the interview, be sure you have everything you need (preferably in a professional-looking briefcase). Anticipate everything you may need for your interview and be sure you have the following items.

- Directions on how to get to the interview (including the interviewer's name)
- Cash (or change) for parking
- Extra copies of your resume (three or four)
- Writing samples, including anything you have ever had published or anything that has been published about you
- Your list of personal references and phone numbers
- Copies of your transcripts
- Letters of recommendation (if you have any)
- A list of questions you would like answered and topics you would like to discuss during the interview

If you have never been to the office where your interview will be held, you may find it helpful and reassuring to drive to the office and locate it several days before your interview. Depending on the size and formality of the firm or company, you may want to go directly to the reception area and pick up any available literature about the firm or company that is offered to clients or customers. If you get a chance to make a dry run to the office, you will know how long it will take you to get there, and it will take some of the stress out of your interview.

HANDLING THE INTERVIEW

Try to relax. When you are introduced to the interviewer, greet him or her with a smile and a handshake. The first impression you want to make is that of being friendly and professional. Try to focus on what the interviewer tells you, especially his or her name.

Everyone is nervous during job interviews, and every interviewer will understand and expect a certain amount of nervousness. Do not let it control you to the point where you are unable to answer questions or ask the questions you would like to ask. That is where being prepared comes in.

Typically the interviewer will begin by telling you about the firm or the corporation in general. You can show that you have researched the firm by asking pertinent questions about the firm at this point.

Next, the interviewer usually will tell you about the position for which you are applying. He or she probably will ask questions about you and your background as they apply to the firm and the position. You may be introduced to others in the firm with whom you may be working.

Be as open and honest as possible with the interviewer, without being overbearing or overly familiar. If the interviewer asks you a question that you are uncomfortable with, keep your answer short and to the point. Do not feel that you have to explain every detail.

Do not lay blame for any past failures or complain about former employers. You can best answer tough questions by being prepared for them. Following is a list of sample questions that are commonly asked at interviews.

1. Tell me about yourself.
2. Why do you feel that you are a good candidate for this position?
3. What are you looking for in a position?
4. What particular strengths do you have to offer this firm?
5. What life accomplishments are you most proud of? Why?
6. What are your weaknesses?
7. Why did you decide to become a paralegal?
8. Why did you leave your last position?
9. How do you cope with pressure on the job?
10. What were your favorite courses in school? Your least favorite? Why?
11. What were your grades in school?
12. What are your salary requirements?
13. What do you plan on doing five years from now? Ten years?
14. Are you available to work overtime?
15. Why should we hire you?

Although it is impossible to anticipate every question an interviewer might ask, you can at least have answers prepared for those listed here, which will give you the added confidence you need to think on your feet for the other questions.

Illegal Interview Questions. Some interview questions are illegal. For instance, it is illegal for employers to discriminate against potential employees by asking questions concerning an applicant's marital status, number of children, childcare situation, age, health, religion, or political affiliation. If you are asked an illegal question, you have several options.

First, do not be rude. Perhaps the interviewer is inexperienced and the turn of the conversation caused him or her to ask an inappropriate question without any intention of breaking the law. Second, do not feel obliged to answer the question if you do not want to. One way to handle an inappropriate question is by answering with a relatively positive statement concerning yourself. For example, if the interviewer asks if you plan on having any children, you may respond by saying that you are committed to a full-time career. You need not say anything further.

Questions for the Interviewer. After the interviewer has finished giving you the prepared information about the firm or company and the position and has finished asking you the pertinent questions, he or she will probably ask if you have any questions. This is the time to show the interviewer that you are prepared by referring to your list of prepared questions. You will probably find that most of your questions have been answered during the interviewing process. If you still have unanswered questions, be sure to ask now. Your questions should focus on the position and the firm, leaving questions regarding salary and benefits for a second interview.

Do not forget that the interview is also your opportunity to interview your next employer. Be sure to ask the questions that are important to you in determining whether the position is one you really want.

Closing the Interview. Try to leave the interview on a positive note. Offer your writing samples and personal references to the interviewer if he or she has not already asked for them. If you are interested in the position, be sure to say so and to say why you are interested. Find out when the interviewer expects a decision to be made on hiring for the position. Usually, promising first interviews are followed by second interviews with the same individual or with other individuals within the firm or company. If you have received other offers, be honest with the interviewer. If he or she knows that you have received another offer, interviewers will often do what they can to speed up the decision-making process and not keep you waiting.

THE SECOND INTERVIEW

Second interviews are often a chance for attorneys and paralegals who will be working with the new hire to meet the best candidates. The second

DO . . .	DON'T . . .
Point out relevant accomplishments when discussing previous experience	Speak poorly of previous employers
Allow the interviewer to speak about half of the time	Dominate the entire conversation
Research salaries and benefits in your area and decide what you will accept	Bring up salary and benefits during the first interview
Make a practice drive to be sure you know where your interview is, where to park and how long it will take you to get there	Show up late for your appointment
Ask relevant questions that demonstrate that you have researched the firm or company	Attend an interview without knowing anything about the firm or company
End the interview on a pleasant note and express your interest in the position	Forget to send a thank-you letter to everyone who took time to meet with you
Bring at least three extra copies of your resume, writing samples, transcripts and references with you	

FIGURE 8–9
Interview do's and don'ts

interview may be a lunch meeting with several individuals from the firm or you may be introduced to several individuals in the office. If you have not met any paralegals in the office by the end of the second interview, you may ask to meet one. No one can give you better insight on the available position than a paralegal in the office.

The second interview usually provides the opportunity for discussion of such matters as pay, benefits, and any other questions not answered during the first interview. If you are offered a position at the second interview, do not feel obligated to give your answer on the spot. It is reasonable to ask for a couple of days to think the offer over (but do not take too long).

You may want to research the going rate of pay for paralegals in similar positions in your area before you attend your second interview so that you will have some idea of what is an acceptable salary to you. See Figure 8–9.

FOLLOWING UP

Your part of the interview is not over when you walk out the office door. Every interview should be followed up with a personal letter to the individual who interviewed you, thanking that individual for his or her time and consideration. Again, be sure to let the interviewer know if you are interested in the position. See Figure 8-10.

JANET WILLIAMS
123 Elm Street
Maplewood, Minnesota 55117
342-435-2845

January 20, 2000

Ms. Linda Evert
Felton, Lindloff and Richards
348 Mendota Road
Clarksville, Ohio 012345

Dear Ms. Evert:

Thank you for meeting with me yesterday. I thoroughly enjoyed our meeting and the tour of your offices. I am very interested in the paralegal position we discussed.

I feel that my education and litigation experience would be a good fit with your firm and that I would be able to make a strong contribution to your paralegal department.

I look forward to hearing from you soon regarding the position you have available.

Sincerely,

Janet Williams

FIGURE 8–10
Sample thank-you letter for interview

SUMMARY

You may be a seasoned job hunter or just starting out looking for your first professional position. Whatever your situation, finding a paralegal position can be a stressful and overwhelming task—but be prepared and you can face up to it. A positive outlook can produce positive results. Look at the job-hunting process as an opportunity for a fresh start with unlimited potential. Be confident and sell yourself every step of the way. Then it is up to you to pick the opportunity that best suits you.

In addition to all the Internet resources listed in this chapter, there are numerous publications that can be of assistance to you during your job search. Here are a few of them.

RESUMES AND COVER LETTERS

- *101 Best Resumes*, Jay A. Block *and Michael Betrus, McGraw* Hill (1997)
- *Cover Letters that Knock 'Em Dead, 3rdEdition*, Martin Yate, Adams Media Corporation (1998)
- *The New Perfect Resume*, Tom Jackson & Ellen Jackson, Doubleday (1996)

RESUMES AND COVER LETTERS—cont'd

- *The Resume Catalog: 200 Damn Good Examples*, Yana Parker, Ten Speed Press (1996)
- *Resumes by The National Business Employment Weekly*, Taunee Besson, John Wiley and Sons (1994)
- *Resumes for Dummies*, Joyce Lain Kennedy, IDG Books Worldwide (1998)
- *Resumes for Law Careers*, Editors of VGM Career Horizons, VGM Career Horizons (1995)

INTERVIEWING

- *101 Dynamite Answers to Interview Questions—Sell Your Strengths*, Caryl Rae Krannich and Ronald L. Krannich, Ph.D.s, Impact Publications (1997)
- *101 Great Answers to the Toughest Interview Questions, 3rd Edition*, Ron Fry, Career Press (1996)
- *Ask the Headhunter*, Nick A. Corcodilos, Plume (1997)
- *The Complete Idiot's Guide to the Perfect Interview*, Marc Dorio, Alpha Books (1997)
- *Interviewing for Success: A Practical Guide to Increasing Job Interviews, Offers, and Salaries*, Caryl Rae Krannich and Ronald L. Krannich, Ph.D.s. Impact Publications (1998)

GENERAL JOB HUNTING ADVICE

- *College Grad Job Hunter—Insider Techniques and Tactics for Finding a Top-Paying Entry Level Job, 4th Edition*, Brian D. Krueger, Adams Media Corporation (1998)
- *Guerrilla Tactics for Getting the Legal Job of Your Dreams*, Kimm Alayne Walton, J.D., Harcourt, Brace Legal and Professional Publications, Inc. (1995)
- *The Guide to Internet Job Searching*, Margaret Riley Dikel, Frances Roehm, Steve Oserman, VGM Career Horizons (1998)
- *Knock Em Dead 1998*, Martin Yate, Adams Media (1998)
- *Resumes in Cyberspace*, Pat Criscito, Barron's (1997)
- *What Color is Your Parachute 2000?*, Richard Nelson Bolles, Ten Speed Press (1999)

CAREER TRACK

When you are looking for a job, the tendency is to focus on potential positions and how best to attain them. With all your attention being focused outward, you run the risk of losing focus on exactly what it is *you* want in a position. Throughout this text, the Career Track sections have asked you to do a little self-evaluation; now it is time to apply that self-evaluation to your job hunt—to find the job you really want.

Before you begin your job search, review what you have learned and decided so far.

1. Look back to Chapter Two of this text. What type of employer did you decide would be your first choice? Your second choice?
2. Which of the specialties in Chapter Three most appealed to you?
3. What type of position has your education prepared you for? Which classes did you most enjoy?
4. Reviewing the information in Chapter Four, what do you feel is a realistic salary expectation for your next position? How important are benefits to you?
5. What skills do you possess, and what are your strengths and weaknesses?

Answering these questions can help you to focus your job hunt and concentrate on the next step, getting the offer you really want.

EVALUATING THE OFFER

When the offer finally comes for a paralegal position, you must decide whether accepting the position is the right move to make. Do not assume that just because you have been offered a position, you must take it. Consider your self-evaluation from above. How many of your expectations and preferences does the position you are being offered fulfill? The following exercise may help you to evaluate any position you are being offered.

Rank each of the following items on a scale from 0 to 5, with 5 being the most desirable and 0 the least.

Consideration	**Rank**
1. Is this the type of employer I want to work for? (law firm vs. corporation, government agency, or nonprofit)	_____
2. How do I like the office atmosphere?	_____
3. How do I like the people I would be working with and for?	_____
4. Do the billing requirements seem reasonable?	_____
5. How will this position blend with my family/social life?	_____
6. Is this the specialty I want to work in?	_____
7. How interesting will the work be?	_____
8. Would this position utilize my best skills?	_____
9. Is there a possibility of advancement with this employer?	_____
10. Does this position offer enough variety?	_____
11. Is the offered salary acceptable?	_____
12. Are the offered benefits acceptable?	_____

13. Will I be eligible for bonuses? _____

14. Is the office location convenient? _____

15. Are the personal office arrangements adequate? _____

16. How does this position fit with my long-range goals? _____

17. How does this position fit with my short-term goals? _____

Total points _____

The score on this test is not nearly as important as the process involved in considering each of the questions and using your best judgment. A poor score on any one or two of the questions may be enough to eliminate the position from consideration. For example, even if the offered position ranks a nearly perfect score, one question ranked poorly could be enough to cause you to turn down the job. If question 5 received a 0 because the position requires extensive travel and your family circumstances will not permit it, you would have to decline the offer.

If you ever find a position that ranks 85 (a perfect score)—take it! Otherwise you can use the score of this exercise to compare the multiple positions you may be offered. Other factors to consider are how quickly you need to be employed, other opportunities, and possibly most important, your best judgment.

GLOSSARY

Blended Resume Resume that uses a combination of the chronological and functional formats to emphasize achievements and skills in the beginning and then provide a chronological listing of your work experience and education.

Chronological Resume Resume that focuses on a chronological description of work experience and education experience, beginning with the current date and working back in time.

Electronic Resume Resume prepared with special formatting specifically for submission over the Internet, via e-mail, or for electronic scanning.

Functional Resume Resume that focuses on your skills and achievements and eliminates or de-emphasizes a precise chronology of all work and education experience.

Informational Interview An interview with the person responsible for hiring for an organization to obtain information about a particular kind of employment even if no positions are currently available.

Networking Meeting and establishing contacts with a relatively large number of people with similar interests who might be helpful to you later. Similarly, you become such a contact for others.

ENDNOTES

[1] National Federation of Paralegal Associations, Inc., *1997 Paralegal Compensation and Benefits Report.*

[2] *Law Office Management and Administration Report,* LOMAR NEWS BRIEF, October 1997.

[3] *Internet World,* April 13, 1998.

[4] *Career Mosaic* Web site, September 28, 1998.

[5] National Federation of Paralegal Associations, Inc., *1997 Paralegal Compensation and Benefits Report.*

State Adopted Definitions of the Terms Paralegal *and* Legal Assistant

---

Note that new definitions are continually being adopted by state legislatures, courts, and bar associations. Check with your local paralegal association or the companion Web site to this text at **www.westlegalstudies.com** for new definitions.

ALASKA
Alaska Bar Association
The Alaska Bar Association has defined legal assistants as qualified and educated individuals working under attorneys' supervision.

COLORADO
Colorado Bar
Legal assistants (also known as paralegals) are a distinguishable group of persons who assist attorneys in the delivery of legal services. Through formal education, training, and experience, legal assistants have knowledge and expertise regarding the legal system, as well assubstantive and procedural law, which will qualify them to do work of a legal nature under the direct supervision of a licensed attorney.

CONNECTICUT
House of Delegates of the Connecticut Bar Association
A legal assistant is a person, qualified through education, training, or work experience, who is employed or retained by a lawyer, law office, governmental agency, or other entity in a capacity or function which involves the performance, under the ultimate direction and supervision of an attorney, of specifically delegated substantive legal work, work which, for the most part, requires a sufficient knowledge of legal concepts that, absent such

assistant, the attorney would perform the task. [As used herein, "legal assistant" and "paralegal" are synonymous terms.]

FLORIDA

Florida Statutes Annotated Sec. 57.014 concerning computation of attorneys' fees

Florida Rules of Professional Conduct, Rule 4-5.3 was amended in 1999 to provide the following. "A person who uses the title of paralegal, legal assistant, or other similar term when offering or providing services to the public must work for or under the direction or supervision of a lawyer or an authorized business entity as defined elsewhere in these Rules Regulating The Florida Bar."

The amendment also provides that "(w)hile paralegals or legal assistants may perform the duties delegated to them by the lawyer without the presence or active involvement of the lawyer, the lawyer shall review and be responsible for the work product of the paralegals or legal assistants."

GEORGIA

Georgia Advisory Opinion No. 21 (Rev. May 20, 1983)

For the purposes of this opinion, the terms "legal assistant," "paraprofessional," and "paralegal" are defined as any lay person not admitted to the practice of law in this state who is an employee of or an assistant to an active member of the State Bar of Georgia or of a partnership or professional corporation . . . of active members of the State Bar . . . and who renders services relating to the law to such member, partnership, or professional corporation under the direct control, supervision, and compensation of a member of the State Bar of Georgia.

ILLINOIS

Illinois Statutes Ch. 5, Section 70/1.35 (1999)

§ 1.35. Paralegal. "Paralegal" means a person who is qualified through education, training, or work experience and is employed by a lawyer, law office, governmental agency, or other entity to work under the direction of an attorney in a capacity that involves the performance of substantive legal work that usually requires a sufficient knowledge of legal concepts and would be performed by the attorney in the absence of the paralegal. A reference in an Act to attorney fees includes paralegal fees, recoverable at market rates.

INDIANA

Indiana Code 1-1-4-6 (1999)

1-1-4-6 Attorney's Fees As Including Paralegal's Fees

Sec. 6. (a) As used in this section, "paralegal" means a person who is: (1) qualified through education, training, or work experience; and (2) employed by a lawyer, law office, governmental agency, or other entity; to work under the direction of an attorney in a capacity that involves the performance of substantive legal work that usually requires a sufficient knowledge of legal concepts and would be performed by the attorney in the absence of the paralegal.

Sec. 6 (b) A reference in the Indiana Code to attorney's fees includes paralegal's fees.

Indiana Supreme Court Rules, Guideline 9.1
Guideline 9.1. Supervision
A legal assistant shall perform services only under the direct supervision of a lawyer authorized to practice in the State of Indiana and in the employ of the lawyer or the lawyer's employer. Independent legal assistants, to-wit, those not employed by a specific firm or by specific lawyers, are prohibited. A lawyer is responsible for all of the professional actions of a legal assistant performing legal assistant services at the lawyer's direction and should take reasonable measures to ensure that the legal assistant's conduct is consistent with the lawyer's obligations under the Rules of Professional Conduct.

IOWA
Iowa State Bar
The Iowa State Bar has defined legal assistants as qualified and educated individuals working under attorney supervision.

KANSAS
Kansas State Bar
The Kansas State Bar Association has defined legal assistants as qualified and educated individuals working under attorneys' supervision.

KENTUCKY
Kentucky Supreme Court Rule 3.700
SCR 3.700 Provisions Relating to Paralegals
For purposes of this rule, a paralegal is a person under the supervision and direction of a licensed lawyer who may apply knowledge of law and legal procedures in rendering direct assistance to lawyers engaged in legal research; design, develop, or plan modifications or new procedures, techniques, services, processes, or applications; prepare or interpret legal documents and write detailed procedures for practicing in certain fields of law; select, compile, and use technical information from such references as digests, encyclopedias, or practice manuals; and analyze and follow procedural problems that involve independent decisions.

MAINE
Maine Revised Statutes Annotated 1.4 c. 18
Sec. 921. Definitions
As used in this chapter, unless the context otherwise indicates, the following terms have the following meanings.

1. Paralegal and legal assistant. "Paralegal" and "legal assistant" mean a person, qualified by education, training, or work experience, who is employed or retained by an attorney, law office, corporation, governmental agency, or other entity and who performs specifically delegated substantive legal work for which an attorney is responsible.

Sec. 922. Restriction On Use of Titles

1. Prohibition. A person may not use the title "paralegal" or "legal assistant" unless the person meets the definition in section 921, subsection 1.
2. Penalty. A person who violates subsection 1 commits a civil violation for which a forfeiture of not more than $1000 may be adjudged.

MASSACHUSETTS
Massachusetts State Bar Association

The Massachusetts State Bar Association has defined legal assistants as qualified and educated individuals working under attorneys' supervision.

MICHIGAN
Michigan State Bar Bylaws

Any person currently employed or retained by a lawyer, law office, governmental agency, or other entity engaged in the practice of law in a capacity or function which involves the performance, under the direction and supervision of an attorney, of specifically delegated substantive legal work, work which, for the most part, requires a sufficient knowledge of legal concepts such that, absent that legal assistant, the attorney would perform the task, and work which is not primarily clerical or secretarial in nature, and:

(a) who has graduated from an ABA-approved program of study for legal assistance and has a baccalaureate degree; or
(b) has received a baccalaureate degree in any field, plus not less than two years of in-house training as a legal assistant; or
(c) who has received an associate degree in the legal assistant field, plus not less than two years of in-house training as a legal assistant; or
(d) who has a minimum of four years of in-house training as a legal assistant;

may upon submitting proof thereof at the time of application and annually thereafter become a Legal Assistant Affiliate Member of the State Bar of Michigan.

MINNESOTA
Minnesota State Bar Association

The Minnesota State Bar Association has defined legal assistants as qualified and educated individuals working under attorneys' supervision.

MISSOURI
Missouri State Bar Association

A legal assistant or paralegal is a person qualified by education, training, or work experience who is employed or retained by a lawyer, law office, corporation, governmental agency, or other entity and who performs specifically delegated substantive legal work for which a lawyer is responsible.

MONTANA
Montana Statutes 37-60-101(12)

"Paralegal" or "legal assistant" means a person qualified through education, training, or work experience to perform substantive legal work that requires knowledge of legal concepts and that is customarily but not exclusively performed by a lawyer and who may be retained or employed by one or more lawyers, law offices, governmental agencies, or other entities or who may be authorized by administrative, statutory, or court authority to perform this work.

NEVADA
Nevada State Bar

A legal assistant (also known as a paralegal) is a person qualified through education, training, or work experience who is employed or retained by a lawyer, law office, governmental agency, or other entity in a capacity or function which involves the performance, under the ultimate direction and supervision of an attorney, of specifically delegated substantive legal work, which, for the most part, requires sufficient knowledge of legal concepts that, absent such an assistant, the attorney would perform the task.

NEW HAMPSHIRE
New Hampshire Supreme Court Administrative Rule 35, Guidelines for the Utilization by Lawyers of the Services of Legal Assistants
C. Definition of "Legal Assistant"

As used in these Guidelines, the term "legal assistant" shall mean a person not admitted to the practice of law in New Hampshire who is an employee of or an assistant to an active member of the New Hampshire Bar, a partnership comprised of active members of the New Hampshire Bar, or a Professional Association within the meaning of RSA chapter 294-A and who, under the control and supervision of an active member of the New Hampshire Bar, renders services related to but not constituting the practice of law.

NEW JERSEY
New Jersey Bar Association

The New Jersey State Bar defines a paralegal/legal assistant as an individual qualified through education, training, or work experience who is retained by a lawyer, law office, governmental agency, or other entity to perform, under the direction and supervision of a lawyer, specifically delegated substantive legal work, which for the most part requires sufficient knowledge of legal concepts and which absent the paralegal or legal assistant would be performed by a lawyer.

NEW MEXICO
Rule 20-102
Rule 20-102. Definitions

As used in these guidelines:

A. a "legal assistant" is a person qualified through education, training, or work experience who is employed or retained by a lawyer, law office, governmental agency, or other entity in a capacity or function which involves the performance, under the ultimate direction and supervision of an attorney, of specifically delegated substantive legal work, which, for the most part, requires a sufficient knowledge of legal concepts that, absent such assistant, the attorney would perform the task; and

B. practice of law, insofar as court proceedings are concerned, includes:

(1) representation of parties before judicial or administrative bodies;

(2) preparation of pleadings and other papers, incident to actions and special proceedings;

(3) management of such actions and proceedings; and

(4) noncourt-related activities, such as:

(a) giving legal advice and counsel;

(b) rendering a service which requires use of legal knowledge or skill; and

(c) preparing instruments and contracts by which legal rights are secured.

Rule 20-112. Accountability

The legal assistant is directly accountable to the lawyer. The lawyer maintains ultimate responsibility for and has an ongoing duty to actively supervise the legal assistant's work performance, conduct, and product.

NEW YORK

New York Bar Association *Report on Nonlawyer Practice*

"Traditional Paralegal" is defined as:

A person who, with supervision by and/or accountability to a lawyer performs specifically delegated substantive legal work. Paralegals are employed or retained by a lawyer, law office, governmental agency, or other entity. The paralegal qualifies for the role through experience, education, training, or any combination of the three. Qualification as a paralegal permits the person to perform work that requires such knowledge of legal work. A paralegal may also perform substantive legal work as permitted by administrative, statutory, or court authority.

"Freelance Paralegal" is defined as:

A paralegal who works as an independent contractor with supervision by and/or accountability to a lawyer.

NORTH CAROLINA

North Carolina State Bar Association

The North Carolina State Bar Association has defined legal assistants as qualified and educated individuals working under attorneys' supervision.

NORTH DAKOTA

North Dakota Rules of Professional Conduct Terms

"Legal Assistant" (or paralegal) means a person who assists lawyers in the delivery of legal services and who through formal education, training, or experience, has knowledge and expertise regarding the legal system and substantive and procedural law which qualifies the person to do work of a legal nature under the direct supervision of a licensed lawyer.

OHIO
Ohio State Bar Association
A legal assistant or paralegal is a person qualified by education, training, or work experience who is employed or retained by a lawyer, law office, corporation, governmental agency, or other entity and who performs specifically delegated substantive legal work for which a lawyer is responsible.

OREGON
Oregon State Bar Association
The Oregon State Bar Association has defined legal assistants as qualified and educated individuals working under attorneys' supervision.

RHODE ISLAND
Rhode Island Supreme Court Rules Art. V, RPC Rule 5.5
Provisional Order NO. 18—Use of Legal Assistants
These guidelines shall apply to the use of legal assistants by members of the Rhode Island Bar Association. A legal assistant is one who, under the supervision of a lawyer, shall apply knowledge of law and legal procedures in rendering direct assistance to lawyers, clients, and courts; design, develop, and modify procedures, techniques, services, and processes; prepare and interpret legal documents; detail procedures for practicing in certain fields of law; research, select, assess, compile, and use information from the law library and other references; and analyze and handle procedural problems that involve independent decisions. More specifically, a legal assistant is one who engages in the functions set forth in Guideline 2. Nothing contained in these guidelines shall be construed as a determination of the competence of any person performing the functions of a legal assistant or as conferring status upon any such person serving as a legal assistant.

Guidelines
1. A lawyer shall not permit a legal assistant to engage in the unauthorized practice of law. Pursuant to Rules 5.3 and 5.5 of the Rhode Island Supreme Court Rules of Professional Conduct, the lawyer shares in the ultimate accountability for a violation of this guideline. The legal assistant remains individually accountable for engaging in the unauthorized practice of law.
2. A legal assistant may perform the following functions, together with other related duties, to assist lawyers in their representation of clients: attend client conferences; correspond with and obtain information from clients; draft legal documents; assist at closings and similar meetings between parties and lawyers; witness execution of documents; prepare transmittal letters; maintain estate/guardianship trust accounts; transfer securities and other assets; assist in the day-to-day administration of trusts and estates; index and organize documents; conduct research; check citations in briefs and

memoranda; draft interrogatories and answers thereto; deposition notices and requests for production; prepare summaries of depositions and trial transcripts; interview witnesses; obtain records from doctors, hospitals, police departments, other agencies and institutions; and obtain information from courts. Legal documents, including, but not limited to, contracts, deeds, leases, mortgages, wills, trusts, probate forms, pleadings, pension plans, and tax returns shall be reviewed by a lawyer before being submitted to a client or another party.

In addition, except where otherwise prohibited by statute, court rule or decision, administrative rule or regulation, or by the Rules of Professional Conduct, a lawyer may permit a legal assistant to perform specific services in representation of a client. Thus, a legal assistant may represent clients before administrative agencies or courts where such representation is permitted by statute or agency or court rules.

Notwithstanding any other part of this Guideline,

(1) Services requiring the exercise of independent professional legal judgment shall be performed by lawyers and shall not be performed by legal assistants.

(2) Legal assistants shall work under the direction and supervision of a lawyer, who shall be ultimately responsible for their work product.

(3) The lawyer maintains direct responsibility for all aspects of the lawyer-client relationship, including responsibility for all actions taken by and errors of omission by the legal assistant, except as modified by Rule 5.3(c) of the Rules of Professional Conduct.

3. A lawyer shall direct a legal assistant to avoid any conduct that if engaged in by a lawyer would violate the Rules of Professional Conduct. In particular, the lawyer shall instruct the legal assistant regarding the confidential nature of the attorney/client relationship and shall direct the legal assistant to refrain from disclosing any confidential information obtained from a client or in connection with representation of a client.

4. A lawyer shall direct a legal assistant to disclose that he or she is not a lawyer at the outset in contacts with client, court, administrative agencies, attorneys, or, when acting in a professional capacity, the public.

5. A lawyer may permit a legal assistant to sign correspondence relating to the legal assistant's work, provided the legal assistant's non-lawyer status is clear and the contents of the letter do not constitute legal advice. Correspondence containing substantive instructions or legal advice to a client shall be signed by an attorney.

6. Except where permitted by statute or court rule or decision, a lawyer shall not permit a legal assistant to appear in court as a legal advocate on behalf of a client. Nothing in this Guideline shall be

construed to bar or limit a legal assistant's right or obligation to appear in any forum as a witness on behalf of a client.

7. A lawyer may permit a legal assistant to use a business card, with the employer's name indicated, provided the card is approved by the employer and the legal assistant's nonlawyer status is clearly indicated.

8. A lawyer shall not form a partnership with a legal assistant if any part of the partnership's activity involves the practice of law.

9. Compensation of legal assistants shall not be in the manner of sharing legal fees, nor shall the legal assistant receive any remuneration for referring legal matters to a lawyer.

10. A lawyer shall not use or employ as a legal assistant any attorney who has been suspended or disbarred pursuant to an order of this court or an attorney who has resigned in this or any other jurisdiction for reasons related to a breach of ethical conduct.

Entered as an order of this court on this 31st day of October, 1990.
Sup. Ct. Rules, Art. V, Rules of Prof. Conduct, Rule 5.5
RI R S CT ART V RPC Rule 5.5

SOUTH CAROLINA
South Carolina Case Law: *In re: Easler, 272 S.E. 2d 32, 32-33 (1980), cited in* **The State of South Carolina v. Robinson, Opinion No. 24391, filed March 18, 1996.**

Paralegals are routinely employed by licensed attorneys to assist in the preparation of legal documents such as deeds and mortgages. The activities of a paralegal do not constitute the practice of law as long as they are limited to work of a preparatory nature, such as legal research, investigation, or the composition of legal documents that enable the licensed attorney-employer to carry a given matter to a conclusion through his or her own examination, approval, or additional effort.

South Carolina Bar Association
The South Carolina Bar Association has defined legal assistants as qualified and educated individuals working under attorneys' supervision.

SOUTH DAKOTA
South Dakota Supreme Court Rule 97-25, SD ST Section 16-18-34
16-18-34 Definition of Legal Assistant.

Legal assistants (also known as paralegals) are a distinguishable group of persons who assist licensed attorneys in the delivery of legal services. Through formal education, training, and experience, legal assistants have knowledge and expertise regarding the legal system, substantive and procedural law, the ethical considerations of the legal profession, and the Rules of Professional Conduct as stated in chapter 16-18, which qualifies them to do work of a legal nature under the employment and direct supervision of a licensed attorney. This rule shall apply to all unlicensed persons employed by a licensed attorney who are represented to the public or clients as possessing training or education which qualifies them to assist in the handling of legal matters or document preparation for the client.

16-18-34.1 Minimum Qualifications.

Any person employed by a licensed attorney as a legal assistant must meet the minimum qualifications of:

(1) Successful completion of the Certified Legal Assistant (CLA) examination of the National Association of Legal Assistants, Inc.; or

(2) Graduation from an ABA-approved program of study for legal assistants; or

(3) Graduation from a course of study for legal assistants which is institutionally accredited but not ABA-approved, and which requires not less than the equivalent of sixty semester hours of classroom study; or

(4) Graduation from a course of study for legal assistants, other than those set forth in (b) and (c) above, plus not less than six months of in-house training as a legal assistant; or

(5) A baccalaureate degree in any field, plus not less than six months in-house training as a legal assistant; or

(6) A minimum of three years of law-related experience under the supervision of a licensed attorney, including at least six months of in-house training as a legal assistant; or

(7) Two years of in-house training as a legal assistant.

Provided, further, that any legal assistant hereunder shall have a high school diploma or general equivalency diploma (GED).

For purposes of these standards, "in-house training as a legal assistant" means legal education of the employee by a licensed attorney concerning legal assistant duties and these guidelines. In addition to review and analysis of assignments, the legal assistant should receive a reasonable amount of instruction directly related to the duties and obligations of the legal assistant and the Rules of Professional Conduct as stated in this chapter.

TENNESSEE
Tennessee State Bar Association

The Tennessee State Bar Association has defined legal assistants as qualified and educated individuals working under attorneys' supervision.

TEXAS
Texas Bar Association

The Texas Bar Association has established the following criteria for membership in its Legal Assistant Division:

To qualify for active membership in the Legal Assistant's Division, one must be working under the supervision of a licensed Texas attorney and qualify under one of the following criteria:

1. certificate of completion from an accredited paralegal program and one (or two years depending on the program) year of work as a legal assistant

2. a bachelors degree and one year of work as a legal assistant

3. a certified legal assistant (CLA), one who has passed the examination offered by the National Association of Legal Assistants located in Tulsa, Oklahoma, and one year of work
4. three years of experience working as a legal assistant

VIRGINIA
Virginia State Bar Association
The Virginia State Bar Association has defined legal assistants as qualified and educated individuals working under attorneys' supervision.

WASHINGTON
Local Court Rules
Various definitions of legal assistant, as well as qualifications for legal assistants, are established in some local court rules.

WISCONSIN
Wisconsin State Bar Paralegal Task Force
A paralegal is an individual qualified through education and training, who is supervised by a lawyer licensed to practice law in this State, to perform substantive legal work requiring a sufficient knowledge of legal concepts that, absent the paralegal, the attorney would perform the work.

How to Choose
a Paralegal Program

If you have decided to enter the exciting paralegal profession, you should consider completion of a paralegal program to help you realize your goal. Because there are many different kinds of paralegal education programs, selecting the one that is best for you can be a challenge. This page will give you the tools you need to identify paralegal programs that you might wish to attend and to assess the quality of these programs.

The following organizations participated in the development of this page:

American Association for Paralegal Education
American Bar Association Standing Committee on Legal Assistants
Association of Legal Administrators
Legal Assistant Management Association
National Association of Legal Assistants
National Federation of Paralegal Associations

These organizations represent approximately 20,000 legal assistants, 500 legal assistant managers, 7,500 legal administrators and 300 paralegal education programs across the country. These groups and their members share the common interests of encouraging high standards in paralegal education and providing information about the field and paralegal education to the public.

INTRODUCTION

The paralegal profession has grown tremendously since it first appeared in the mid-1960s. There are now more than 120,000 paralegals in the United States. Presently, paralegals are involved in sophisticated legal work in traditional law office settings and in the corporate, government and public arenas. The occupation has achieved great recognition and has moved rapidly to professional stature.

Obtaining a quality paralegal education is the best way to prepare for the paralegal profession. Since a paralegal education requires a substantial commitment of time, effort and money, the decision about which program to choose should be made with as much information and care as possible.

Regulation of paralegals has been and continues to be discussed at a national level and by many jurisdictions. However, no state currently requires paralegals to be licensed and, as a result, no standardization of educational programs or criteria for employment has been established. This is another reason why a prospective paralegal student should examine carefully different programs before making a final selection.

Your choice of a paralegal program will have a profound impact on your opportunities for success in the career. Since there is a wide range in the quality of programs, choose carefully. Give yourself the best possible chance to succeed in this exciting profession.

TYPES OF PROGRAMS

Having a formal paralegal education has become increasingly important. Even though there are an estimated 600 paralegal education programs in the United States, paralegal education is not standardized.

Paralegal education programs are offered in many formats and lengths. Various kinds of public and private institutions offer paralegal education, including community colleges, four-year colleges and universities, business colleges and proprietary institutions.

These various institutions make it possible for persons with diverse backgrounds to enter the profession.

The most common types of programs are:

Associate Degree Programs

These programs are offered by two-year community colleges, some four-year colleges and universities, and some business schools.

Upon successful completion of 60 to 70 semester units, a student earns an associate degree. The curriculum usually consists of approximately one-half paralegal courses and one-half courses in general education and related areas. In selecting a program, prospective students should consider whether they might continue their education to earn a four-year degree at another college and, if so, should investigate the transferability of courses in the programs they are considering.

Baccalaureate Degree Programs

Paralegal education is also offered by four-year colleges and universities which have a paralegal studies major, minor, or concentration within a major. These programs are usually about 120 to 130 semester units, including 30 to 60 semester units in paralegal and related courses. Upon successful completion of the program, the student is awarded a baccalaureate degree.

Certificate Programs

Various kinds of educational institutions offer paralegal certificate programs ranging from 18 to 60 semester units. Longer programs usually include both general education and paralegal courses, similar to associate degree programs. Certificate programs are usually designed for students who already hold an associate or a baccalaureate degree.

Master's Degree Programs

A few colleges and universities that offer undergraduate paralegal degree programs are now offering an advanced degree in paralegal studies. Other universities offer advanced degree programs in law-related areas such as legal administration and legal studies.

EDUCATIONAL STANDARDS

American Bar Association

The American Bar Association has been involved in promoting the paralegal career since 1968 and has been approving paralegal education programs since 1975. The approval process is voluntary since it is not required by any governmental agency. To be approved, a program must be offered by an institution that is accredited by an accrediting agency on an approved list and must meet standards relating to administration, resources, curriculum and academic policies, faculty and program direction, admissions standards and practices, student services including placement and counseling, library, and facilities. Programs seeking approval must submit a detailed self-evaluation report with supporting documents and are visited by an evaluation team. Approval is granted for a period of seven years. As of February 1999, the paralegal programs at 232 institutions across the country have been approved. A few new programs are usually approved each year. In some metropolitan areas, employers require potential candidates to possess a credential from an ABA-approved program.

American Association for Paralegal Education

The American Association for Paralegal Education, established in 1981, is an organization that represents paralegal education programs and has 285 institutional members. Its primary mission is to promote high standards in paralegal education. In its Statement of Academic Quality, AAfPE acknowledges that the education of a paralegal requires a unique curriculum that covers both substantive legal knowledge and practical skills. This intellectually demanding course of study should be designed to provide instruction in the competencies that paralegals need as professionals. AAfPE recognizes seven essential components of a quality paralegal education program: curriculum development, facilities, faculty, marketing and promotion, paralegal instruction, student services and related competencies.

EVALUATING PARALEGAL PROGRAMS

Here are some important factors to consider in evaluating the quality of paralegal programs:

1. **What is the reputation of the institution and the paralegal program?**
   The general public and the legal community should hold the institution offering the program and the program itself in high regard. Check with people you know in the community, in the legal field and in higher education for information.

2. **What services are offered to students?** Assistance should be offered in these areas: orientation, tutoring, academic counseling, financial aid, career information and counseling, and placement assistance. Information on the placement rate and job satisfaction of graduates should be available.

3. **What facilities are available to students?** Programs should have a legal research library, computer laboratories, and properly furnished classrooms. Facilities should accommodate students with disabilities.

4. **What activities are available to students?** Students should have the opportunity to participate in such activities as honor societies and volunteer work in the legal community. Information about paralegal associations and continuing paralegal education should be available.

5. **What is the mission of the institution and what are the goals of the paralegal program?** The mission and goals should be clearly stated in the institutional and program literature. You should assess whether the mission and goals match your individual needs.

6. **What is the content and nature of the curriculum?** The courses should teach practical job skills in conjunction with the underlying legal theory. The curriculum should cover legal research and writing, litigation, ethics, contracts, business organizations and torts. Courses should develop students' critical thinking, communication, computational, computer and organizational skills, and competency to handle ethical issues. Programs should offer an experiential learning component such as an internship, practicum or clinical experience.

7. **What are the graduation requirements?** Students should be required to take both paralegal and general education courses unless students have completed general education prior to enrollment.

8. **What are the backgrounds of the program director and faculty?** The program director and members of the faculty should possess appropriate academic credentials. Most program directors have a law degree or formal paralegal education; some have advanced degrees in related areas. Many have experience in the legal field. Faculty members should have expertise and experience in the subject areas they teach and experience working with or as paralegals. The program director and faculty must be committed to the role of the paralegal in the delivery of legal services.

9. **What are the special considerations of enrolling in a distance education program?** A growing number of educational institutions and other providers are offering paralegal courses and/or entire paralegal programs through distance education. Prospective students need to supplement the above criteria with additional factors when evaluating these offerings. You should find out the type of distance delivery system used, such as interactive video broadcasts to distant sites, telecourses, or web-based courses on the Internet and determine whether the institution provides training to students in using the system and technical assistance throughout the course. You should find out how much interaction takes

place among teachers and students during courses and through what medium. Additionally you should assess whether you are well suited to learn through a distance delivery system which requires a high degree of self-discipline, self-motivation and independence.

FINDING A QUALITY PARALEGAL PROGRAM

Once you have made your career decision, assistance in identifying the program in your area can be obtained from a number of sources:

- Local colleges and universities
- Paralegal associations. Two national associations are the National Association of Legal Assistants (NALA) and the National Federation of Paralegal Associations (NFPA). There may be local chapters in your area. Contact their headquarters or websites.
- Paralegal placement agencies. There are employment agencies which specialize in placing legal assistants.
- Practicing paralegals
- Graduates of local paralegal programs
- American Bar Association Standing Committee on Legal Assistants (SCOLA). This committee has a list of programs which is available on its website.
- American Association for Paralegal Education (AAFPE). AAfPE has a membership directory which is available from AAfPE's headquarters and information is available through AAfPE's website.
- Legal Assistant Management Association (LAMA) has members in law firms and corporate law departments throughout the United States and Canada. Information about LAMA can be obtained from their headquarters and is available at LAMA's website.
- Local bar associations
- Law firms and individual attorneys who have worked with paralegals

Directory of Paralegal Associations

NATIONAL ORGANIZATIONS

American Association For Paralegal Education
2965 Flowers Road South, Suite 105
Atlanta, GA 30341
Phone: (770) 452-9877
Fax: (770) 458-3314
E-mail: **info@aafpe.org**
Internet: **www.aafpe.org**

American Bar Association
750 N. Lakeshore Dr.,
Chicago, IL 60611
Phone: (312) 988-5000
E-mail: **info@abanet.org**
Internet: **www.abanet.org**

Association of Legal Administrators
175 E. Hawthorne Parkway, Suite 325
Vernon Hills, IL 60061-1428
Phone: (847) 816-1212
Fax: (847) 816-1213
Internet: **www.alanet.org**

Legal Assistant Management Association
LAMA Headquarters
2965 Flowers Road South, Suite 105
Atlanta, GA 30341
Phone: (770) 457-7746
Fax: (770) 458-3314
E-mail: **lamaoffice@aol.com**
Internet: **www.lamanet.org**

National Association of Legal Assistants
1516 S. Boston, #200
Tulsa, OK 74119
Phone: (918) 587-6828
Fax: (918) 582-6772
E-mail: **nalanet@nala.org**
Internet: **www.nala.org**

National Federation of Paralegal Associations
P.O. Box 33108
Kansas City, MO 64114
Phone: (816) 941-4000
Fax: (816) 941-2725
E-mail: **info@paralegals.org**
Internet: **www.paralegals.org**

DIRECTORY OF STATE AND LOCAL PARALEGAL ASSOCIATIONS

Please note that the contact information of several of the following associations changes with each change of officers and directors. For that reason, not all addresses are included in this list, and some of the following addresses may be out of date.

NFPA Affiliates

NALA Affiliates

Alabama

Mobile Association of Legal Assistants
P.O. Box 1852
Mobile, AL 36633

Alabama Association of Legal Assistants
P.O. Box 55921
Birmingham, AL 35255
E-mail: **president@aala.net**
Internet: **www.aala.net**

Legal Assistant Society of Southern Institute

Samford University Paralegal Association

Alaska

Alaska Association of Legal Assistants
P.O. Box 101956
Anchorage, AK 99510-1956
E-mail: Alaska@paralegals.org

Fairbanks Association of Legal Assistants

Arizona

Arizona Association of Professional
Paralegals, Inc.
P.O. Box 430
Phoenix, AZ 85001
E-mail: **Arizona@paralegals.org**

Arizona Paralegal Association

Legal Assistants of Metropolitan Phoenix

Tucson Association of Legal Assistants
P.O. Box 257
Tucson, AZ 85702
E-mail: **tala@azstarnet.com**
Internet: **www.azstarnet.com/nonprofit/tala**

Arkansas

Arkansas Association of Legal Assistants

California

California Association of Independent
   Paralegals
39120 Argonaut Way, #114
Fremont, CA 94538

Legal Assistants Association of Santa Barbara
P.O. Box 2695
Santa Barbara, CA 93120-2695

NFPA Affiliates

NALA Affiliates

California—cont'd

Sacramento Association of Legal Assistants
P.O. Box 453
Sacramento, CA 95812-0453
Phone: (916) 763-7851
E-mail: **Sacramento@paralegals.org**
Internet:
www.paralegals.org/Sacramento/sala.htm

San Diego Association of Legal Assistants
P.O. Box 87449
San Diego, CA 92138-7449
Phone: (619) 491-1994
E-mail: **SanDiego@paralegals.org**
Internet:
www.paralegals.org/SanDiego/sdala1.htm

San Francisco Paralegal Association
P.O. Box 2110
San Francisco, CA 94126-2110
Phone: (415) 777-2390
Fax: (415) 586-6606
E-mail: **SanFrancisco@paralegals.org**
Internet: **www.sfpa.com/**

Los Angeles Paralegal Association
P.O. Box 8788
Calabasas, CA 91372
Phone: (818) 347-1001
Fax: (818) 222-1336
E-mail: **DavidR7944@AOL.COM**
Internet: **www.lapa.org**

Orange County Paralegal Association
P.O. Box 8512
Newport Beach, CA 92658-8215
Internet: **www.OCPARALEGAL.org**

Palomar College Paralegal Studies Club (San Marcos)

Paralegal Association of Santa Clara County
P.O. Box 26736
San Jose, CA 95159-6736
Phone: (408) 235-0301
Internet: **www.sccba.com/PASCCO**

San Joaquin Association of Legal Assistants
P.O. Box 1306
Fresno, CA 93716
Internet: **www.caparalegal.org/sjala.html**

Ventura County Association of Legal Assistants
P.O. Box 24229
Ventura, CA 93002
Internet: **www.caparalegal.org/vala.html**

Colorado

Rocky Mountain Paralegal Association
P.O. Box 481864
Denver, CO 80248-1834
Phone: (303) 370-9444
E-mail: **rmpa@rockymtnparalegal.org**
Internet:
   www.rockymtnparalegal.org/index.html

Association of Legal Assistants of Colorado
606 South Nevada Avenue
Colorado Springs, CO 80903
Phone: (719) 475-0026
Fax: (719) 475-8671
E-mail: **swoop137@netzero.net**
Internet: **firms.findlaw.com/ALAC**

NFPA Affiliates   **NALA Affiliates**

Connecticut

Central Connecticut Paralegal Association, Inc.
P.O. Box 230594
Hartford, CT 06123-0594
E-mail: **CentralConnecticut@paralegals.org**
Internet: **www.paralegals.org/Central Connecticut/home.html**

Connecticut Association of Paralegals, Inc.
P.O. Box 134
Bridgeport, CT 06601-0134
E-mail: **Connecticut@paralegals.org**
Internet: **www.paralegals.org/Connecticut/home. html**

New Haven County Association of Paralegals, Inc.
P.O. Box 862
New Haven, CT 06504-0862
E-mail: **NewHaven@paralegals.org**
Internet: **www.paralegals.org/NewHaven/home. html**

Delaware

Delaware Paralegal Association
P.O. Box 1362
Wilmington, DE 19899
Phone: (302) 426-1362
E-mail: **Delaware@paralegals.org**
Internet: **paralegals.org/Delaware/home.html**

District of Columbia

National Capital Area Paralegal Association
P.O. Box 27607
Washington, DC 20038-7607
Phone: (202) 659-0243
E-mail: **NationalCapital@paralegals.org**
Internet: **paralegals.org/NationalCapital/home. html**

Florida

Florida Paralegal Association, Inc.
P.O. Box 7479
Seminole, FL 33775
E-mail: **Florida@paralegals.org**

Central Florida Paralegal Association
Orlando, FL

Dade Association of Legal Assistants
Bay Harbor Island, FL

<table>
<tr><td>

NFPA Affiliates

</td><td>

NALA Affiliates

</td></tr>
</table>

Florida—cont'd

Gainesville Association of Legal Assistants
P.O. Box 2519
Gainesville, FL 32602
Phone: (352) 367-9088
Fax: (352) 367-0720

Jacksonville Legal Assistants
P.O. Box 52264
Jacksonville, FL 32201
Phone: (904) 366-8440
E-mail: **Info@jaxla.org**
Internet: **www.jaxla.org**

Legal Assistants of Southwest Florida, Inc.

Florida Legal Assistants, Inc.
Clearwater, FL

Northwest Florida Paralegal Association
P.O. Box 1333
Pensacola, FL 32596
Internet: **www.pla-net.org**

Phi Lambda Alpha Legal Assisting Society of
Southwest Florida

Tampa College-Brandon Student Association
Tampa, FL

Volusia Association of Legal Assistants
Ormond Beach, FL

Georgia

Georgia Association of Paralegals, Inc.
1199 Euclid Ave., NE
Atlanta, GA 30307
Phone: (404) 522-1457
Fax: (404) 522-0132
E-mail: **Georgia@paralegals.org**
Internet: **paralegals.org/Georgia/home.htm**

Georgia Legal Assistants
Alma, GA

Professional Paralegals of Georgia

South Georgia Association of Legal Assistants
Nashville, GA

Southeastern Association of Legal Assistants
of Georgia
Pooler, GA

NFPA Affiliates	**NALA Affiliates**

Hawaii

Hawaii Paralegal Association
P.O. Box 674
Honolulu, HI 96809
E-mail: **Hawaii@paralegals.org**
Internet: **paralegals.org/Hawaii/home.html**

Idaho

Gem State Association of Legal Assistants
Hailey, ID

Illinois

Illinois Paralegal Association
P.O. Box 8089
Bartlett, IL 60103-8089
Phone: (630) 837-8088
Fax: (630) 837-8096
E-mail: **Illinois@paralegals.org**
Internet: **www.ipaonline.org/**

Central Illinois Paralegal Association
Bloomington, IL

Heart of Illinois Paralegal Association
Peoria, IL

Indiana

Indiana Paralegal Association
Federal Station
P.O. Box 44518
Indianapolis, IN 46204
Phone: (317) 767-7798
E-mail: **Indiana@paralegals.org**
Internet: **www.paralegals.org/Indiana/
   home.html**

Indiana Legal Assistants
c/o The Indiana State Bar Association
230 East Ohio Street, 4th Floor
Indianapolis, Indiana 47204
Internet: **www.freeyellow.com:8080/
members/ila**

Michiana Paralegal Association
P.O. Box 11458
South Bend, IN 46634
E-mail: **Michiana@paralegals.org**
Internet: **www.paralegals.org/Michiana/home.
   html**

Northeast Indiana Paralegal Association, Inc.
P.O. Box 13646
Fort Wayne, IN 46865
E-mail: **NortheastIndiana@paralegals.org**
Internet: **www.paralegals.org/NortheastIndiana/
   home.html**

NFPA Affiliates

NALA Affiliates

Iowa

Iowa Association of Legal Assistants
P.O. Box 93153
Des Moines, IA 50393
E-mail: **ialanet@forbin.com**
Internet: **www.ialanet.org**

Kansas

Kansas City Paralegal Association
P.O. Box 344
Lee's Summit, MO 64063-0344
Phone: (816) 524-6078
E-mail: **KansasCity@paralegals.org**
Internet: **www.paralegals.org/KansasCity/home.html**

Kansas Association of Legal Assistants
P.O. Box 47031
Wichita, KS 67201
Internet:
www.ink.org/public/kala/main.html

Kansas Paralegal Association
P.O. Box 1675
Topeka, KS 66601
E-mail: **Kansas@paralegals.org**
Internet: **www.ink.org/public/ksparalegals/**

Kentucky

Greater Lexington Paralegal Association, Inc.
P.O. Box 574
Lexington, KY 40586
E-mail: **Lexington@paralegals.org**

Western Kentucky Paralegals
Murray, KY

Louisiana

New Orleans Paralegal Association
P.O. Box 30604
New Orleans, LA 70190
Phone: (504) 467-3136
E-mail: **NewOrleans@paralegals.org**
Internet:
paralegals.org/NewOrleans/home.html

Louisiana State Paralegal Association
Monroe, LA

Northwest Louisiana Paralegal Association
Shreveport, LA

Maine

Maine State Association of Legal Assistants
E-mail: **mrroy@unum.com**
Internet: **www.msala.org**

NFPA Affiliates   **NALA Affiliates**

Maryland

Maryland Association of Paralegals
P.O. Box 13244
Baltimore, MD 21203
Phone: (410) 576-2252
E-mail: **Maryland@paralegals.org**
Internet: **paralegals.org/Maryland/home.html**

Massachusetts

Central Massachusetts Paralegal Association
P.O. Box 444
Worcester, MA 01614
E-mail: **CentralMassachusetts@paralegals.org**

Massachusetts Paralegal Association
c/o Offtech Management Services
99 Summer Street, Suite L-150
Boston, MA 02110
Phone: (800) 637-4311
Fax: (617) 439-8639
E-mail: **Massachusetts@paralegals.org**
Internet: **www.paralegals.org/Massachusetts/
    home.html**

Western Massachusetts Paralegal Association
P.O. Box 30005
Springfield, MA 01103
E-mail: **WesternMassachusetts@paralegals.org**

Michigan

Michiana Paralegal Association   Legal Assistants Association of Michigan
P.O. Box 11458   Dearborn, MI
South Bend, IN 46634   E-mail: **goLAAM@aol.com**
E-mail: **Michiana@paralegals.org**

Minnesota

Minnesota Paralegal Association
1711 W. County Rd. B, #300N
Roseville, MN 55113
Phone: (612) 633-2778
Fax: (612) 635-0307
E-mail: **info@mnparalegals.org**
Internet: **mnparalegals.org/**

NFPA Affiliates

NALA Affiliates

NALA Affiliates

Mississippi

Mississippi Association of Legal Assistants
Post Office Box 996
Jackson, MS 39205
Internet: **www.mslawyer.com/MALA**

University of Southern Mississippi Society
for Paralegal Studies
Hattiesburg, MS

Missouri

St. Louis Association of Legal Assistants
P.O. Box 69218
St. Louis, MO 63169-0218
Internet:
www.nwmissouri.edu/~bdye/slalapage

Montana

Montana Association of Legal Assistants
E-mail: **mala@montana.com**
Internet: **www.montana.com/mala**

Nebraska

Nebraska Association of Legal Assistants
E-mail: **webmaster@meala.org**
Internet: **www.neala.org**

Nevada

Clark County Organization of Legal
Assistants
Las Vegas, NV

Sierra Nevada Association of Paralegals
Reno, NV

New Hampshire

Paralegal Association of New Hampshire
Henniker, NH

| **NFPA Affiliates** | **NALA Affiliates** |

New Jersey

Prudential Insurance Company of America-
Paralegal Council
751 Broad Street
Newark, NJ 07102
E-mail: **Prudential@paralegals.org**

South Jersey Paralegal Association
P.O. Box 355
Haddonfield, NJ 08033
E-mail: **SouthJersey@paralegals.org**
Internet: **www.paralegals.org/SouthJersey/
 home.html**

Legal Assistants Association of New Jersey
P.O. Box 142
Caldwell, NJ 07006
Internet:
www.geocities.com/CapitolHill/2716

New Mexico

Southwestern Association of Legal Assistants
P.O. Box 8042
Roswell, NM 88202-8042
Internet: **homepages.infoseek.com/
 ~shewolf2/sala.html**

New York

Long Island Paralegal Association
1877 Bly Road
East Meadow, NY 11554-1158
E-mail: **LongIsland@paralegals.org**

Manhattan Paralegal Association, Inc.
521 Fifth Ave., 17th Floor
New York, NY 10175
Phone: (212) 330-8213
E-mail: Manhattan
Internet: **www.paralegals.org/Manhattan/
 home.html**

Paralegal Association of Rochester
P.O. Box 40567
Rochester, NY 14604
Phone: (716) 234-5923
E-mail: **Rochesterparalegals.org**

NFPA Affiliates

NALA Affiliates

New York—cont'd

Southern Tier Paralegal Association
P.O. Box 2555
Binghamton, NY 13903-2555
E-mail: **SouthernTier@paralegals.org**
Internet: **www.paralegals.org/SouthernTier/home.html**

West/Rock Paralegal Association
P.O. Box 668
New City, NY 10956
Phone: (914) 786-6184
E-mail: **WestRockparalegals.org**

Western New York Paralegal Association
P.O. Box 207, Niagara Square Station
Buffalo, NY 14201
Phone: (716) 635-8250
E-mail: **WesternNewYork@paralegals.org**
Internet: **www.paralegals.org/WesternNewYork/home.html**

North Carolina

Coastal Carolina Paralegal Club
Jacksonville, NC

Metrolina Paralegal Association
Charlotte, NC

North Carolina Paralegal Association
NCPA
P.O. Box 28554
Raleigh, NC 27611
Phone: (800) 479-1905, (919) 779-1903
Fax: (919) 779-1685
E-mail: **info@ncparalegal.org**
Internet: **www.ncparalegal.org**

North Dakota

Red River Valley Legal Assistants
Moorhead, MN

Western Dakota Association of Legal
Assistants
Minot, ND

NFPA Affiliates   **NALA Affiliates**
Ohio

Cincinnati Paralegal Association
P.O. Box 1515
Cincinnati, OH 45201
Phone: (513) 244-1266
E-mail: **Cincinnati@paralegals.org**
Internet: **www.paralegals.org/Cincinnati/
   home.html**

Cleveland Association of Paralegals
P.O. Box 14517
Cleveland, OH 44114-0517
Phone: (216) 556-5437
E-mail: **Cleveland@paralegals.org**

Greater Dayton Paralegal Association
P.O. Box 515, Mid-City Station
Dayton, OH 45402
E-mail: **Dayton@paralegals.org**
Internet: **www.paralegals.org/GreaterDayton/
   home.html**

Northeastern Ohio Paralegal Association
P.O. Box 80068
Akron, OH 44308-0068
E-mail: **NorthEasternOhio@paralegals.org**
Internet: **www.paralegals.org/NortheasternOhio/
   home.html**

Paralegal Association of Central Ohio
P.O. Box 15182
Columbus, OH 43215-0182
Phone: (614) 224-9700
E-mail: **CentralOhio@paralegals.org**

Toledo Association of Legal Assistants
Toledo, OH

Oklahoma

Oklahoma Paralegal Association
Norman, OK

Rogers State College Association of Legal
   Assistants
Claremore, OK

Rose State Paralegal Association
Midwest City, OK

NFPA Affiliates	**NALA Affiliates**

Oklahoma—cont'd

TCC Student Association of Legal Assistants
Tulsa, OK

Tulsa Association of Legal Assistants
Tulsa, OK

Oregon

Oregon Paralegal Association
P.O. Box 8523
Portland, OR 97207
Phone: (503) 796-1671
E-mail: **Oregon@paralegals.org**
Internet: **paralegals.org/Oregon/home.html**

Pacific Northwest Legal Assistants
Eugene, OR

Pennsylvania

Central Pennsylvania Paralegal Association
P.O. Box 11814
Harrisburg, PA 17108
E-mail: **CentralPennsylvania@paralegals.org**
Internet: **www.paralegals.org/**
   CentralPennsylvania/home.html

Keystone Legal Assistant Association
Summerdale, PA

Chester County Paralegal Association
P.O. Box 295
West Chester, PA 19381-0295
E-mail: **ChesterCounty@paralegals.org**

Lycoming County Paralegal Association
P.O. Box 991
Williamsport, PA 17701
E-mail: **Lycoming@paralegals.org**

Philadelphia Association of Paralegals
P.O. Box 59179
Philadelphia, PA 19102-9179
Phone: (215) 545-5395
E-mail: **Philadelphia@paralegals.org**

Pittsburgh Paralegal Association
P.O. Box 2845
Pittsburgh, PA 15230
Phone: (412) 344-3904
E-mail: **Pittsburgh@paralegals.org**
Internet: **www.paralegals.org/**
CentralPennsylvania/home.html

NFPA Affiliates   **NALA Affiliates**

Rhode Island

Rhode Island Paralegal Association
P.O. Box 1003
Providence, RI 02901
E-mail: **RhodeIsland@paralegals.org**
Internet: **paralegals.org/RhodeIsland/home.html**

South Carolina

Palmetto Paralegal Association   Central Carolina Technical College Paralegal
P.O. Box 11634   Association
Columbia, SC 29211-1634   Sumter, SC
E-mail: **Palmetto@paralegals.org**
Internet: **paralegals.org/Palmetto/home.html**   Charleston Association of Legal Assistants
                                        P.O. Box 1511
                                        Charleston, SC 29402

                                        Grand Strand Paralegal Association (GSPA)
                                        743 Hemlock Avenue
                                        Myrtle Beach, SC 29577

                                        Greenville Association of Legal Assistants
                                        P.O. Box 10491
                                        Greenville, SC 29603

                                        Paralegal Association of Beaufort County
                                        South Carolina
                                        Beaufort, SC

                                        Tri-County Paralegal Association, Inc. (TCPA)
                                        P.O. Box 62691
                                        North Charleston, SC 29419-2691

South Dakota

                                        South Dakota Legal Assistants Association
                                        Aberdeen, SD

                                        National College Student Association of
                                        Legal Assistants
                                        Rapid City, SD

NFPA Affiliates

Memphis Paralegal Association
P.O. Box 3646
Memphis, TN 38173-0646
E-mail: **Memphis@paralegals.org**
Internet:
  paralegals.org/Memphis/home.html

Dallas Area Paralegal Association
P.O. Box 12533
Dallas, TX 75225-0533
Phone: (972) 991-0853
E-mail: **Dallas@paralegals.org**
Internet: **paralegals.org/Dallas/home.html**

NALA Affiliates

Tennessee

Greater Memphis Paralegal Alliance, Inc.
Memphis, TN
E-mail: **pcobb@tlblaw.com**

Tennessee Paralegal Association

Texas

Capitol Area Paralegal Association
Austin, TX

El Paso Association of Legal Assistants
El Paso, TX

Legal Assistants Association/Permian Basin
Midland, Texas

Northeast Texas Association of Legal
  Assistants
Longview, TX

Nueces County Association of Legal
  Assistants
Corpus Christi, TX

Southeast Texas Association of Legal
  Assistants
Beaumont, TX

Texas Panhandle Association of Legal
  Assistants
Amarillo, TX

Tyler Area Association of Legal Assistants
Tyler, TX

West Texas Association of Legal Assistants
Lubbock, TX

Wichita County Student Association
Wichita Falls, TX

Utah

Legal Assistants Association of Utah

<table>
<tr><td>**NFPA Affiliates**</td><td>**NALA Affiliates**</td></tr>
</table>

Vermont

Vermont Paralegal Organization
P.O. Box 5755
Burlington, VT 05402
E-mail: **Vermont@paralegals.org**

Virgin Islands

Virgin Islands Paralegal Association

Virginia

Peninsula Legal Assistants, Inc.
Poquoson, VA

Richmond Association of Legal Assistants
P.O. Box 384
Richmond, VA 23218-0384
E mail: **rala@geocities.com**
Internet:
  www.geocities.com/CapitolHill/7082

Tidewater Association of Legal Assistants
Norfolk, VA

Washington

Washington State Paralegal Association
P.O. Box 48153
Burien, WA 98148
Phone: (800) 288-WSPA
E-mail: **Washington@paralegals.org**
Internet: **paralegals.org/Washington/home.html**

West Virginia

Legal Assistants of West Virginia
Huntington, WV
E-mail: **lawvlawv.org**

Wisconsin

Paralegal Association of Wisconsin, Inc.
P.O. Box 510892
Milwaukee, WI 53203-0151
Phone: (414) 272-7168
E-mail: **Wisconsin@paralegals.org**
Internet: **paralegals.org/Wisconsin/home.html**

Madison Area Paralegal Association
Madison, WI
E-mail: **ckorth@foleylaw.com**
Internet: **www.califex.com/mapa/index.html**

NFPA Affiliates

NALA Affiliates

Wyoming

Legal Assistants of Wyoming
Casper, WY

NALA's Model Standards and Guidelines for Utilization of Legal Assistants

INTRODUCTION

The purpose of this annotated version of the National Association of Legal Assistants, Inc. Model Standards and Guidelines for the Utilization of Legal Assistants (the "Model," "Standards" and/or the "Guidelines") is to provide references to the existing case law and other authorities where the underlying issues have been considered. The authorities cited will serve as a basis upon which conduct of a legal assistant may be analyzed as proper or improper.

The Guidelines represent a statement of how the legal assistant may function. The Guidelines are not intended to be a comprehensive or exhaustive list of the proper duties of a legal assistant. Rather, they are designed as guides to what may or may not be proper conduct for the legal assistant. In formulating the Guidelines, the reasoning and rules of law in many reported decisions of disciplinary cases and unauthorized practice of law cases have been analyzed and considered. In addition, the provisions of the American Bar Association's Model Rules of Professional Conduct, as well as the ethical promulgations of various state courts and bar associations have been considered in the development of the Guidelines.

These Guidelines form a sound basis for the legal assistant and the supervising attorney to follow. This Model will serve as a comprehensive resource document and as a definitive, well-reasoned guide to those considering voluntary standards and guidelines for legal assistants.

I. PREAMBLE

Proper utilization of the services of legal assistants contributes to the delivery of cost-effective, high-quality legal services. Legal assistants and the legal profession should be assured that measures exist for identifying legal assistants and their role in assisting attorneys in the delivery of legal services. Therefore, the National Association of Legal Assistants, Inc.., hereby adopts these Standards and Guidelines as an educational document for the benefit of legal assistants and the legal profession.

COMMENT

The three most frequently raised questions concerning legal assistants are (1) How do you define a legal assistant; (2) Who is qualified to be identified as a legal assistant; and (3) What duties may a legal assistant perform? The definition adopted in 1984 by the National Association of Legal Assistants answers the first question. The Model sets forth minimum education, training and experience through standards which will assure that an individual utilizing the title "legal assistant" has the qualifications to be held out to the legal community and the public in that capacity. The Guidelines identify those acts which the reported cases hold to be proscribed and give examples of services which the legal assistant may perform under the supervision of a licensed attorney.

These Guidelines constitute a statement relating to services performed by legal assistants, as defined herein, as approved by court decisions and other sources of authority. The purpose of the Guidelines is not to place limitations or restrictions on the legal assistant profession. Rather, the Guidelines are intended to outline for the legal profession an acceptable course of conduct. Voluntary recognition and utilization of the Standards and Guidelines will benefit the entire legal profession and the public it serves.

II. DEFINITION

The National Association of Legal Assistants adopted the following definition in 1984:

> Legal assistants, also known as paralegals, are a distinguishable group of persons who assist attorneys in the delivery of legal services. Through formal education, training, and experience, legal assistants have knowledge and expertise regarding the legal system and substantive and procedural law which qualify them to do work of a legal nature under the supervision of an attorney.

COMMENT

This definition emphasizes the knowledge and expertise of legal assistants in substantive and procedural law obtained through education and work experience. It further defines the legal assistant or paralegal as a professional working under the supervision of an attorney as distinguished from a non-lawyer who delivers services directly to the public without any intervention or review of work product by an attorney. Statutes, court rules, case law and bar associations are additional sources for legal assistant or paralegal definitions. In applying the Standards and Guidelines, it is important to remember that they were developed to apply to the legal assistant as defined herein.

Lawyers should refrain from labeling those who do not meet the criteria set forth in this definition, such as secretaries and other administrative staff, as legal assistants.

For billing purposes, the services of a legal secretary are considered part of overhead costs and are not recoverable in fee awards. However, the courts have held that fees for paralegal services are recoverable as long as they are not clerical functions, such as organizing files, copying documents, checking docket, updating files, checking court dates and delivering papers. As established in *Missouri v. Jenkins,* 491 U.S.274, 109 S.Ct. 2463, 2471, n.10 (1989) tasks performed by legal assistants must be substantive in nature which, absent the legal assistant, the attorney would perform.

There are also case law and Supreme Court Rules addressing the issue of a disbarred attorney serving in the capacity of a legal assistant.

III. STANDARDS

A legal assistant should meet certain minimum qualifications. The following standards may be used to determine an individual's qualifications as a legal assistant:

1. Successful completion of the Certified Legal Assistant ("CLA") certifying examination of the National Association of Legal Assistants, Inc.;
2. Graduation from an ABA approved program of study for legal assistants;
3. Graduation from a course of study for legal assistants which is institutionally accredited but not ABA approved, and which requires not less than the equivalent of 60 semester hours of classroom study;
4. Graduation from a course of study for legal assistants, other than those set forth in (2) and (3) above, plus not less than six months of in-house training as a legal assistant;
5. A baccalaureate degree in any field, plus not less than six months in-house training as a legal assistant;
6. A minimum of three years of law-related experience under the supervision of an attorney, including at least six months of in-house training as a legal assistant; or
7. Two years of in-house training as a legal assistant.

For purposes of these Standards, "in-house training as a legal assistant" means attorney education of the employee concerning legal assistant duties and these Guidelines. In addition to review and analysis of assignments, the legal assistant should receive a reasonable amount of instruction directly related to the duties and obligations of the legal assistant.

COMMENT

The Standards set forth suggest minimum qualifications for a legal assistant. These minimum qualifications, as adopted, recognize legal related work backgrounds and formal education backgrounds, both of which provide the legal assistant with a broad base in exposure to and knowledge of the legal profession. This background is necessary to assure the public and the legal profession that the employee identified as a legal assistant is qualified.

The Certified Legal Assistant ("CLA") examination established by NALA in 1976 is a voluntary nationwide certification program for legal assistants. The CLA designation is a statement to the legal profession and the public that the legal assistant has met the high levels of knowledge and professionalism required by NALA's certification program. Continuing education requirements, which all certified legal assistants must meet, assure that high standards are maintained. The CLA designation has been recognized as a means of establishing the qualifications of a legal assistant in supreme court rules, state court and bar association standards and utilization guidelines.

Certification through NALA is available to all legal assistants meeting the educational and experience requirements. Certified Legal Assistants may also pursue advanced specialty certification ("CLAS") in the areas of bankruptcy, civil litigation, probate and estate planning, corporate and business law, criminal law and procedure, real estate, intellectual property, and may also pursue state certification based on state laws and procedures in California, Florida, Louisiana and Texas.

IV. GUIDELINES

These Guidelines relating to standards of performance and professional responsibility are intended to aid legal assistants and attorneys. The ultimate responsibility rests with an attorney who employs legal assistants to educate them with respect to the duties they are assigned and to supervise the manner in which such duties are accomplished.

COMMENT

In general, a legal assistant is allowed to perform any task which is properly delegated and supervised by an attorney, as long as the attorney is ultimately responsible to the client and assumes complete professional responsibility for the work product.

ABA Model Rules of Professional Conduct, Rule 5.3 provides:

> With respect to a non-lawyer employed or retained by or associated with a lawyer:
> (a) a partner in a law firm shall make reasonable efforts to ensure that the firm has in effect measures giving reasonable assurance that the person's conduct is compatible with the professional obligations of the lawyer;
> (b) a lawyer having direct supervisory authority over the non-lawyer shall make reasonable efforts to ensure that the

person's conduct is compatible with the professional obligations of the lawyer; and

(c) a lawyer shall be responsible for conduct of such a person that would be a violation of the rules of professional conduct if engaged in by a lawyer if:

(1) the lawyer orders or, with the knowledge of the specific conduct ratifies the conduct involved; or

(2) the lawyer is a partner in the law firm in which the person is employed, or has direct supervisory authority over the person, and knows of the conduct at a time when its consequences can be avoided or mitigated but fails to take remedial action.

There are many interesting and complex issues involving the use of legal assistants. In any discussion of the proper role of a legal assistant, attention must be directed to what constitutes the practice of law. Proper delegation to legal assistants is further complicated and confused by the lack of an adequate definition of the practice of law.

Kentucky became the first state to adopt a Paralegal Code by Supreme Court Rule. This Code sets forth certain exclusions to the unauthorized practice of law:

For purposes of this rule, the unauthorized practice of law shall not include any service rendered involving legal knowledge or advice, whether representation, counsel or advocacy, in or out of court, rendered in respect to the acts, duties, obligations, liabilities or business relations of the one requiring services where:

A. The client understands that the paralegal is not a lawyer;

B. The lawyer supervises the paralegal in the performance of his or her duties; and

C. The lawyer remains fully responsible for such representation including all actions taken or not taken in connection therewith by the paralegal to the same extent as if such representation had been furnished entirely by the lawyer and all such actions had been taken or not taken directly by the attorney. Paralegal Code, Ky.S.Ct.R3.700, Sub-Rule 2.

South Dakota Supreme Court Rule 97-25 Utilization Rule a(4) states:

The attorney remains responsible for the services performed by the legal assistant to the same extent as though such services had been furnished entirely by the attorney and such actions were those of the attorney.

Guideline 1
Legal assistants should:

1. Disclose their status as legal assistants at the outset of any professional relationship with a client, other attorneys, a court or admin-

istrative agency or personnel thereof, or members of the general public;

2. Preserve the confidences and secrets of all clients; and
3. Understand the attorney's Rules of Professional Responsibility and these Guidelines in order to avoid any action which would involve the attorney in a violation of the Rules, or give the appearance of professional impropriety.

COMMENT

Routine early disclosure of the legal assistant's status when dealing with persons outside the attorney's office is necessary to assure that there will be no misunderstanding as to the responsibilities and role of the legal assistant. Disclosure may be made in any way that avoids confusion. If the person dealing with the legal assistant already knows of his/her status, further disclosure is unnecessary. If at any time in written or oral communication the legal assistant becomes aware that the other person may believe the legal assistant is an attorney, immediate disclosure should be made as to the legal assistant's status.

The attorney should exercise care that the legal assistant preserves and refrains from using any confidence or secrets of a client, and should instruct the legal assistant not to disclose or use any such confidences or secrets.

The legal assistant must take any and all steps necessary to prevent conflicts of interest and fully disclose such conflicts to the supervising attorney. Failure to do so may jeopardize both the attorney's representation of the client and the case itself.

Guidelines for the Utilization of Legal Assistant Services adopted December 3, 1994 by the Washington State Bar Association Board of Governors states:

> "Guideline 7: A lawyer shall take reasonable measures to prevent conflicts of interest resulting from a legal assistant's other employment or interest insofar as such other employment or interests would present a conflict of interest if it were that of the lawyer."

In Re Complex Asbestos Litigation, 232 Cal. App. 3d 572 (Cal. 1991), addresses the issue wherein a law firm was disqualified due to possession of attorney-client confidences by a legal assistant employee resulting from previous employment by opposing counsel.

The ultimate responsibility for compliance with approved standards of professional conduct rests with the supervising attorney. The burden rests upon the attorney who employs a legal assistant to educate the latter with respect to the duties which may be assigned and then to supervise the manner in which the legal assistant carries out such duties. However, this does not relieve the legal assistant from an independent obligation to refrain from illegal conduct. Additionally, and notwithstanding that the Rules are not binding upon non-lawyers, the very nature of a legal assistant's employment imposes an obligation not to engage in conduct which would involve the supervising attorney in a violation of the Rules.

The attorney must make sufficient background investigation of the prior activities and character and integrity of his or her legal assistants.

Further, the attorney must take all measures necessary to avoid and fully disclose conflicts of interest due to other employment or interests. Failure to do so may jeopardize both the attorney's representation of the client and the case itself.

Legal assistant associations strive to maintain the high level of integrity and competence expected of the legal profession and, further, strive to uphold the high standards of ethics.

NALA's Code of Ethics and Professional Responsibility states "A legal assistant's conduct is guided by bar associations' codes of professional responsibility and rules of professional conduct."

Guideline 2

Legal assistants should not:

1. Establish attorney-client relationships; set legal fees; give legal opinions or advice; or represent a client before a court, unless authorized to do so by said court; nor
2. Engage in, encourage, or contribute to any act which could constitute the unauthorized practice law.

COMMENT:

Case law, court rules, codes of ethics and professional responsibilities, as well as bar ethics opinions now hold which acts can and cannot be performed by a legal assistant. Generally, the determination of what acts constitute the unauthorized practice of law is made by State Supreme Courts.

Numerous cases exist relating to the unauthorized practice of law. Courts have gone so far as to prohibit the legal assistant from preparation of divorce kits and assisting in preparation of bankruptcy forms and, more specifically, from providing basic information about procedures and requirements, deciding where information should be placed on forms, and responding to questions from debtors regarding the interpretation or definition of terms.

Cases have identified certain areas in which an attorney has a duty to act, but it is interesting to note that none of these cases state that it is improper for an attorney to have the initial work performed by the legal assistant. This again points out the importance of adequate supervision by the employing attorney.

An attorney can be found to have aided in the unauthorized practice of law when delegating acts which cannot be performed by a legal assistant.

Guideline 3

Legal assistants may perform services for an attorney in the representation of a client, provided:

1. The services performed by the legal assistant do not require the exercise of independent professional legal judgment;
2. The attorney maintains a direct relationship with the client and maintains control of all client matters;

3. The attorney supervises the legal assistant;
4. The attorney remains professionally responsible for all work on behalf of the client, including any actions taken or not taken by the legal assistant in connection therewith; and
5. The services performed supplement, merge with and become the attorney's work product.

COMMENT:

Legal assistants, whether employees or independent contractors, perform services for the attorney in the representation of a client. Attorneys should delegate work to legal assistants commensurate with their knowledge and experience and provide appropriate instruction and supervision concerning the delegated work, as well as ethical acts of their employment. Ultimate responsibility for the work product of a legal assistant rests with the attorney. However, a legal assistant must use discretion and professional judgment and must not render independent legal judgment in place of an attorney.

The work product of a legal assistant is subject to civil rules governing discovery of materials prepared in anticipation of litigation, whether the legal assistant is viewed as an extension of the attorney or as another representative of the party itself. Fed. R. Civ. P. 26 (b)(2).

Guideline 4

In the supervision of a legal assistant, consideration should be given to:

1. Designating work assignments that correspond to the legal assistant's abilities, knowledge, training and experience;
2. Educating and training the legal assistant with respect to professional responsibility, local rules and practices, and firm policies;
3. Monitoring the work and professional conduct of the legal assistant to ensure that the work is substantively correct and timely performed;
4. Providing continuing education for the legal assistant in substantive matters through courses, institutes, workshops, seminars and in-house training; and
5. Encouraging and supporting membership and active participation in professional organizations.

COMMENT:

Attorneys are responsible for the actions of their employees in both malpractice and disciplinary proceedings. In the vast majority of cases, the courts have not censured attorneys for a particular act delegated to the legal assistant, but rather, have been critical of and imposed sanctions against attorneys for failure to adequately supervise the legal assistant. The attorney's responsibility for supervision of his or her legal assistant must be more than a willingness to accept responsibility and liability for the legal assistant's work. Supervision of a legal assistant must be offered in both the procedural and substantive legal areas. The attorney must delegate work based upon the education, knowledge and abilities of the legal assistant and must monitor the work product and conduct of the legal assistant to insure that the work performed is substantively correct and competently performed in a professional manner.

Michigan State Board of Commissioners has adopted Guidelines for the Utilization of Legal Assistants (April 23, 1993). These guidelines, in part, encourage employers to support legal assistant participation in continuing education programs to ensure that the legal assistant remains competent in the fields of practice in which the legal assistant is assigned.

The working relationship between the lawyer and the legal assistant should extend to cooperative efforts on public service activities wherever possible. Participation in pro bono activities is encouraged in ABA Guideline 10.

Guideline 5

Except as otherwise provided by statute, court rule or decision, administrative rule or regulation, or the attorney's rules of professional responsibility, and within the preceding parameters and proscriptions, a legal assistant may perform any function delegated by an attorney, including, but not limited to the following:

1. Conduct client interviews and maintain general contact with the client after the establishment of the attorney-client relationship, so long as the client is aware of the status and function of the legal assistant, and the client contact is under the supervision of the attorney.
2. Locate and interview witnesses, so long as the witnesses are aware of the status and function of the legal assistant.
3. Conduct investigations and statistical and documentary research for review by the attorney.
4. Conduct legal research for review by the attorney.
5. Draft legal documents for review by the attorney.
6. Draft correspondence and pleadings for review by and signature of the attorney.
7. Summarize depositions, interrogatories and testimony for review by the attorney.
8. Attend executions of wills, real estate closings, depositions, court or administrative hearings and trials with the attorney.
9. Author and sign letters providing the legal assistant's status is clearly indicated and the correspondence does not contain independent legal opinions or legal advice.

COMMENT:

The United States Supreme Court has recognized the variety of tasks being performed by legal assistants and has noted that use of legal assistants encourages cost-effective delivery of legal services, *Missouri v. Jenkins,* 491 U.S.274, 109 S.Ct. 2463, 2471, n.10 (1989). In *Jenkins,* the court further held that legal assistant time should be included in compensation for attorney fee awards at the rate in the relevant community to bill legal assistant time.

Courts have held that legal assistant fees are not a part of the overall overhead of a law firm. Legal assistant services are billed separately by attorneys, and decrease litigation expenses. Tasks performed by legal assistants must contain substantive legal work under the direction or supervision of an attorney, such that if the legal assistant were not present, the work would be performed by the attorney.

In *Taylor v. Chubb,* 874 P.2d 806 (Okla. 1994), the Court ruled that attorney fees awarded should include fees for services performed by legal assistants and, further, defined tasks which may be performed by the legal assistant under the supervision of an attorney including, among others: interview clients; draft pleadings and other documents; carry on legal research, both conventional and computer aided; research public records; prepare discovery requests and responses; schedule depositions and prepare notices and subpoenas; summarize depositions and other discovery responses; coordinate and manage document production; locate and interview witnesses; organize pleadings, trial exhibits and other documents; prepare witness and exhibit lists; prepare trial notebooks; prepare for the attendance of witnesses at trial; and assist lawyers at trials.

Except for the specific proscription contained in Guideline 1, the reported cases do not limit the duties which may be performed by a legal assistant under the supervision of the attorney.

An attorney may not split legal fees with a legal assistant, nor pay a legal assistant for the referral of legal business. An attorney may compensate a legal assistant based on the quantity and quality of the legal assistant's work and value of that work to a law practice.

CONCLUSION

These Standards and Guidelines were developed from generally accepted practices. Each supervising attorney must be aware of the specific rules, decisions and statutes applicable to legal assistants within his/her jurisdiction.

Addendum

For further information, the following cases may be helpful to you:

Duties:
Taylor v. Chubb, 874 P.2d 806 (Okla. 1994)
McMackin v. McMackin, 651 A.2d 778 (Del.Fam Ct 1993)

Work Product:
Fine v. Facet Aerospace Products Co., 133 F.R.D. 439 (S.D.N.Y. 1990)

Unauthorized Practice of Law
Akron Bar Assn. V. Green, 673 N.E.2d 1307 (Ohio 1997)
In Re Hessinger & Associates, 192 B.R. 211 (N.D. Calif. 1996)
In the Matter of Bright, 171 B.R. 799 (Bkrtcy. E.D. Mich)
Louisiana State Bar Assn v. Edwins, 540 So.2d 294 (La. 1989)

Attorney/Client Privilege
In Re Complex Asbestos Litigation, 232 Cal. App. 3d 572 (Calif. 1991)
Makita Corp. V. U.S., 819 F.Supp. 1099 (CIT 1993)

Conflicts

In Re Complex Asbestos Litigation, 232 Cal. App. 3d 572 (Calif. 1991)
Makita Corp. V. U.S., 819 F.Supp. 1099 (CIT 1993)
Phoenix Founders, Inc., v. Marshall, 887 S.W.2d 831 (Tex. 1994)
Smart Industries v. Superior Court, 876 P.2d 1176 (Ariz. App. Div.1 1994)

Supervision

Matter of Martinez, 754 P.2d 842 (N.M. 1988)
State v. Barrett, 483 P.2d 1106 (Kan. 1971)

Fee Awards

In Re Bicoastal Corp., 121 B.R. 653 (Bktrcy.M.D.Fla. 1990)
In Re Carter, 101 B.R. 170 (Bkrtcy.D.S.D. 1989)
Taylor v. Chubb, 874 P.2d 806 (Okla.1994)
Missouri v. Jenkins, 491 U.S. 274, 109 S.Ct. 2463, 105 L.Ed.2d 229 (1989)
 11 U.S.C.A. '330
McMackin v. McMackin, Del.Fam.Ct. 651 A.2d 778 (1993)
Miller v. Alamo, 983 F.2d 856 (8th Cir. 1993)
Stewart v.Sullivan, 810 F.Supp. 1102 (D.Hawaii 1993)
In Re Yankton College, 101 B.R. 151 (Bkrtcy. D.S.D. 1989)
Stacey v. Stroud, 845 F.Supp. 1135 (S.D.W.Va. 1993)

Court Appearances

Louisiana State Bar Assn v. Edwins, 540 So.2d 294 (La. 1989)

In addition to the above referenced cases, you may contact your state bar association for information regarding guidelines for the utilization of legal assistants that may have been adopted by the bar, or ethical opinions concerning the utilization of legal assistants. The following states have adopted a definition of "legal assistant"or "paralegal" either through bar association guidelines, ethical opinions, legislation or case law:

Legislation:

California	Illinois	Pennsylvania
Florida	Indiana	

Supreme Court Cases or Rules:

Kentucky	North Dakota	Virginia
New Hampshire	Rhode Island	
New Mexico	South Dakota	

Guidelines:

Colorado	Idaho	Utah
Connecticut	New York	Wisconsin
Georgia	Oregon	

Bar Associations:

Alaska
Arizona
Colorado
Connecticut
Florida
Illinois
Iowa
Kansas
Kentucky

Massachusetts
Michigan
Minnesota
Missouri
Nevada
New Mexico
New Hampshire
North Carolina
North Dakota

Ohio
Oregon
Rhode Island
South Carolina
South Dakota
Tennessee
Texas
Virginia
Wisconsin

> # National Federation of Paralegal Associations, Inc. Model Code of Ethics and Professional Responsibility and Guidelines for Enforcement

PREAMBLE

The National Federation of Paralegal Associations, Inc. ("NFPA") is a professional organization comprised of paralegal associations and individual paralegals throughout the United States and Canada. Members of NFPA have varying backgrounds, experiences, education and job responsibilities that reflect the diversity of the paralegal profession. NFPA promotes the growth, development and recognition of the paralegal profession as an integral partner in the delivery of legal services.

In May 1993 NFPA adopted its Model Code of Ethics and Professional Responsibility ("Model Code") to delineate the principles for ethics and conduct to which every paralegal should aspire.

Many paralegal associations throughout the United States have endorsed the concept and content of NFPA's Model Code through the adoption of their own ethical codes. In doing so, paralegals have confirmed the profession's commitment to increase the quality and efficiency of legal services, as well as recognized its responsibilities to the public, the legal community, and colleagues.

Paralegals have recognized, and will continue to recognize, that the profession must continue to evolve to enhance their roles in the delivery of legal services. With increased levels of responsibility comes the need to define and enforce mandatory rules of professional conduct. Enforcement of codes of paralegal conduct is a logical and necessary step to enhance and ensure the confidence of the legal community and the public in the integrity and professional responsibility of paralegals.

In April 1997 NFPA adopted the Model Disciplinary Rules ("Model Rules") to make possible the enforcement of the Canons and Ethical Considerations contained in the NFPA Model Code. A concurrent determination was made that the Model Code of Ethics and Professional Responsibility, formerly aspirational in nature, should be recognized as setting forth the enforceable obligations of all paralegals.

The Model Code and Model Rules offer a framework for professional discipline, either voluntarily or through formal regulatory programs.

§1.   NFPA MODEL DISCIPLINARY RULES AND ETHICAL CONSIDERATIONS

1.1   A PARALEGAL SHALL ACHIEVE AND MAINTAIN A HIGH LEVEL OF COMPETENCE.

Ethical Considerations

EC-1.1(a)   A paralegal shall achieve competency through education, training, and work experience.

EC-1.1(b)   A paralegal shall participate in continuing education in order to keep informed of current legal, technical and general developments.

EC-1.1(c)   A paralegal shall perform all assignments promptly and efficiently.

1.2   A PARALEGAL SHALL MAINTAIN A HIGH LEVEL OF PERSONAL AND PROFESSIONAL INTEGRITY.

Ethical Considerations

EC-1.2(a)   A paralegal shall not engage in any ex parte communications involving the courts or any other adjudicatory body in an attempt to exert undue influence or to obtain advantage or the benefit of only one party.

EC-1.2(b)   A paralegal shall not communicate, or cause another to communicate, with a party the paralegal knows to be represented by a lawyer in a pending matter without the prior consent of the lawyer representing such other party.

EC-1.2(c)   A paralegal shall ensure that all timekeeping and billing records prepared by the paralegal are thorough, accurate, honest, and complete.

EC-1.2(d)   A paralegal shall not knowingly engage in fraudulent billing practices. Such practices may include, but are not limited to: inflation of hours billed to a client or employer; misrepresentation of the nature of tasks performed; and/or submission of fraudulent expense and disbursement documentation.

EC-1.2(e)   A paralegal shall be scrupulous, thorough and honest in the identification and maintenance of all funds, securities, and other assets of a client and shall provide accurate accounting as appropriate.

EC-1.2(f)   A paralegal shall advise the proper authority of non-confidential knowledge of any dishonest or fraudulent acts by any person pertaining to the handling of the funds, securities or other assets of a client. The authority to whom the report is made shall depend on the nature and circumstances of the possible misconduct, (e.g., ethics committees of law firms, corporations and/or paralegal associations, local or state bar associations, local prosecutors, administrative agencies, etc.). Failure to report such knowledge is in itself misconduct and shall be treated as such under these rules.

1.3   **A PARALEGAL SHALL MAINTAIN A HIGH STANDARD OF PROFESSIONAL CONDUCT.**

Ethical Considerations

EC-1.3(a)   A paralegal shall refrain from engaging in any conduct that offends the dignity and decorum of proceedings before a court or other adjudicatory body and shall be respectful of all rules and procedures.

EC-1.3(b)   A paralegal shall avoid impropriety and the appearance of impropriety and shall not engage in any conduct that would adversely affect his/her fitness to practice. Such conduct may include, but is not limited to: violence, dishonesty, interference with the administration of justice, and/or abuse of a professional position or public office.

EC-1.3(c)   Should a paralegal's fitness to practice be compromised by physical or mental illness, causing that paralegal to commit an act that is in direct violation of the Model Code/Model Rules and/or the rules and/or laws governing the jurisdiction in which the paralegal practices, that paralegal may be protected from sanction upon review of the nature and circumstances of that illness.

EC-1.3(d)   A paralegal shall advise the proper authority of non-confidential knowledge of any action of another legal professional that clearly demonstrates fraud, deceit, dishonesty, or misrepresentation. The authority to whom the report is made shall depend on the nature and circumstances of the possible misconduct, (e.g., ethics committees of law firms, corporations and/or paralegal associations, local or state bar associations, local prosecutors, administrative agencies, etc.). Failure to report such knowledge is in itself misconduct and shall be treated as such under these rules.

EC-1.3(e)   A paralegal shall not knowingly assist any individual with the commission of an act that is in direct violation of the Model Code/Model Rules and/or the rules and/or laws governing the jurisdiction in which the paralegal practices.

EC-1.3(f)   If a paralegal possesses knowledge of future criminal activity, that knowledge must be reported to the appropriate authority immediately.

1.4   **A PARALEGAL SHALL SERVE THE PUBLIC INTEREST BY CONTRIBUTING TO THE DELIVERY OF QUALITY LEGAL SERVICES AND THE IMPROVEMENT OF THE LEGAL SYSTEM.**

Ethical Considerations

EC-1.4(a)   A paralegal shall be sensitive to the legal needs of the public and shall promote the development and implementation of programs that address those needs.

EC-1.4(b)   A paralegal shall support efforts to improve the legal system and access thereto and shall assist in making changes.

EC-1.4(c)   A paralegal shall support and participate in the delivery of Pro Bono Publico services directed toward implementing and improving access to justice, the law, the legal system or the paralegal and legal professions.

EC-1.4(d) A paralegal should aspire annually to contribute twenty-four (24) hours of Pro Bono Publico services under the supervision of an attorney or as authorized by administrative, statutory or court authority to:

1. Persons of limited mans; or
2. Charitable, religious, civic, community, governmental and educational organizations in matters that are designed primarily to address the legal needs of persons with limited means; or
3. Individuals, groups or organizations seeking to secure or protect civil rights, civil liberties or public rights.

1.5 **A PARALEGAL SHALL PRESERVE ALL CONFIDENTIAL INFORMATION PROVIDED BY THE CLIENT OR ACQUIRED FROM OTHER SOURCES BEFORE, DURING, AND AFTER THE COURSE OF THE PROFESSIONAL RELATIONSHIP.**

Ethical Considerations

EC-1.5(a) A paralegal shall be aware of and abide by all legal authority governing confidential information in the jurisdiction in which the paralegal practices.

EC-1.5(b) A paralegal shall not use confidential information to the disadvantage of the client.

EC-1.5(c) A paralegal shall not use confidential information to the advantage of the paralegal or of a third person.

EC-1.5(d) A paralegal may reveal confidential information only after full disclosure and with the client's written consent; or, when required by law or court order; or, when necessary to prevent the client from committing an act that could result in death or serious bodily harm.

EC-1.5(e) A paralegal shall keep those individuals responsible for the legal representation of a client fully informed of any confidential information the paralegal may have pertaining to that client.

EC-1.5(f) A paralegal shall not engage in any indiscreet communications concerning clients.

1.6 **A PARALEGAL SHALL AVOID CONFLICTS OF INTEREST AND SHALL DISCLOSE ANY POSSIBLE CONFLICT TO THE EMPLOYER OR CLIENT, AS WELL AS TO THE PROSPECTIVE EMPLOYERS OR CLIENTS.**

Ethical Considerations

EC-1.6(a) A paralegal shall act within the bounds of the law, solely for the benefit of the client, and shall be free of compromising influences and loyalties. Neither the paralegal's personal or business interest, nor those of other clients or third persons, should compromise the paralegal's professional judgment and loyalty to the client.

EC-1.6(b) A paralegal shall avoid conflicts of interest that may arise from previous assignments, whether for a present or past employer or client.

EC-1.6(c) A paralegal shall avoid conflicts of interest that may arise from family relationships and from personal and business interests.

EC-1.6(d) In order to be able to determine whether an actual or potential conflict of interest exists a paralegal shall create and maintain an effective recordkeeping system that identifies clients, matters, and parties with which the paralegal has worked.

EC-1.6(e) A paralegal shall reveal sufficient non-confidential information about a client or former client to reasonably ascertain if an actual or potential conflict of interest exists.

EC-1.6(f) A paralegal shall not participate in or conduct work on any matter where a conflict of interest has been identified.

EC-1.6(g) In matters where a conflict of interest has been identified and the client consents to continued representation, a paralegal shall comply fully with the implementation and maintenance of an Ethical Wall.

1.7 A PARALEGAL'S TITLE SHALL BE FULLY DISCLOSED.

Ethical Considerations

EC-1.7(a) A paralegal's title shall clearly indicate the individual's status and shall be disclosed in all business and professional communications to avoid misunderstandings and misconceptions about the paralegal's role and responsibilities.

EC-1.7(b) A paralegal's title shall be included if the paralegal's name appears on business cards, letterhead, brochures, directories, and advertisements.

EC-1.7(c) A paralegal shall not use letterhead, business cards or other promotional materials to create a fraudulent impression of his/her status or ability to practice in the jurisdiction in which the paralegal practices.

EC-1.7(d) A paralegal shall not practice under color of any record, diploma, or certificate that has been illegally or fraudulently obtained or issued or which is misrepresentative in any way.

EC-1.7(e) A paralegal shall not participate in the creation, issuance, or dissemination of fraudulent records, diplomas, or certificates.

1.8 A PARALEGAL SHALL NOT ENGAGE IN THE UNAUTHORIZED PRACTICE OF LAW.

Ethical Considerations

EC-1.8(a) A paralegal shall comply with the applicable legal authority governing the unauthorized practice of law in the jurisdiction in which the paralegal practices.

§2. NFPA GUIDELINES FOR THE ENFORCEMENT OF THE MODEL CODE OF ETHICS AND PROFESSIONAL RESPONSIBILITY

2.1 BASIS FOR DISCIPLINE

2.1(a) Disciplinary investigations and proceedings brought under authority of the Rules shall be conducted in accord with obligations imposed on the paralegal professional by the Model Code of Ethics and Professional Responsibility.

2.2 STRUCTURE OF DISCIPLINARY COMMITTEE

2.2(a) The Disciplinary Committee ("Committee") shall be made up of nine (9) members including the Chair.

2.2(b) Each member of the Committee, including any temporary replacement members, shall have demonstrated working knowledge of ethics/professional responsibility-related issues and activities.

2.2(c)   The Committee shall represent a cross-section of practice areas and work experience. The following recommendations are made regarding the members of the Committee.

1) At least one paralegal with one to three years of law-related work experience.
2) At least one paralegal with five to seven years of law related work experience.
3) At least one paralegal with over ten years of law related work experience.
4) One paralegal educator with five to seven years of work experience; preferably in the area of ethics/professional responsibility.
5) One paralegal manager.
6) One lawyer with five to seven years of law-related work experience.
7) One lay member.

2.2(d)   The Chair of the Committee shall be appointed within thirty (30) days of its members' induction. The Chair shall have no fewer than ten (10) years of law-related work experience.

2.2(e)   The terms of all members of the Committee shall be staggered. Of those members initially appointed, a simple majority plus one shall be appointed to a term of one year, and the remaining members shall be appointed to a term of two years. Thereafter, all members of the Committee shall be appointed to terms of two years.

2.2(f)   If for any reason the terms of a majority of the Committee will expire at the same time, members may be appointed to terms of one year to maintain continuity of the Committee.

2.2(g)   The Committee shall organize from its members a three-tiered structure to investigate, prosecute and/or adjudicate charges of misconduct. The members shall be rotated among the tiers.

2.3   OPERATION OF COMMITTEE

2.3(a)   The Committee shall meet on an as-needed basis to discuss, investigate, and/or adjudicate alleged violations of the Model Code/Model Rules.

2.3(b)   A majority of the members of the Committee present at a meeting shall constitute a quorum.

2.3(c)   A Recording Secretary shall be designated to maintain complete and accurate minutes of all Committee meetings. All such minutes shall be kept confidential until a decision has been made that the matter will be set for hearing as set forth in Section 6.1 below.

2.3(d)   If any member of the Committee has a conflict of interest with the Charging Party, the Responding Party, or the allegations of misconduct, that member shall not take part in any hearing or deliberations concerning those allegations. If the absence of that member creates a lack of a quorum for the Committee, then a temporary replacement for the member shall be appointed.

2.3(e)   Either the Charging Party or the Responding Party may request that, for good cause shown, any member of the Committee not participate in a hearing or deliberation. All such requests shall be honored. If the absence of a Committee member under those circumstances creates a lack of a quorum for the Committee, then a temporary replacement for that member shall be appointed.

2.3(f)   All discussions and correspondence of the Committee shall be kept confidential until a decision has been made that the matter will be set for hearing as set forth in Section 6.1 below.

2.3(g)   All correspondence from the Committee to the Responding Party regarding any charge of misconduct and any decisions made regarding the charge shall be mailed certified mail, return receipt requested, to the Responding Party's last known address and shall be clearly marked with a "Confidential" designation.

2.4   PROCEDURE FOR THE REPORTING OF ALLEGED VIOLATIONS OF THE MODEL CODE/DISCIPLINARY RULES

2.4(a)   An individual or entity in possession of non-confidential knowledge or information concerning possible instances of misconduct shall make a confidential written report to the Committee within thirty (30) days of obtaining same. This report shall include all details of the alleged misconduct.

2.4(b)   The Committee so notified shall inform the Responding Party of the allegation(s) of misconduct no later than ten (10) business days after receiving the confidential written report from the Charging Party.

2.4(c)   Notification to the Responding Party shall include the identity of the Charging Party, unless, for good cause shown, the Charging Party requests anonymity.

2.4(d)   The Responding Party shall reply to the allegations within ten (10) business days of notification.

2.5   PROCEDURE FOR THE INVESTIGATION OF A CHARGE OF MISCONDUCT

2.5(a)   Upon receipt of a Charge of Misconduct ("Charge"), or on its own initiative, the Committee shall initiate an investigation.

2.5(b)   If, upon initial or preliminary review, the Committee makes a determination that the charges are either without basis in fact or, if proven, would not constitute professional misconduct, the Committee shall dismiss the allegations of misconduct. If such determination of dismissal cannot be made, a formal investigation shall be initiated.

2.5(c)   Upon the decision to conduct a formal investigation, the Committee shall:
1) mail to the Charging and Responding Parties within three (3) business days of that decision notice of the commencement of a formal investigation. That notification shall be in writing and shall contain a complete explanation of all Charge(s), as well as the reasons for a formal investigation and shall cite the applicable codes and rules;
2) allow the Responding Party thirty (30) days to prepare and submit a confidential response to the Committee, which response shall address each charge specifically and shall be in writing; and
3) upon receipt of the response to the notification, have thirty (30) days to investigate the Charge(s). If an extension of time is deemed necessary, that extension shall not exceed ninety (90) days.

2.5(d)   Upon conclusion of the investigation, the Committee may:
1) dismiss the Charge upon the finding that it has no basis in fact;
2) dismiss the Charge upon the finding that, if proven, the Charge would not constitute Misconduct;
3) refer the matter for hearing by the Tribunal; or

4) in the case of criminal activity, refer the Charge(s) and all investigation results to the appropriate authority.

2.6   **PROCEDURE FOR A MISCONDUCT HEARING BEFORE A TRIBUNAL**

2.6(a)   Upon the decision by the Committee that a matter should be heard, all parties shall be notified and a hearing date shall be set. The hearing shall take place no more than thirty (30) days from the conclusion of the formal investigation.

2.6(b)   The Responding Party shall have the right to counsel. The parties and the Tribunal shall have the right to call any witnesses and introduce any documentation that they believe will lead to the fair and reasonable resolution of the matter.

2.6(c)   Upon completion of the hearing, the Tribunal shall deliberate and present a written decision to the parties in accordance with procedures as set forth by the Tribunal.

2.6(d)   Notice of the decision of the Tribunal shall be appropriately published.

2.7   **SANCTIONS**

2.7(a)   Upon a finding of the Tribunal that misconduct has occurred, any of the following sanctions, or others as may be deemed appropriate, may be imposed upon the Responding Party, either singularly or in combination:

     1) letter of reprimand to the Responding Party; counseling;

     2) attendance at an ethics course approved by the Tribunal; probation;

     3) suspension of license/authority to practice; revocation of license/authority to practice;

     4) imposition of a fine; assessment of costs; or

     5) in the instance of criminal activity, referral to the appropriate authority.

2.7(b)   Upon the expiration of any period of probation, suspension, or revocation, the Responding Party may make application for reinstatement. With the application for reinstatement, the Responding Party must show proof of having complied with all aspects of the sanctions imposed by the Tribunal.

2.8   **APPELLATE PROCEDURES**

2.8(a)   The parties shall have the right to appeal the decision of the Tribunal in accordance with the procedure as set forth by the Tribunal.

DEFINITIONS

"Appellate Body" means a body established to adjudicate an appeal to any decision made by a Tribunal or other decision-making body with respect to formally-heard Charges of Misconduct.

"Charge of Misconduct" means a written submission by any individual or entity to an ethics committee, paralegal association, bar association, law enforcement agency, judicial body, government agency, or other appropriate body or entity, that sets forth non-confidential information regarding any instance of alleged misconduct by an individual paralegal or paralegal entity.

"Charging Party" means any individual or entity who submits a Charge of Misconduct against an individual paralegal or paralegal entity.

"Competency" means the demonstration of: diligence, education, skill, and mental, emotional, and physical fitness reasonably necessary for the performance of paralegal services.

"**Confidential Information**" means information relating to a client, whatever its source, that is not public knowledge nor available to the public. ("Non-Confidential Information" would generally include the name of the client and the identity of the matter for which the paralegal provided services.)

"**Disciplinary Hearing**" means the confidential proceeding conducted by a committee or other designated body or entity concerning any instance of alleged misconduct by an individual paralegal or paralegal entity.

"**Disciplinary Committee**" means any committee that has been established by an entity such as a paralegal association, bar association, judicial body, or government agency to: (a) identify, define and investigate general ethical considerations and concerns with respect to paralegal practice; (b) administer and enforce the Model Code and Model Rules and; (c) discipline any individual paralegal or paralegal entity found to be in violation of same.

"**Disclose**" means communication of information reasonably sufficient to permit identification of the significance of the matter in question.

"**Ethical Wall**" means the screening method implemented in order to protect a client from a conflict of interest. An Ethical Wall generally includes, but is not limited to, the following elements: (1) prohibit the paralegal from having any connection with the matter; (2) ban discussions with or the transfer of documents to or from the paralegal; (3) restrict access to files; and (4) educate all members of the firm, corporation, or entity as to the separation of the paralegal (both organizationally and physically) from the pending matter. For more information regarding the Ethical Wall, see the NFPA publication entitled "The Ethical Wall - Its Application to Paralegals."

"**Ex parte**" means actions or communications conducted at the instance and for the benefit of one party only, and without notice to, or contestation by, any person adversely interested.

"**Investigation**" means the investigation of any charge(s) of misconduct filed against an individual paralegal or paralegal entity by a Committee.

"**Letter of Reprimand**" means a written notice of formal censure or severe reproof administered to an individual paralegal or paralegal entity for unethical or improper conduct.

"**Misconduct**" means the knowing or unknowing commission of an act that is in direct violation of those Canons and Ethical Considerations of any and all applicable codes and/or rules of conduct.

"**Paralegal**" is synonymous with "Legal Assistant" and is defined as a person qualified through education, training, or work experience to perform substantive legal work that requires knowledge of legal concepts and is customarily, but not exclusively performed by a lawyer. This person may be retained or employed by a lawyer, law office, governmental agency, or other entity or may be authorized by administrative, statutory, or court authority to perform this work.

"**Pro Bono Publico**" means providing or assisting to provide quality legal services in order to enhance access to justice for persons of limited means; charitable, religious, civic, community, governmental and educational organizations in matters that are designed primarily to address the legal needs of persons with limited means; or individuals, groups or organizations seeking to secure or protect civil rights, civil liberties or public rights.

"**Proper Authority**" means the local paralegal association, the local or state bar association, Committee(s) of the local paralegal or bar association(s), local prosecutor, administrative agency, or other tribunal empowered to investigate or act upon an instance of alleged misconduct.

"**Responding Party**" means an individual paralegal or paralegal entity against whom a Charge of Misconduct has been submitted.

"**Revocation**" means the recision of the license, certificate or other authority to practice of an individual paralegal or paralegal entity found in violation of those Canons and Ethical Considerations of any and all applicable codes and/or rules of conduct.

"**Suspension**" means the suspension of the license, certificate or other authority to practice of an individual paralegal or paralegal entity found in violation of those Canons and Ethical Considerations of any and all applicable codes and/or rules of conduct.

"**Tribunal**" means the body designated to adjudicate allegations of misconduct.

Sample Resumes

F-1 SAMPLE CHRONOLOGICAL RESUMES

KAREN KITTELSON
3850 PACIFIC STREET
SANTA BARBARA, CA 93120
805-837-5748

SUMMARY OF QUALIFICATIONS

- Bachelors Degree, with honors, in Paralegal Studies from The Santa Barbara and Ventura Colleges of Law
- Successful completion of 12-month internship at Klebber, James & Howard
- Experience in bankruptcy, family law, personal injury, and criminal law areas
- Excellent legal research and writing skills
- Proficient in Westlaw and Lexis

WORK EXPERIENCE

Klebber, James & Howard   **May 1999 to May 2000**
Paralegal Intern

Assisted two attorneys and one senior paralegal in firm specializing in bankruptcy law; prepared bankruptcy notices to banks and financial institutions; coordinated appraisals of debtors' assets; prepared all types of bankruptcy documents.

Santa Barbara Legal Clinic   **January 1997 to May 1999**
Volunteer Administrative Assistant

Assisted with administrative tasks for legal clinic. Interviewed clients and completed client intake forms for attorney review; performed legal research in the areas of family law, bankruptcy, personal injury, and criminal law. Drafted legal documents and legal memoranda concerning legal research and analysis. Organized office files.

EDUCATION

B.S. Legal Studies
Santa Barbara and Ventura Colleges of Law
Graduated with Honors, May 2000

Coursework included classes in Legal Writing, Legal Research, Basic Law, Business Law, Legal Applications of Computers, Litigation and Advanced Litigation, Bankruptcy Law, Family Law, Criminal Law, and Procedure and Business Organizations.

AFFILIATIONS

- Student Member of the Legal Assistants Association of Santa Barbara

ANDREA STOFFEL
1100 Grand Avenue
Overland Park, KS 66212
913-889-0922

OBJECTIVE

A paralegal position in a corporate legal department or the corporate department of a law firm in the Kansas City area.

SUMMARY OF QUALIFICATIONS

- Over 5 years experience working in the corporate setting
- Certified Legal Assistant
- Bachelor of Arts in English from University of Minnesota
- Excellent Communication Skills
- Paralegal Certificate from Johnson County Community College, an ABA-approved program

WORK EXPERIENCE

Lambert Technologies   **May 1995 to September 1999**
Administrative Assistant

Assistant to Chief Executive Officer of Fortune 1000 Corporation; drafted correspondence and corporate documents; maintained files for executives; coordinated travel arrangements for domestic and international travel; scheduled meetings for executives; presented documents and reports at meetings of the board of directors.

Brixon Computers   **January 1991 to May 1995**
Secretary

Part-time secretary while attending school; drafted and typed correspondence; maintained department files; filed documents; scheduled meetings with executives and customers.

EDUCATION

Paralegal Certificate
Johnson Community College Paralegal Program
An ABA-Approved Program
Certificate Awarded May 2000

Coursework included classes in Legal Research and Writing, Introduction to Law, Business Law, Legal Applications of Computers, Business Organizations I, Business Organizations II, Litigation and Advanced Litigation, Bankruptcy Law, Family Law, Criminal Law and Procedure.

Bachelor of Arts – English Major
Berkeley College
Graduated with Honors May 1995

AFFILIATION

- Member of the Kansas City Paralegal Association
- Paralegal Member of the Kansas Bar Association

References, writing samples and transcripts available upon request.

F-1

JANET WILLIAMS

123 Elm Street
Maplewood, Minnesota 55117
342-435-2845

Objective: Position as a litigation paralegal in a litigation department of a large law firm.

Education

1999   The Paralegal Institute (ABA-Approved); Minneapolis, MN
              Legal Assistant Certificate Received May 1999
              Legal Specialty Courses Completed: Fundamentals of American Law, Litigation,
              Advanced Litigation for Paralegals, Legal Writing and Research, Business Law,
              Contracts Law, Torts, Computers in the Law Firm

1998   University of Minnesota
              Bachelor of Science in Business Administration Received
              June 1998

Work Experience

1999   Brown, McKinley and Johanson
              Maplewood, Minnesota
              Summer Legal Assistant Internship
              Drafted pleadings and other legal documents; reviewed and summarized
              depositions

1996 – 1998   Top Temporary Service, Inc.
              Minneapolis, Minnesota
              Part-Time Temporary Clerical Worker
              Assignments included: Secretarial—drafted and typed routine correspondence
              and reports; Receptionist—greeted clients, scheduled appointments, and
              handled busy switchboard

Professional Associations

Member of the Minnesota Paralegal Association
References, transcripts, and writing samples available upon request.

F-2 SAMPLE FUNCTIONAL RESUME

BRIAN HOLDEN
442 Elkhorn
Great Falls, MT 59405
406-872-3598

SUMMARY OF QUALIFICATIONS

- Certified Legal Assistant
- Bachelor of Science in Business Administration and Paralegal Certificate from the College of Great Falls
- Knowledge of all types of law office procedures
- Over 5 years experience in the legal field
- Excellent legal research and writing skills

Education

Paralegal Certificate
College of Great Falls, Paralegal Studies Program
Legal Specialty Courses Completed: Fundamentals of American law, Litigation, Advanced Litigation, Legal Writing and Research, Business Law, Contracts law, Torts, Computers in the Law Firm

Bachelor of Science in Business Administration
College of Great Falls
Grade Point Average 3.75

Work Experience

Little, Elvers and Samson
Great Falls, MT
Legal Secretary
Assisted busy litigation attorney by drafting and typing correspondence, pleadings, and other legal documents; answered telephone calls from clients; scheduled depositions and other appointments; prepared client bills

Special Skills

- Fluent in Spanish, written and spoken
- Knowledge of several word processing and accounting software programs, including WordPerfect and Lotus 1-2-3
- Excellent communication skills
- Excellent organizational skills

Professional Associations

Member of the Montana Association of Legal Assistants

F-3 SAMPLE BLENDED RESUMES

ALEXANDER MICHAELS
CERTIFIED LEGAL ASSISTANT
1238 Elm Street, Burlington VT 02314
(201) 873-4732

SUMMARY OF QUALIFICATIONS

- 1999 Graduate of Burlington College Paralegal Program with a 3.75 GPA
- Completed Internship with Adams County Attorney's Office, Assisted in Bringing a Successful Conclusion to Numerous Criminal Prosecution Cases
- Excellent Interviewing, Research and Writing Skills
- Proficient with Westlaw and Lexis Nexis

RELEVANT EXPERIENCE

PARALEGAL INTERN
Completed paralegal internship at Adams County Attorney's Office, working with County Attorney Brian Zeblowski:
- Researching criminal law and procedure
- Interviewing police officers, witnesses, and crime victims
- Writing reports for review by County Attorney and Assistant County Attorneys
- Drafting motions for criminal court
- Assisting in court with pre-trial motions

LEGAL FILE CLERK
File clerk for Brown & Jablonski Law Firm, a 20-attorney firm specializing in personal injury.
- Designed efficient filing system
- Drafted procedures for maintaining filing system
- Implemented filing system, tracking and storing over 20,000 files for 20 attorneys.
- Supervised assistant file clerk

LEGAL COURSEWORK
- Legal Writing
- Legal Research
- Basic Law
- Business Law
- Legal Applications of Computers
- Litigation and Advanced Litigation
- Probate and Estate Planning
- Family Law
- Criminal Law and Procedure
- Corporate Law and Business Organizations

WORK HISTORY

May 1998 – May 1999	Paralegal Intern	Adams County Attorney's Office Adams, Vermont
May 1996 – May 1998	Legal File Clerk	Brown & Jablonski Law Firm Adams, Vermont

EDUCATION

September 1994 – May 1999	Bachelor of Science Paralegal Studies	Burlington College Burlington, Vermont
June 1994	High School Diploma	Linden High School Linden, Vermont

AFFILIATIONS

Voting Member of the Vermont Legal Assistant Association.

JASON BANNING
3777 Sherburne Avenue
Seattle, WA 98105
206-881-2233

Objective: Legal Administrator for a Mid-Sized Law Firm.

Relevant Skills and Abilities

Management Expertise
- Train attorneys and support staff in the use of computers
- Monitor work flow for all law firm support staff
- Hire and supervise law firm management staff
- Research, organize, and manage relocation of office

Computer Knowledge
- Installed Local Area Network computer system
- Research and purchase computer software
- Use WordPerfect, Westlaw, PC-File, MS-DOS, ZyIndex
- Wrote reference manual for hundreds of macros and dozens of forms and letters

Legal Experience
- Interview clients and witnesses
- Experience with federal and state courts
- Worked with collections, judgments, and real estate matters

Professional Experience
1990 to present	Smith & Smith, Seattle, Washington Systems and Office Manager/Paralegal
1985 – 1990	Legal secretary for various Seattle small and mid-sized law firms

Education
Bachelor of Arts Degree in Sociology, Stanford University; Stanford, California

Affiliations
- American Bar Association, Legal Assistants Division
- Seattle Paralegal Association
- Association of Legal Administrators
- YMCA National Fundraising Group
- Community Counsel Services, Board of Directors

SAMPLE ELECTRONIC FORMAT RESUME

ALEXANDER MICHAELS
CERTIFIED LEGAL ASSISTANT
1238 Elm Street, Burlington VT 02314
(201) 873-4732
_____

SUMMARY OF QUALIFICATIONS

¨ 1999 Graduate of Burlington College Paralegal Program with a 3.75 GPA

¨ Completed Internship with Adams County Attorney's Office, Assisted in Bringing a Successful Conclusion to Numerous Criminal Prosecution Cases

¨ Excellent Interviewing, Research and Writing Skills

¨ Proficient with Westlaw and Lexis/Nexis

RELEVANT EXPERIENCE

PARALEGAL INTERN
Completed paralegal internship at Adams County Attorney's Office, working with County Attorney Brian Zeblowski:

¨ Researching criminal law and procedure
¨ Interviewing police officers, witnesses, and crime victims
¨ Writing reports for review by County Attorney and Assistant County Attorneys
¨ Drafting motions for criminal court
¨ Assisting in court with pre-trial motions

LEGAL FILE CLERK
File clerk for Brown & Jablonski Law Firm, a 20-attorney firm specializing in personal injury.

¨ Designed efficient filing system
¨ Drafted procedures for maintaining filing system
¨ Implemented filing system, tracking and storing over 20,000 files for 20 attorneys.
¨ Supervised assistant file clerk

LEGAL COURSEWORK
¨ Legal Writing
¨ Legal Research
¨ Basic Law
¨ Business Law
¨ Legal Applications of Computers
¨ Litigation and Advanced Litigation
¨ Probate and Estate Planning
¨ Family Law

¨ Criminal Law and Procedure
¨ Corporate Law and Business Organizations

WORK HISTORY

May 1998 - May 1999	Paralegal Intern	Adams County Attorney's Office Adams, Vermont
May 1996 - May 1998	Legal File Clerk	Brown & Jablonski Law Firm Adams, Vermont

EDUCATION

September 1994 - May 1999 Paralegal Studies	Bachelor of Science	Burlington College Burlington, Vermont
June 1994	High School Diploma	Linden High School Linden, Vermont

AFFILIATIONS

Voting Member of the Vermont Legal Assistant Association.

Sample
Cover Letters

JANET WILLIAMS
123 Elm Street
Maplewood, Illinois 59244

Date

Ms. Kathleen Hunt
Personnel Director
Alberts, Nixon & Robertson, Ltd.
4865 Main Street
Chicago, IL 58474

Dear Ms. Hunt:

I am very interested in the position you had advertised in the *Chicago Times.* My resume is enclosed for your consideration.

I am a recent graduate of the Paralegal Institute, an ABA-approved institution. I also have a Bachelor of Science Degree in Business Administration from the University of Minnesota. As you will note from my resume, I have completed an internship working in the area of litigation. I feel that with my education and litigation experience, I could make a significant contribution to your firm.

Please call me at (234) 555-3948 to schedule an interview at your convenience. I look forward to hearing from you soon.

Sincerely,

Janet Williams

Enclosure

ROBERT LESTER
23 South 9th Street,
Philadelphia, PA 19106
(216) 455-3425

December 10, 2000

Ms. Katherine Laurence
Office Administrator
Michaels & Waldman
35 Pine Street
Philadelphia, PA 19103

Dear Ms. Laurence:

David Hines told me of the paralegal position soon to become available in your corporate law department. My experience interning in the law department of Walton Manufacturing and my education as a paralegal has prepared me well to fulfill the duties your position requires.

As you will note from my enclosed resume, I will be graduating from the Peirce College in January 2001, and my internship at Walton Manufacturing will end at that time as well. During my internship I have had the opportunity to experience several aspects of corporate law, including the maintenance of the corporate minute book and assisting with mergers and acquisitions. I feel that my corporate law experience and my paralegal education would allow me to make a valuable contribution to your corporate law department.

Thank you for the opportunity to be considered for this position. Please contact me at (216) 455-3425 if you would like set up an interview. I look forward to your reply.

Sincerely,

Robert Lester

ANNA RUIZ

439 – 8th Avenue
Eau Claire, Wisconsin 54701
715-555-7655

June 20, 2000

Blankenship & Lowell, PLC
947 Elm Street
Eau Claire, Wisconsin 54701

Attention: Cindy Stemple, Personnel Manager

Dear Ms. Stemple:

I am writing in response to your advertisement for an estate planning paralegal, which was posted on the job-listing page of the NFPA web site.

As you will see from my enclosed resume, I have just recently completed my education at Chippewa Valley Technical College, where I received my Legal Assistant Certificate. As part of that program, I successfully completed a course on estate planning and probate, which I found to be very interesting and informative. Because I enjoy working with the elderly, have excellent writing skills, and a knowledge of estate planning procedures, I feel that I am well qualified for the estate planning paralegal position you are seeking to fill.

I welcome the opportunity to discuss with you the position you are seeking to fill. Please call me at 715-555-7655 to schedule an appointment at your convenience.

Thank you for your consideration.

Sincerely yours,

Anna Ruiz

Glossary

Administrative Law Law, including rules, regulations, orders, and decisions, to carry out regulatory powers and duties of administrative agencies.

Alternative Dispute Resolution (ADR) A procedure for settling a dispute by means other than litigation, such as arbitration, mediation, or minitrial. *(Black's Law Dictionary, Seventh Edition)*

American Association for Paralegal Education (AAfPE) Association of paralegal educators and institutions that educate paralegals formed in 1981. The AAfPE currently has approximately 285 members.

American Bar Association (ABA) A voluntary national organization of lawyers. Among other things, it participates in law reform, law-school accreditation, and continuing legal education in an effort to improve legal services and the administration of justice. *(Black's Law Dictionary, Seventh Edition)*

Amicus Curiae A person who is not a party to a lawsuit but who petitions the court or is requested by the court to file a brief in the action because that person has a strong interest in the subject matter. Often shortened to *amicus*. Also termed *friend of the court*. *(Black's Law Dictionary, Seventh Edition)*

Arbitration A method of dispute resolution involving one or more neutral third parties who are usually agreed to by the disputing parties and whose decision is binding. *(Black's Law Dictionary, Seventh Edition)*

Associate An attorney who is an employee of a law firm but does not have an ownership interest.

Bankruptcy The system under which a debtor may come into court, or be brought into court by his or her creditors, either seeking to have his or her assets administered and sold for the benefit of creditors and to be discharged from his or her debts, or to have his or her debts reorganized.

Bar Association An association of members of the legal profession. [Several state bar associations sponsor superb CLE programs.] *(Black's Law Dictionary, Seventh Edition)*

Billable Hour Hours billed to a client for legal services performed by each attorney, paralegal, or other timekeeper.

Binding (Mandatory) Authority Previous decisions of a higher court in the same jurisdiction or statutes that a judge must follow in reaching a decision or a case.

Blended Resume Resume that uses a combination of the chronological and functional formats to emphasize achievements and skills in the beginning and then provide a chronological listing of your work experience and education.

Case Law The collection of reported cases that form the body of law within a given jurisdiction. Also written case law; case-law. Also termed *decisional law; adjudicative law; jurisprudence; organic law. (Black's Law Dictionary, Seventh Edition)*

Certification Form of self-regulation whereby an organization grants recognition to an individual who has met qualifications specified by that organization.

Certified Legal Assistant (CLA) Title granted by the National Association of Legal Assistants to paralegals who have passed the CLA examination and met other criteria of NALA.

Chronological Resume Resume that focuses on a chronological description of work experience and education experience, beginning with the current date and working back in time.

Contract Paralegal A paralegal who works for several different attorneys, law firms, or corporations, either as a freelance paralegal or through one or more temporary agencies.

Copyright A property right in an original work of authorship (such as a literary, musical, artistic, photographic, or film work) fixed in any tangible medium of expression, giving the holder the exclusive right to produce, adapt, distribute, perform, and display the work. *(Black's Law Dictionary, Seventh Edition)*

Credentials Documentary evidence of a person's qualifications; commonly in the form of letters, licenses, or certificates.

Defendant A person sued in a civil proceeding or accused in a criminal proceeding. *(Black's Law Dictionary, Seventh Edition)*

Demonstrative Evidence Physical evidence offered for viewing by the judge or jury.

Documentary Evidence A document or other writing that tends to establish the truth or falsity of a matter at issue. When oral evidence is given, it is the person (usually the witness) who speaks; when documentary evidence is involved, it is the document that "speaks."

Document Preparer An individual who prepares or assists in the preparation of legal documents at the direction of an individual who is representing himself or herself in a legal matter.

Electronic Resume Resume prepared with special formatting specifically for submission over the Internet, via e-mail, or for electronic scanning.

Employee Benefit Plans Area of law dealing with the drafting, implementation, maintenance, and compliance of all types of employee benefit plans, including pension plans, profit sharing plans, and welfare benefit plans.

Environmental Law Area of law dealing with implementation and enforcement of laws and regulations concerning environmental issues affecting the use of air, water, and land.

Estate Planning The preparation for the distribution and management of a person's estate at death through the use of wills, trusts, insurance policies, and other arrangements, especially to reduce estate-tax liability. *(Black's Law Dictionary, Seventh Edition)*

Evidence The means by which any matter of fact may be established or disproved. Such means include testimony, documents, and physical objects. The law of evidence is made up of rules that determine what evidence is to be admitted or rejected in the trial of a civil action or a criminal prosecution and what weight is to be given to admitted evidence.

Freelance Paralegal A self-employed paralegal who works for several different attorneys, law firms, or corporations under the supervision of an attorney.

Functional Resume Resume that focuses on your skills and achievements and eliminates or de-emphasizes a precise chronology of all work and education experience.

General Counsel The lead attorney of a corporate law department.

Immigration The act of entering a country with the intention of settling there permanently. *(Black's Law Dictionary, Seventh Edition)*

Independent Paralegal A self-employed paralegal who works directly for the public to provide legal services not considered the practice of law. Also known as a *legal technician.*

Informational Interview An interview with the person responsible for hiring for an organization to obtain information about a particular kind of employment even if no positions are currently available.

Intellectual Property Law The law governing copyrights, patents, trademarks, and trade names.

Investigate To inquire; to look into; to make an investigation.

IRAC An acronym used to refer to a common legal analysis process. It is composed of the first letter of the descriptive term for each step of the process—*Issue, Rule, Analysis/Application, Conclusion.* This process is the identification of the issue, followed by the presentation of the governing rule of law, the analysis/application of the rule of law, and the conclusion.

Law Clerk An employee of a law firm or legal department who is in law school studying to become an attorney or who has graduated from law school and is waiting to pass the bar examination.

Law Office Administrator An individual with responsibility for administrative and management functions of the law firm, including personnel, marketing, and budgeting.

Legal Analysis The process of applying the law to a given set of facts.

Legal Assistant A person with specialized knowledge gained through education and training who performs substative legal work not considered to be the practice of law, under the supervision of an attorney, or within the law through administrative, statutory, or court authority. Also known as a *paralegal.*

Legal Document Assistant Individuals recognized in California who are authorized to provide or assist in providing, for compensation, self-help legal services to the public.

Legalese Legal jargon, including specialized words or phrases, used by lawyers instead of plain talk, when it serves no purpose.

Legal Nurse Consultant An individual who has training both as a nurse and a paralegal who often works for personal injury law firms, medical malpractice law firms, or the legal department of insurance companies.

Legal Secretary An employee in a law office whose responsibilities include typing legal documents and correspondence, keeping records and files, and performing other duties supportive of the employer's law practice. Legal secretaries usually are more highly skilled, and therefore more highly compensated, than secretaries in general business. *(Black's Law Dictionary, Seventh Edition)*

Legal Technician A self-employed paralegal who works directly for the public to provide legal services not considered the practice of law. Also known as an *independent paralegal.*

License Permission by competent authority, usually the government, to do an act which, without such permission would be illegal or otherwise not allowable. Permission to exercise a certain privilege, to carry on a particular business, or to pursue a certain occupation.

Litigation The process of carrying on a lawsuit (the attorney advised his client to make a generous settlement offer in order to avoid litigation). A lawsuit itself (several litigations pending before the court). *(Black's Law Dictionary, Seventh Edition)*

Maritime Law The body of law governing marine commerce and navigation, the transportation at sea of persons and property, and marine affairs in general; the rules governing contract, tort, and workers' compensation claims arising out of commerce on or over water. Also termed *admiralty; admiralty law*. *(Black's Law Dictionary, Seventh Edition)*

Mediation An alternative dispute resolution process in which a neutral third person, the mediator, helps disputing parties to reach an agreement. The mediator has no power to impose a decision on the parties, unless participation is voluntary.

Model Guidelines for the Utilization of Legal Assistant Services Guidelines adopted by the American Bar Association's Standing Committee on Legal Assistants in 1991 to provide guidance to attorneys for the effective utilization for paralegals.

National Association of Legal Assistants (NALA) National association of legal assistants (paralegals) formed in 1975; currently represents over 18,000 members through individual memberships and 90 state- and local-affiliated associations.

National Federation of Paralegal Associations (NFPA) National association of paralegals formed in 1974; currently has more than 55 association members representing more than 17,000 individual members.

Networking Meeting and establishing contacts with a relatively large number of people with similar interests who might be helpful to you later. Similarly, you become such a contact for others.

Paralegal A person with specialized knowledge gained through education and training, who performs substantive legal work not considered to be the practice of law, under the supervision of an attorney, or within the law through administrative, statutory, or court authority. Also known as a *legal assistant*.

Paralegal Advanced Competency Examination (PACE) Test developed for the NFPA as a means of validating the knowledge and experience of paralegals who pass the test and meet with certain other criteria. Paralegals who pass the PACE are granted the title of Registered Paralegal (RP).

Paralegal Manager A person responsible for hiring and supervising paralegals who spends little or no time working on client cases as a paralegal. Also known as a *legal assistant manager*.

Partner An owner and a member of a partnership.

Partnership A voluntary association of two or more persons who jointly own and carry on a business for profit. Under the Uniform Partnership Act, a partnership is presumed to exist if the persons agree to share proportionally the business's profits or losses. *(Black's Law Dictionary, Seventh Edition)*

Patent The governmental grant of a right, privilege, or authority. The official document so granting. *(Black's Law Dictionary, Seventh Edition)*

Personal Injury In a negligence action, any harm caused to a person, such as broken bone, a cut, or a bruise; bodily injury. Any invasion of a personal right, including mental suffering and false imprisonment. For purposes of workers' compensation, any harm (including worsened preexisting condition) that arises in the scope of employment. (*Black's Law Dictionary, Seventh Edition*)

Plaintiff The party who brings a civil suit in a court of law. Abbr. Pltf. (*Black's Law Dictionary, Seventh Edition*)

Probate To admit a will to proof. To administer a decedent's estate. (*Black's Law Dictionary, Seventh Edition*)

Pro Bono (Latin *pro bono publico* "for the public good") Being or involving uncompensated legal services performed especially for the public good [took the case pro bono] [50 hours of pro bono work each year]. (*Black's Law Dictionary, Seventh Edition*)

Professional Corporation (PC) A corporation that provides services of a type that requires a professional license. A professional corporation may be made up of architects, accountants, physicians, veterinarians, or the like. (*Black's Law Dictionary, Seventh Edition*)

Professional Limited Liability Company Entity similar to a professional corporation that allows limited liability and partnership taxation status to its members, who must be professionals.

Pro Se For oneself; on one's own behalf; without a lawyer (the defendant pro se) (a pro se defendant). Also termed *pro persona; in propria persona*. (*Black's Law Dictionary, Seventh Edition*)

Real Evidence Physical evidence, as opposed to testimony; demonstrative evidence.

Registration The process by which individuals or institutions meeting with certain requirements list their names on a roster kept by an agency of government or by a nongovernmental organization. Registration provides the public with a list of individuals or institutions who have met with certain requirements.

Regulatory Agency Agency that receives its power from the legislative branch of the government to oversee and regulate certain industries and professions.

Securities Instruments such as stocks, bonds, notes, convertible debentures, warrants, or other documents that represent a share in a company or a debt owed by a company or government entity.

Self-Represented Person A person who represents himself or herself for the purpose of resolving or completing a process in which the law is involved.

Shareholder One who owns or holds a share or shares in a company, especially a corporation. Also termed *shareowner*, (in a corporation) *stockholder*. (*Black's Law Dictionary, Seventh Edition*)

Skill Ability to use one's knowledge effectively in doing something; developed or acquired ability.

Sole Practitioner A single attorney who owns and manages his or her own practice of law.

Standing Committee on Legal Assistants Committee formed by the American Bar Association, which currently oversees the ABA approval process for paralegal education programs.

Statutory Law That body of law created by acts of the legislature in contrast to constitutional law and law generated by decisions of courts and administrative bodies.

Testimonial Evidence Oral evidence elicited from a witness.

Trademark A word, phrase, logo, or other graphic symbol used by a manufacturer or seller to distinguish its product or products from those of others. (*Black's Law Dictionary, Seventh Edition*)

Traditional Paralegal An individual who works as a paralegal under the direct supervision of an attorney.

Treatise A book or set of books that provide an overview, analysis, or summary of a particular type of law.

Unauthorized Practice of Law (UPL) The practice of law by a person, typically a nonlawyer, who has not been licensed or admitted to practice law in a given jurisdiction. *(Black's Law Dictionary, Seventh Edition)*

Workers' Compensation A system of providing benefits to an employee for injuries occurring in the scope of employment. Most workers' compensation statutes both hold the employer strictly liable and bar the employee from suing in tort. Also termed *workmen's compensation; employers' liability.* *(Black's Law Dictionary, Seventh Edition)*

Index

C

Career America Connection, 43–44
Careers
  nontraditional paths in, 89–90
  objectives for, 218
Case assistants, 30
Case law, 201
Certification, 157, 174
Certified Legal Assistant (CLA), 133
Character traits, 197–199
Charging part, 291
City attorneys' offices, 48
CLA. *See* Certified Legal Assistant
Classified ads, 208–209
Clerical personnel, 32, 39
Client(s)
  confidentiality of, 51–53
  interview forms for, 196
Commission on Nonlawyer Practice, 9
Communication, 21
  in-person, 184–185
  skills, 183–187
  written, 185–187
Compensation
  billable hours and, 121–122
  Bureaus of Labor Statistics data, 102–103
  CLA and RP designation and, 112–114
  data on, 100–103
  education, training, credentials and, 110–114
  employer type and, 114
  experience and, 107–110
  geographic location and, 103–105
  by geographic region, 105–107
  increasing levels of, 13–14
  by law firm size, 115–118
  Legal Assistant Today data, 101–102
  in metropolitan areas, 103–104
  NALA data, 101
  NFPA data, 100–101
  salary, starting, 109–110
  salary surveys, access to, 142
  specialty and, 118–121
Competency, 199–200, 291–292
Computer skills, 188–189
Confidentiality, 51–53

Conflicts of interest, 91–92
Continuing education, 143
Contract paralegals, 6, 15
Conventions, national, 144
Copyrights, 77
Corporate employers, 40
Corporate law, 70–71
Corporate law departments, 36–39
  organizational chart, 37
  paralegal functions within, 37
  pros and cons of working for, 39
Courtesy, 20
Cover letters, 225–226, 306–308
Credentials, 174
Criminal law
  defense, 79–80
  prosecution, 80
Current events, 143–144

D

Defense, 69–70
Diligence, 199–200
Directory of Corporate Counsel, 53
Disciplinary rules, 125
Documents, organizing, 182

E

Education, 220
  continuing, 143
  standards, 252
Elder law, 81–82
E-mail, 222–223
Employee benefits law, 82–84
Employee Retirement Income Security Act (ERISA), 83
Employers
  corporate law departments, 36–39
  federal government agencies, 40–44
  local governments, 44–49
  of paralegals, 23
  researching potential, 215–216
  salary and, 114–118. *See also* Compensation
  state governments, 44–49
  targeting potential, 213–215
Employment
  agencies, 215
  priorities, 54–57
Environmental law, 84–85